THE CANOER'S BIBLE

By the same author

Reunion; A Personal History of the Middle Generation
Hellas and Rome
New Promised Land
Europe Reborn

Robert Douglas Mead

THE
CANOER'S BIBLE

Doubleday & Company, Inc., Garden City, New York

Library of Congress Cataloging in Publication Data
Mead, Robert Douglas.
The canoer's bible.
Includes bibliographies.
1. Canoes and canoeing.   2. Canoes and
canoeing—North America—Directories.   I. Title.
GV783.M4   797.1′22
ISBN 0-385-07276-7
Library of Congress Catalog Card Number 74–33610

9

To James E. Mead

my father
who, so far as I am concerned,
began it all.

CONTENTS

Introduction. WHY CANOE?   xi

Chapter 1. THE CANOER'S WORLD   I
Canoe Travel   I
Who Canoes   4
Canoeing and Camping   4

Chapter 2. CANOES AND PADDLES   6

Buy or Rent?   6
Choosing Your Own Canoe   6
  Size and Capacity   7
  Weight   7
  Materials   8
  Costs   I I
  Design   I 2
Canoe Makers   I 4
  Alumacraft Boat Co.   I 5
  Chestnut Canoe Co., Ltd.   I 5
  The Chicagoland Canoe Base, Inc.   I 5
  Great World, Inc.   I 7
  Grumman Boats   I 7
  Mad River Canoe   I 7
  Old Town Canoe Company   I 7
  Sawyer Canoe Company   I 8
  Voyageur Canoe Company, Ltd.   I 8

Choosing the Right Paddle 19
    Cannon Products, Inc. 22
    Clement Paddles 22
    Grumman Boats 22
    Iliad, Inc. 22
    Old Town Canoe Company 22
    Sawyer Canoe Company 23
    Smoker Lumber Company, Inc. 24
    Sports Equipment, Inc. 24

Chapter 3. HANDLING YOUR CANOE 25

Getting In and Out 25
Seats and Stability 30
Basic Paddling Strokes 31
    Paddling Bow 31
    Paddling Stern 33
    Turning Strokes 36
Lifting and Carrying 36
Special Conditions and Techniques 40
    Waves 40
    Wind and Current 42
    Rapids 42
Emergencies 44
Some Options 47

Chapter 4. EQUIPPING YOUR CANOE 49

Protection 49
Transportation 53
Propulsion 54
Comforts 55

Chapter 5. GEAR 57

Clothing the Canoer 57
Tents 58
Sleeping Bags 60
Between You and the Ground 61

Food and Cooking 62

    Pots, Pans, and Other Vital Matters 62

    Fires and Fire Making 64

    Stoves 67

And a Few of the Comforts 68

    Lighting the Night 70

    First Aid, Repairs, and Personal Care 70

    Living Off the Land 72

Packs and Packing 72

    The Duluth Pack 72

    In and Out of the Canoe 75

Chapter 6. TRAVELING FREE 78

Planning a Canoe Trip 78

On the Move 81

Making and Breaking Camp 84

Chapter 7. VOICES OF EXPERIENCE 89

Where to Go 89

Getting Organized 92

Outfitters' Services 94

Chapter 8. ON YOUR OWN 97

Maps and Map Sources 97

Canoe Equipment 100

Clothing 100

Sleeping Gear 103

Personal Accessories; Repairs and Emergencies 103

Food 104

    General 105

    Breakfast 106

    Lunch 106

    Dinner 107

Cooking and Related Equipment 108

Packs 109

Chapter 9. CANOE COUNTRY　　　　　　　111

Mid-Continent　　　　　　　113
    Boundary Waters-Quetico　　　　　113
    Elsewhere in Ontario　　　　　116
    Upper Midwest　　　　　117
Northeastern United States　　　　　118
Southeastern United States　　　　　122
The Central Midwest　　　　　125
Western United States　　　　　126
Wild Waters of the Far North　　　　　129
    Quebec　　　　　130
    Across the Prairie Provinces　　　　　132
The Far Northwest　　　　　136

Appendixes　　　　　　　142

1. National Associations　　　　　142
2. Local Canoe Clubs　　　　　142
3. Books About Canoeing　　　　　149
4. Sources for U.S. and Canadian Maps　　　　　151
5. Local Sources of Canoeing Information　　　　　151
6. Canoe Manufacturers　　　　　158
7. Paddles and Other Canoe Equipment　　　　　158
8. Camping Equipment Manufacturers　　　　　159
9. Retail Sources for Canoe-Camping Equipment　　　　　159
10. Freeze-Dried Foods　　　　　160
11. Outfitters　　　　　161

Introduction

WHY CANOE?

Something like two million Americans, individuals and families, own canoes today. Another six million rent canoes from time to time. Both figures are on the rise. What is it about canoeing that attracts people in such numbers?

The reasons why people take to the water with canoe and paddle are probably as various as the people themselves. Speaking as one among the millions, I would put at the top of my own list a delight in the waterside country itself, as experienced from the seat of a canoe. That delight connects country as different as the desert canyons of the Rio Grande and the lush pine and hardwood forests of northern Minnesota, the remote, almost unpeopled wilderness of the Canadian North and the populous environment of the Delaware River. Linked with that pleasure, fed by all the senses, is another, which you can cultivate equally in the half-forgotten stream on the edge of town or the mightiest river system of the continent: self-reliance. For the time that you are on the water in your canoe, you depend on no one but yourself, your own combination of strength, skill, experience. The canoe itself, slipping in silken silence through the water, is the intimate source of that feeling of independence. Of all the vehicles human inventiveness has evolved, none is more perfectly adapted to its physical medium.

One immediate consequence of that adaptation is that canoeing—viewed simply as a sport, a form of exercise—is remarkably democratic. You needn't, that is, be endowed with great physical strength to do it, nor do you need to develop a high degree of skill before you can engage in it with pleasure and satisfaction. Canoe and paddle respond equally to the very young and to those past middle age, to heavily muscled men and delicately constructed women. A husband-and-wife team is among the recent U.S. national canoeing champions; at other times, middle-aged fathers and their teen-aged sons (or mothers and daughters) have been winners. In practice, that means that canoeing is one of the small number of things a family can do together on pretty much even terms and with appropriate satisfaction for all concerned—husband and wife, boys and girls, young and half-grown or adult-size children. To be a parent is also necessarily to be, consciously and unconsciously, one's children's first teacher—a role that the society we live in, with its reverence for professionalism and its superstitious bias toward technical arrangements in place of personal relationships, has made immeasurably more difficult than it once was. In the context of a canoe trip, however, whatever competence and wisdom one has communicate themselves immediately to one's children, without having to be asserted—and vice versa; and what you learn from each other and value is a good deal broader than simply how to take a canoe safely through rough water or build a fire that lights when all the wood is wet.

There's another thing about canoeing that recommends it to families and to anyone else who lives on a budget (and who doesn't?): simply, it doesn't cost very much. My own canoeing experience goes back to the Depression years of the early thirties. As a family—father, mother, my two brothers and myself—more than part of our reason for getting started was that a canoe trip was a vacation we could afford to take together.

These reasons for canoeing, which, with varying emphasis, most canoeists share, are also the reasons for the content of this book. You'll find a heavily illustrated outline of paddling technique and of canoe handling generally (Chapter 3), starting from the beginning, but useful (I hope) even to those who already know more than a little about these matters. Obviously, no physical skill can be learned solely from pictures and a written description. With this information, however, and with lots of practice graduated through increasingly demanding conditions—plus the kind of in-person tips you can pick up from other, more experienced canoers—you should be ready when the time and opportunity come for you to shove off on a canoe trip of your own. And that is the goal of this book: to assemble between two covers the knowledge and information essential to safe and enjoyable canoe travel on your own, whether that means a long weekend on the nearest river or a summer-long odyssey through the farthest wilderness.

Given that goal, three chapters of this book (2, 4, and 5) are concerned with kinds of equipment and supplies suited to canoe travel and camping in varied conditions and climates, beginning with the canoes and paddles. These chapters can serve as a buying guide as you assemble your own canoeing gear, but in many areas canoes and other basic equipment can be rented—an inexpensive way for first-time canoe travelers to check my suggestions against their own preferences. U.S. and Canadian sources for purchase and rental of all equipment and supplies discussed are listed in the Appendixes, along with much other useful information.

And when you've mastered your canoe and collected your equipment? You shove off and travel, of course—as far as time and energy will carry you. The book's final chapters, then, have to do with planning and organizing a canoe trip, whether for one canoeload or a group, on your own or with the help that's available from canoe outfitters and guides—and with how to conduct the trip itself for everyone's safety and enjoyment. The book closes with an introduction, region by region, to the major canoeing areas throughout the continent, with sources for further information about each, which, again, are summarized in the Appendixes. All of these are areas where extended canoe trips are possible, from a week or so to, in some cases, an entire season. Wherever you happen to live, there's no limit to the possibilities.

In all of this, I've tried to share with you the things I've learned in forty years of canoeing, first with my parents and brothers, later with friends, and now with my wife and our four sons. I've tried, that is, to set forth as plainly as possible how *I* do things, and why. This is not to say that I consider my way of canoeing the only one possible. You'll meet other experienced canoeists who do things a little differently or with different emphases. You'll have, in time, your own ideas. Indeed, I've never made a trip without learning something about canoeing or camping that, often, has seemed fundamental in retrospect. Nor do I consider myself the kind of superskilled canoeman who seeks out steep-pitched rapids for the fun of it or who will ever bring home a blue ribbon for flatwater or downriver racing. What I do know, however, is that my particular combination of experience and skill has carried me and the people I've canoed with through most of the kinds of conditions that canoers can meet with on this continent—and we've met them with enjoyment and assurance and without serious hazard even when, at the time, the going seemed toughest. That, I think, is the essential requirement any time you set out by canoe: to enjoy the trip; and to surmount whatever difficulties present themselves along the way, so that you, your party, your canoe and equipment come back again in safety. The two go together.

This is the place for saying thanks, and I do so. My father, to whom this book is dedicated, heads the list; his ways as a canoer and camper became mine, duly modified by the difference in our temperaments. My wife and, later, our sons have been tolerant companions on canoe trips that go back to the early months of our marriage. My wife also took many of the pictures in this book not otherwise credited, my son Jim others; both my wife and my son Matthew have surrendered countless weekends to helping me illustrate this book, particularly in Chapter 3. Jim Hansen produced the prints from which many of these pictures are reproduced. Nancy Ulrich survived the typing of the manuscript. Among the several people who have shared their expert knowledge in several fields connected with canoeing, I particularly thank Ralph Frese—canoeist and canoe builder, proprietor of the Chicagoland Canoe Base. And finally, I express my thanks to the editors at Doubleday, Sandy Richardson and Bill Thompson, who in the first place suggested that I undertake this book and who have provided the encouragement needed in its writing and publication.

Chapter 1

THE CANOER'S WORLD

A few years ago, two of my sons and I headed our canoe down the eight miles of river that connects two lakes called Darky and Minn, in the Quetico country, north of the Minnesota-Ontario border. It was a bright morning in early June, and on the river, sheltered from the wind by big pines thick on either bank, the weather was almost sultry, as on a meandering tidal stream of the far South. At times, the river elbowed out in a little lake, with dense growths of wild rice and white and yellow flowering lilies surrounding the channel, and squads of young ducks and loons feeding among them. Again, the river narrowed, cutting its way through indestructible rock, and there were the half a dozen rapids marked on the map for the boys to watch for and skim through, exercising skills they'd been practicing in the two weeks of our trip—though at this season the rapids turned out to be no more than momentary riffles in the smooth flow of the water. But, miles as we were from any other people, any town, we treated them with respect all the same.

Toward noon, with a final rush around a last bend, the river current broke against the deeper waters of a new lake, made choppy by a freshening breeze. We worked our way down it, pushing against the wind and waves, portaged into the next lake, and camped for the night on a tiny island a mile from shore, with just room for our tent, a fireplace, a dozen stunted pines and birches, and the two big rocks—one to fish from, the other for swimming—around which the island itself had grown, like a pearl. Another day and we were crossing an arm of a lake that still carries its *voyageur* name, Lac La Croix, the biggest in this border country, with water vistas of five miles or more in any direction. From our vantage point,

hugging the water, feeling every pressure of wind and wave in the movement of the canoe and the muscles of our bodies, it was like putting out on an ocean. Our route that afternoon took us on portages around two waterfalls (where we paused to gather tiny wild strawberries growing cool in the spray, and ripe blueberries from a sunny outcropping above). We camped that night on an island dividing a third, much bigger fall and slept to its roaring lullaby: a ceaseless tumbling of waters like an image of irresistible force, pounding against smooth granite cubes of living rock that are its immovable object and its channel.

The next day—and next-to-last of our trip—was twenty miles of a long, narrow lake, with the wind building behind us until the following waves were breaking over the stern of the canoe. After the effort of keeping headed, we faced another river, sheltered now, but this time upstream, with the current against us and a series of rapids to push up and falls to portage around. Another day, and we were back at our starting point, the village of Winton, ninety miles north of Duluth—where roads end and the hundred or so people are mostly Finns whose parents or grandparents came there as loggers; their speech still sings with the music of that other northland of lakes and pines and rocky streams thousands of miles to the east.

Canoe Travel

The few days at the end of that canoe trip with my sons form a kind of small-scale model of the subject of this book: canoe travel. Call it tripping if you like, cruising, flat-water canoeing (the white-water enthusiasts' term, to set it apart from what *they* do), the elements are the same. Whether for a day or two at a time or for months, you are *traveling:* you have a sequence of places to get to and an objective at the end, even if it is only to complete the circuit and return to your starting point. Whatever help you may have in setting out or after you get back, while you are on your route you are *on your own: you* supply the power that drives you along. And whatever you require to sustain you on the way—food and cooking gear, tent and sleeping bags, clothes—you carry with you in your canoe and pack on your back over the portage trails between waters, which may be anywhere from a few feet to a mile or more. Traveling by canoe, you can, if you like, reach parts of this continent that are not in fact accessible by any other means. On the other hand, even when you are not traveling to or through actual wilderness—and there are literally thousands of fine, canoeable lakes and rivers within a few miles of major cities from Boston to Los Angeles—the effect will be much the same. The nameless stream that you flash past on the turnpike with hardly a glance looks entirely different when seen from a canoe. By returning to this older mode of travel—as old as the Indians who preceded us on this continent—you return to an earlier viewpoint, a simpler and more basic way of doing things, and that is part of the lure of canoeing and one of its rewards. In either case, whether you are canoeing through deepest wilderness or within sight and sound of a million people, the effect is the same: you travel with the freedom that comes of being self-sustaining, dependent on no one but yourself.

That canoe trip of ours was typical in another way of what a new-time canoer can look forward to: it took us through most of the kinds of waters one is likely to encounter in traveling by canoe. There were lakes ranging in size from beaver ponds, no more than dots on our maps and too small to be named, to big lakes five or six miles across and thirty miles long, where the waves can build up almost like ocean combers to test the canoer's heart and nerves and skill. There were rivers connecting some of these lakes, to glide down or battle up with hard paddling, rivers that might spread lake-like, a mile at a stretch, half marshy at the edges, and then narrow around the next bend, running deep and swift, punctuated by rapids. And there was, finally, that succession of waterfalls to negotiate, from both directions—paddling through the turbulent eddies at the bottom to reach the

carrying place, approaching from above with a different but equal caution.

The variety of water and weather that I led my boys through was no accident, of course. I had been canoeing that country with my father, brothers, mother, friends since I was a child smaller than my sons, and for their first sampling I picked from all those memories a route that would show them a little of every kind of thing that country has to offer. It's varied country—and big: the Boundary Waters Canoe Area, created in 1965 after decades of evolution and growth, runs for two hundred miles along the top of Minnesota—more than a million acres, thousands of lakes, thousands of miles of canoe routes; and Quetico Park, across the border, is on the same scale. You could spend a lifetime canoeing that country and never know all of it.

The BWCA-Quetico long ago implanted my own notions of what canoeing might be, like a boy's first experience of the possibilities of love. But any canoe travel you're likely to do will partake of that variousness. Indeed, the possible combinations of the canoer's pair of elements, water and weather, must be infinite, and they can vary in one place from year to year, season to season, so that, even following the same route, no canoe trip is likely ever to be twice the same. Hence, if canoers had a motto, it might well be the Coast Guard's *Semper Paratus*—"ready for anything." Taking you the first steps toward being ready for anything when you step into your canoe is what this book is about.

Any canoe trip you make will involve you in a variety of waters, calling on several different specific canoeing skills, but, depending on where you live, one or another kind is going to predominate. We'll look at the possibilities in greater detail in a later chapter. Here, we'll be thinking ahead, since the kind of country you'll be canoeing determines not only the skills you need to master but a whole series of choices in equipment and clothing and in the canoe itself.

Anywhere in the Midwest, you're within fairly easy reach of canoe country like the BWCA-Quetico—more or less connected lakes, short streams, and rivers, the scourings of successive ice ages. Similar country fans out from central Wisconsin north through Minnesota and northern Michigan, spreading in a great network of lake and river routes whose only limits are Hudson Bay and the Arctic Ocean. These were the canoe routes of the fur-trading voyageurs until near the end of the nineteenth century, built on much older Indian foundations, a comprehensive system covering much of the continent. You can still, like them, put your canoe in at any point in this vast system and reach any other point, from Buffalo or Montreal to the Arctic outlet of the Mackenzie River or the mouth of the Yukon on Alaska's Pacific coast. With a summer to spare and sufficient hardihood, it's possible to cross the continent by canoe—and people do.

There is comparable lake-and-river canoeing farther east: in Algonquin Park in southeastern Ontario, in the Adirondacks of New York State (where Thoreau is among one's distinguished predecessors), and, on a more limited scale, in the lakes and rivers of northwestern Maine. To the south, in the Ozarks of southern Missouri and northern Arkansas, dams over the past thirty years have created some interesting long lakes for distance canoeing, interspersed with the fast waters of the rivers from which they were formed.

Historically, the Great Lakes and the Ohio and Mississippi rivers were also canoe routes, and the voyageurs' French records their passage at key points from Detroit to Isle Royale to Eau Claire and Fond du Lac. Today, the canoers have pretty well abandoned these big waters to the tugs and barges, but the narrow headwaters of the Mississippi, above Minneapolis-St. Paul, remain attractive and fairly wild, and the routes themselves exist as ineradicable facts of midwestern geography. You can, for instance, follow the voyageur route through the islands of Lake Huron's Georgian Bay, the Straits of Mackinac, and along the forbidding black-rock north shore of Lake Superior to Grand Portage, the fur traders' summer transfer point to the Quetico and the farthest west and north—and canoers do. Or from Mackinac you can follow Jolliet's track, swinging south along the western shore of Lake Michigan to Green Bay, the Fox and Wisconsin rivers and, at Prairie du Chien, the Mississippi, which will carry you as far to the south as you care to go. Again, it's done. In this dare-anything age of ours, there are also races *across* the Great Lakes—Lake Michigan, for instance—for covered canoes and tireless paddlers impervious to cold and wet; a venture, for most canoe travelers, on a par with a Newfoundland-to-Iceland dinghy race.

There is notable canoe travel to be had in every state of the Union, every Canadian province. East and west of the great central basin walled off by the Appalachians and the Rockies, river canoeing predominates. The range is from such big and comparatively gentle streams as the Hudson, the Delaware, and Oregon's Willamette, where you can make rewarding canoe trips of a week or two, to hair-raising roller coasters like Maine's Dead River and parts of the Connecticut in New Hampshire that reach or surpass the limits of what's possible in a canoe. In the East particularly, the horizons of the canoer's world tend to be seasonal. In the Northeast, rivers that fill in spring with melting snow and rain may be too shallow and rocky to afford much fun in summer; from Pennsylvania south, the season is earlier, and winter and early-spring canoeing has much to recommend it. Dams on these rivers present a hazard in the shape of unpredictable rise and fall in the water level—or, if you like, a welcome change of pace in the form of portages. Yet, for the general public one of the surprises of the energy shortage was something canoers knew all along: just how little of our power comes from water—and hence how few of our canoeable waterways are interrupted by the dams that produce it.

All these waters that form the canoe traveler's world are what is known as "flat." This is not to say millpond-smooth, but with a current slow enough—under four miles an hour—that the canoer can usually travel at will in any direction, up, down, or across. Water flows because it follows a natural slope; the steeper the grade, the swifter the current. The difference between flat-water and white-water canoeing is very much like the difference between cross-country and downhill skiing. For the canoe traveler, white water is a part of the whole, an aspect of his sport. He knows how to handle it—and knows what is beyond the limits of himself and his canoe. Relying on himself even when in a party with several other canoes, he reads the water ahead and scouts the banks of rapids he has not tried. Knowing that he must depend on the gear in his canoe for days or weeks to come, he does not risk depositing it at the bottom of an impassable stream; he portages around the hazards he's not sure of or uses poles or a rope from the bank to let his canoe down the descent, under control. Any river he can go down he can also come up again, though the going against the current may be slow and wearying.

The white-water canoer, in contrast, seeks out

the swiftest rapids, the steepest gradients, for a few hours or a day of split-second action—and plans his runs around cars or buses to carry him back by road to his starting point. Since his gear need be no more than a rucksack of lunch (and perhaps a change of clothes against the chance of a dunking), his canoe or kayak will be built light, fast, and nimble. In the past twenty years, the demands of white water have stimulated radical experiments in the design of canoes and paddles and in the materials they're made from, and the white-water canoers have developed the techniques to match them. Today, with the right equipment and careful training, it is possible to canoe—in control and with reasonable safety—streams that would have been suicidal for canoers of the past or their Indian predecessors. Many of these innovations in design and technique have become part of the flat-water canoer's arsenal—like the technical advances that from time to time come out of Watkins Glen or the Indianapolis 500—and we'll be looking at them in later chapters. Nevertheless, for the canoe traveler, white water—exhilarating, scary, or both together—remains only a part of the whole. His world is larger and more varied.

Who Canoes

On canoe trips over the years I've seen just about the entire spectrum of human age and physical prowess. We've come across parties of boys in their middle or early teens . . . lissome girls who raced us over the portages . . . a young man and woman on their wedding trip . . . a pair of elderly ladies canoeing together, who looked like your favorite high school English teachers . . . whole families, mother at the bow, father at the stern, a crowd of children and a dog in between, among the packs. I was six or seven when my father let me take my turn at helping paddle our canoe (not *much* help, probably—my arms got tired). He was seventy when we made our last canoe trip together, with my four- and five-year-old eldest sons as passengers. The point is that you don't have to be an eighteen-year-old football player to canoe well and pleasurably. In a world of seven-foot basketball stars and three-hundred-pound tackles, canoeing is one of the equalizers. One of my boys, who's five and a half feet tall and has the weight of a wombat dripping wet, handles a canoe as effectively in

the water and on the portage trail as his brother who's six feet plus and growing.

The reason for this is that, in whatever modern-design variants, canoe and paddle are among man's great adaptations to his physical environment: knowing how to use them effectively in getting through the waters makes it possible for one who is not so young or strong or big to keep up with those who are. That explains, I think, another fact of the canoer's world. Of all the forms of more or less strenuous exercise, canoeing is among the most gradual. *You* set the pace, adapting your body to paddle and canoe. You may feel tired on the first day or two, but you won't wake up stiff in the morning, with muscles that feel as if they'd been soaked overnight in epoxy. Hence, canoeing is not a sport that requires special conditioning. If you're snowbound in a city apartment and like busywork, do sit-ups for the sake of your back and stomach muscles; flex your arms and shoulders with dumbbells in your hands. But, above all, study and practice the basic skills in calm waters before you venture into the wilderness. The best conditioning for canoeing is *canoeing,* and the mere strength will come. On the first day out, plowing against wind and waves, you may regret every cigarette you ever smoked—and you can count them off against your paddle strokes. By the end of the trip, you'll wonder why the first day seemed so tough. Such is the steady and unfailing process by which canoeing rebuilds your muscles and your mind.

Canoeing and Camping

Whether for a weekend or a spell of weeks, any canoe travel you do is going to include camping along the way. In its camping aspect, canoeing falls somewhere between backpacking and trailering. The differences are in what you can carry and the distances you can expect to cover.

For hiking any distance, the usual recommendation is a load of not more than forty pounds. Whatever your personal limit, you're going to select what goes in your pack with extreme care and an eye to the bulk and the ounces. The hiker's tent, if he uses one at all, must be light and compact. Weight will also be an important factor in his choice of sleeping bag, and an air mattress or a foam-rubber pad to go under it may well be a luxury that won't fit in his pack. Cooking gear will have to be on the same small scale; food will be exclusively freeze-dried, weighing only a few ounces for a serving for two or four people, and the variety and speed of preparation offered by heavier and bulkier canned goods will be out of bounds.

For the canoe camper, the limits are a good deal less stringent. It still takes planning. Unlike his station-wagon-and-trailer counterpart, he can't pack up the contents of his house (as it often looks) and move it to the nearest lake or mountain, but there's no necessity or minor camping comfort that he has to exclude, either. Depending on its length and design, his canoe will have a load capacity of anywhere from six hundred to a thousand pounds or more. With two people in the canoe, that translates into room for at least three hundred pounds of gear—more than you'll ever need or want; even with a passenger, you still have, with a little care, adequate capacity without serious overloading. That means, for instance, that you can carry a tent big enough to avoid the claustrophobic sensation of trying to change your clothes lying flat on your back, as in the old-time Pullman upper berth. It means you can carry a full range of cooking equipment and eat your meals from a plate rather than a bowl or the common pot. It means you can use the bulkier—and less expensive—sleeping bags and stretch out at night on an air mattress or foam-rubber pad (unless you're accustomed to sleeping on mattresses as firm as Mother Earth and can't nod off any other way). And it means, finally, that you can allow yourself a few of those heavy little luxuries that come in cans.

To put this a little more concretely: on the canoe trip described at the beginning of this chapter, we carried food for the three of us, sleeping bags, and spare clothes in two large packs that weighed fifty or sixty pounds each at the start—the more you eat, the lighter they get, and of course we supplemented our diet with fresh-caught fish. Our cooking gear was in a small, separate pack, and

our old balloon-cloth tent, weighing about twenty-five pounds, portaged handily on top of one of the big packs. The weights were not enough to be tiring over the fifteen or twenty minutes of a typical portage (in the old days, before the dried foods came along, we thought nothing of a pack weighing a hundred pounds or more). Actually, weight alone is less important than bulk. When it comes to portaging, it's very much worth some care in pre-planning so as to fit your outfit into as few packs as possible. Trying to thread your way along a portage trail with a lot of small, loose articles dangling from your hands and arms and neck is a refined form of torture, and it's just such encumbrances that tend to get left behind when you shove off at the other end. How to avoid such nuisances and the lost time that goes with them will be taken up in a later chapter.

The canoer's distances, like his equipment and supplies, are also on the generous side compared with hiking. In country like the Boundary Waters Canoe Area-Quetico, you'll travel fifteen or twenty miles a day, with portages, without feeling pushed—and have time to explore, take pictures, perhaps do a little lunchtime fishing, and still stop early enough in the afternoon to make camp, have a swim, eat dinner in daylight, and take your canoe out afterward, unloaded, to match wits with the local fish in the magical twilight calm of their feeding time. On that trip with my sons, our loosely planned itinerary took us through a generous 120-mile loop of the Quetico, and even at that we spent four or five days of our two weeks in stopovers, loafing, fishing, exploring. Going downstream, you may well cover two or three times these average distances with no greater effort; the speed of the current is a bonus added onto the four miles an hour you earn by paddling.

Canoe travel is, in a word, a life of leisure, provided you've mastered the basic skills. Getting those skills is what we'll be doing in this book, beginning with the gentle art of paddling.

Chapter 2

CANOES AND PADDLES

On our family canoe trips back in the thirties and early forties, we never used anything but wood-and-canvas canoes built in Maine, where canoeing as a white man's sport began. After World War II, when some genius in the Grumman Aircraft Company had the idea of switching a surplus plant to canoe building, using techniques developed for planes, we began using the aluminum canoes that resulted. Quite recently, I've been converted to fiberglass canoes.

My personal experience with the various types of canoes is, in effect, a capsule history of canoe building over the past forty years. Yet I believe that, in all that time, I never gave more than two minutes' thought to the many variables in the design of canoes and the materials they're made of or to the differences these might make in handling or durability. If that sounds a bit stupid, I can only say that to me a canoe was a canoe and that was all there was to it.

It wasn't until about a year ago, when I had to decide on the ideal canoe for a long and potentially hazardous trip to the Arctic, that I began seriously to investigate and think about the real differences in canoe design and materials. Then—with the realization that in the remote reaches of the Canadian Northwest I would be betting my life on the choice I made—I discovered that the range of possibilities was so huge as to make a really confident decision seem nearly impossible. There are at least eighty canoe builders in the United States, each offering from two or three to a dozen or more different canoe designs in several different sizes—say a thousand different canoes to choose from. I can't pretend to have studied or tested more than a tenth of these. In what follows, therefore, we'll be looking at a few makes that represent the main possibilities and the practical factors you'll want to consider in any canoe you choose for your own use. Your reasons for deciding on any particular canoe may be entirely different from mine, but the principles involved will be the same, and in that sense the solution to my quandary should make yours a little easier.

Buy or Rent?

You don't have to own a canoe, and if you're a first-time canoer, renting is probably your best way of finding out if you really like the sport—and what to look for when and if you do decide to buy your own canoe. Then, too, renting means you don't have to haul the canoe around with you on top of your car—or store, repair, and maintain it when you're not canoeing. Outfitters in towns around the major canoe areas all rent canoes (see Appendixes for a selected list). With the proliferation of general rental services, by calling around in your area you'll probably be able to find an agency that will rent you a canoe to try out for a day or two on a local lake or river. The cost will generally be between five and ten dollars per day, usually plus a refundable deposit—not a lot of money anyway, though a two-week rental will go a fair way toward paying for a canoe of your own. Any canoe you rent will almost invariably be aluminum, and in the canoe country most outfitters use Grummans.

Choosing Your Own Canoe

The Indians, who invented the canoe, evolved dozens of distinct designs, from the shallow-draft dugouts of the southeastern United States to the ocean-going giants of the Pacific Northwest and the kayak-form canoes of the Arctic and sub-Arctic. Even the birch-bark craft of the central forest lands had almost as many variants as there were tribes, some heavily built, with keels, others light and keel-less, sometimes covered with bark other than birch. As canoeing, in the nineteenth century, changed from a means of commerce to a sport, canoe designs multiplied, and modern materials and manufacturing methods have still further complicated the picture. Faced with this bewildering variety and the contradictory claims that go with it, I've sometimes thought that a skilled pair of paddlers would manage equally well in a tin bathtub—that subtle differences in design matter less than who's using them. But that's a very partial truth, at best. The real point is that some canoe designs are better suited to some conditions than to others; and, since all will be used in a variety of conditions, each is to some degree a compromise among competing possibilities. From your standpoint as a canoe user and potential canoe buyer, the essential factors, in order of importance, are size and capacity, weight, cost, materials, general stability, and that half-tangible, design, which I'll try to illustrate. Just how you balance these factors will depend on the uses you expect to make of your canoe.

Size and Capacity. Traditionally, canoes have been built in lengths ranging, in one-foot increments, from thirteen to eighteen feet. A few models are built as short as eleven or twelve feet, and a few makers offer canoes as long as twenty feet or more. Recently, racing standards established by the canoe associations have encouraged the makers to produce an 18½-foot canoe, comparatively long and narrow across the beam (*beam:* the distance between the sides at the center of the canoe, usually around three feet). Not all sizes, of course, are available in all designs or from all makers. From the standpoint of handling, the 17-foot version of the traditional design (represented by most aluminum and wood-and-canvas canoes) was supposed to provide the best ratio of beam to length. In general, the longer the canoe, the easier it will paddle and the more it will carry. Conversely, the short canoes will be broad in relation to their length, comparatively harder to paddle but a little more maneuverable—and they'll carry appreciably less.

Many makers specify the capacity of their canoes in pounds. By that standard, the theoretical load you can expect to carry will range from around four hundred pounds for a 12-footer to about eight hundred pounds in a typical 17-foot canoe and as much as one thousand pounds in a few 18- or 18½-foot canoes. These capacities represent a limit of safety which in some places is a matter of law. All allow for four to six inches of freeboard (*freeboard:* the distance between the water and the gunwales at the lowest point). The differences in what different canoes of the same length will carry—and the differences are considerable—are due to a combination of several factors: beam, the center depth of the canoe, the natural buoyancy of the materials it's made from, the size of its flotation tanks (in aluminum or fiberglass canoes).

These theoretical load capacities are, of course, no more than that—theory. What counts is your own ability and experience, the kind of waters you'll be traveling, and whether you're aiming for canoe trips of a couple of weeks or more or only a few days at a time. So, to translate theory into practical terms, you can figure that any canoe shorter than fifteen feet is essentially for one person and his gear—or two not very big people and their lunch and tackle, out for a day's fishing. A 15- or 16-footer should be adequate in most conditions for two people with reasonable baggage. (On our family canoe trips when I was a kid, we sometimes traveled safely with a canoe as short as fifteen feet, which with a passenger—myself—and a fair amount of baggage meant only an inch or two of freeboard; but I *don't* recommend it to you.) In New England, where a big canoe is unhandy to maneuver on rivers that are typically narrow, fast, sharp-turning, and shallow, and a canoe trip as long as a week is unusual, the smaller sizes seem to be preferred for general use. Elsewhere, if you want to make your canoeing a family affair, you'll choose one of the bigger canoes, with room for a couple of children as passengers and as much in the way of food and camping gear as you're likely to need. The more traveling you do—and hence, the more varied conditions you'll meet and the bigger your loads—the longer the canoe you'll want; it will give you a little extra freeboard, which at times you'll be mighty glad to have. But there's a limit: weight.

Weight. Not being a big guy myself, I rank weight high on my list of what's important about a canoe, and, other things being more or less equal, I'll usually prefer the lightest canoe I can get. The difference is not so much in paddling as in portaging. If you're under six feet, an extra fifteen or twenty pounds may not mean much on a flat, broad portage, but you'll find it a lot more tiring to lift and put down again, more awkward to maneuver through narrow spots or over fallen trees. When the going gets tough—steep, rocky, muddy —the added weight might sometime mean a fall and a damaged canoe or a twisted ankle. (If you're stuck with a canoe that's a bit heavier than you feel you can manage, you can use one of the two- or three-man carries described in the following chapter, but they'll make your portaging a little more time-consuming.) Before you buy your canoe, by all means get your dealer to put a yoke on it and let you try it out for weight. That's the best way to decide, if you have any doubts.

Leaving aside the small canoes, most 15-footers will weigh in at something like fifty pounds, and each foot will add another ten pounds or so, give or take five pounds either way, depending on the design. Particularly in fiberglass hulls, additional weight doesn't necessarily mean greater strength; it may simply mean the maker is not very smart in his use of materials and his manufacturing techniques. One fiberglass canoe that I've used a lot and consider well designed and sturdily built is an 18½-foot Sawyer that comes in at just seventy pounds on the family scale. We'll look more specifically at weight and other differences when we consider the various representative makes, and you'll have your own ideas about which is going to be best for you. But keep the weight factor in mind; it can be important.

Materials. Today, the choice of canoe materials is essentially three: wood-and-canvas, aluminum, and fiberglass. In addition, before the builders began using canvas, in the nineties, solid wood was used, with the planks flush or sometimes lapped (as in a rowboat); a few all-wood canoes are still built, but they're so rare that we needn't consider them here. Finally, a few makers now use vinyl and a hard plastic (ABS) laminated over a buoyant core. The design possibilities of this laminated material are, I think, similar to fiberglass, but it has other possibilities that make it worth a separate look.

We'll take the materials in the order in which they were developed.

Wood-and-canvas was for nearly fifty years vir-

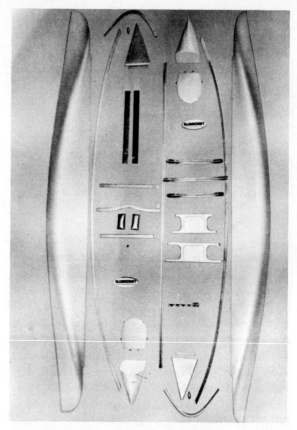

The parts of an aluminum canoe, ready for assembling: the two halves of the stretch-formed hull, with gunwales, stems, decks, and foam flotation; seats and ribs (above, center); thwarts and carrying pads (below, center); with the keel in the middle. (Credit: Alumacraft Boat Company)

tually the only type of canoe made. Cedar is the most usual wood for ribs and planking; various hardwoods are used for gunwales, decks, and seats. The hull is built up around a wooden form that determines its basic shape, then covered with a tightly stretched heavy grade of canvas. The canvas is finished with a marine paint topped by varnish, and all exposed woodwork is varnished. Since a wood-and-canvas canoe is much more fully handmade all through than other types, it lends itself, in theory, to subtle refinements of design that some purists consider superior to any other; in practice, the builders have, I think, been a little unadventurous.

Contrary to what you might suppose, I don't believe that a wood-and-canvas canoe is any more likely than aluminum or fiberglass to smash if you

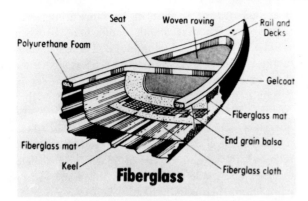

Fiberglass

Fiberglass canoe construction: layers of gelcoat, fiberglass cloth and fiberglass mat, and woven roving. Not all makers build their canoes around a balsa core, and the use of foam in the gunwales to provide flotation is unique to Old Town. (Credit: Old Town Canoe Company)

drive against a rock; nor is it significantly easier, in my experience, to cause a leak in (by gashing through the canvas). If you do get a leak, you can use tape for a quick repair, as with other canoes, and patch in a square of canvas when you get home. However, if you were using a wood-and-canvas canoe much in rapids, the chances are that you'd scratch up the canvas enough, even without cutting it, to require repainting and revarnishing after every trip. Maintenance in general is a problem. Using the canoe a lot, you might have to put on a new coat of varnish as often as once a year, and you wouldn't want to store it outdoors, as you can aluminum and most fiberglass canoes. Storing it indoors would take up a considerable chunk of your basement or as much room in your garage as a car. (For other methods of storage, see Chapter 4.)

There are other disadvantages to wood-and-canvas canoes. Although it's possible to build them very light (and hence a bit fragile under hard use), most are rather heavier than typical aluminum or fiberglass canoes of the same size. In addition, if you have the misfortune to capsize one, the interior wood will soak up the water, takes days to dry out again, and weigh like lead until it does. Nevertheless, if you admire (as I do) fine hand craftsmanship and traditional designs, you'll think seriously about wood-and-canvas. Don't rule it out.

When the aluminum canoes came along, after World War II, they opened up fast-water rivers that in the past had been out of reach to all but the most skilled and venturesome canoeists. The

metal will take a lot of scratching without showing or requiring the kind of protective repairs that canvas would need. Dents can be pounded out with a rubber hammer, like the dents in the fenders of your car, though the resultant stretching of the metal will leave a weak point. (You can't just leave the dents; they create drag in the water, which makes the canoe hard to paddle and difficult to hold on course.) In the flat-water canoe country, the outfitters standardized on aluminum. In normal use, such canoes are virtually maintenance-free, and they'll stand quite a lot of knocking around before they start to look bad. If you decide on one for yourself, you'd do well to avoid a fancy paint job, which will scratch and have to be redone periodically. The bare metal is best, though some owners use a coat of wax on the theory that it will cut water resistance and let the canoe slide off a rock a little more easily.

An aluminum canoe hull is stretch-formed over a metal pattern in two symmetrical halves, which are then joined together with rivets and/or spot welds running along both sides of the keel (there's a fair amount of debate—see **Design**, below—about how a keel or the lack of it affects handling, but in an aluminum canoe it's first of all a structural necessity). Ribs, thwarts, seats, and other fittings are riveted into place. In the course of manufacture, the better makers toughen the metal by baking the half-finished hulls in an oven. The standard gauge of marine aluminum (.050″) produces a canoe weighing about the same as wood-and-canvas—seventy-five pounds, for instance, for a 17-

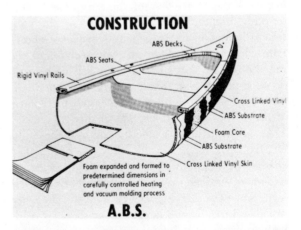

CONSTRUCTION

A.B.S.

ABS canoe construction: layers of vinyl and ABS, vacuum-formed over a foam core, which makes the hull as naturally buoyant as wood-and-canvas. (Credit: Old Town Canoe Company)

footer. With thinner aluminum (.032″ or .040″, depending on the maker), it's possible to shave ten or fifteen pounds from a canoe of the same length. In the lightweights, extra ribs help provide the right balance between rigidity and flexibility; too much of either makes for awkward handling and in some situations could be dangerous. The saving in weight is an obvious advantage, and I think the lightweights are entirely adequate for most canoe travel. On the other hand, if you're going to be using your canoe mainly on fast rivers with moderate rapids, a standard model might be worth the extra weight, perhaps further reinforced with extra ribs (adding another five or six pounds)— but I don't think that, with reasonable care and caution, it's a necessity.

While it's probably no more indestructible, finally, than any other canoe, a well-made aluminum canoe is clearly a good bet for all-around use. There are, however, a few things some people *don't* like about aluminum canoes. For one thing, the lapping of the waves or your own wake as you slice through the water reverberates along the canoe with a muffled bass-drum sound; except perhaps in a dead calm, it's just about impossible to paddle in silence, and some fishermen claim the noise scares fish; or maybe they simply don't like it. In addition, on a bright day the bare aluminum will glare a bit, and in any weather it rubs off, a leaden gray, on your hands or the seat of your pants. The answer to these complaints is woven nylon seats (supplied by some manufacturers); and painted or anodized aluminum, but paint scratches off, and anodization is said to weaken the metal to some degree. I don't take any of these arguments very seriously, but you'll hear them. Probably the most serious limitation in the generally available aluminum canoes is one of design: you won't find the range of choice that's available in either fiberglass or wood-and-canvas. The forms that shape aluminum canoes are presumably expensive to replace. If you're onto a good thing, why change it?

As the white-water canoeists extended the limits of what's possible in a canoe, they also encouraged changes in the traditional canoe design. Racers, on flat water and steep rivers, made demands of their own. Since the early sixties, it's been the fiberglass canoe builders, by and large, who've shown a readiness to experiment in responding to these changing styles in canoeing. The result has been a multiplication of new designs, many of which are well suited to general canoe travel.

The reason for this wealth and diversity of fiberglass designs is that in its fabricating techniques the material stands somewhere between wood-and-canvas and aluminum. There's considerably less hand work in making a fiberglass canoe than in one of wood-and-canvas, but changes in design aren't limited by the costly metal forms that permit relative mass production in aluminum. The fiberglass canoe is formed within a rigid shell, starting with a layer of colored resin or paint, followed by several layers of glass fabric (held together and made rigid by resin that's sprayed or painted on, then usually hand-rolled to remove air bubbles and excess liquid) and ending (the inside of the finished canoe) with a final layer of colored resin and/or paint. When all is dry, the canoe is taken out of the form, and thwarts, gunwales, seats, and decks (or end caps, another term) are riveted into place. The glass fabric supplies the canoe's strength. Beyond a point, the resin, which bonds the layers of fabric together, simply adds weight. Hence, when the process is skillfully done, it's possible to produce a fiberglass canoe that's appreciably lighter and probably stronger than the same size in wood-and-canvas or standard-weight aluminum—and often a touch lighter than lightweight aluminum as well. As a matter of physics, fiberglass and resin formed by the process described test at twice the strength of tempered aluminum of the same weight. Hence, in theory, a fiberglass canoe should be twice as strong as an aluminum one of the same size and weight (theory again—in fact, the differences in weight and strength are less). Never having smashed a canoe of either kind, I can't tell you exactly what that difference in strength means in practice—how much more abuse one will stand than the other before it gives up. I *can* tell you that in fast rivers fiberglass will flex and rebound against blows from rocks that would dent an aluminum canoe and impede its performance.

As my description implies, unitary construction is the desirable norm for a fiberglass canoe—that is, it's made in one piece, built up within a single, undivided form. Some makers, however, mold fiberglass canoes in two symmetrical halves, either divided down the middle from bow to stern, as in aluminum construction, or occasionally from side to side amidships, and then hold them together with fiberglass-and-resin laminations, inner or outer keels, or the equivalent. Such two-part construction isn't necessarily a sign of poor quality— some hull shapes couldn't be made any other way without destroying the mold each time—but I'd be wary of it; in selecting a canoe, look for seams that indicate two-part assembly and ask the dealer or manufacturer about this specific point.

In fiberglass canoes, excessive weight—a difference of as much as ten to twenty pounds for the same size—may indicate a cheaper and less effective manufacturing technique: resin sprayed on rather than brushed (the better makers also squeeze out the excess by hand with rollers to make the finished product lighter). Another short cut is the use of "chopped" fiberglass, which can be sprayed on (and will need more resin to hold it together), rather than single, all-over fiberglass mats. Inspect the floor of the canoe. You should be able to see and feel the weave of the glass fabric. If not, beware!

The most obvious drawback to fiberglass is that it scratches. Not only rocks but waterlogged tree branches jammed below the surface and even sand will leave their marks on the canoe's smooth, shiny skin. (Aluminum also scratches, but the marks aren't nearly as visible.) Since these abrasions are on the underside, you don't have to look at them when you're paddling, but they're ugly and in time will cut through to the glass fabric underneath. At that point, although the canoe won't leak, a repair is in order, using either the old standby, waterproof tape, or epoxy or resin, sanded smooth. Even fairly small irregularities in the surface may impede handling. Since a keel-less fiberglass canoe is most vulnerable to damage at bow and stern just below the water line, some makers offer protective aluminum or stainless-steel bang strips at those points, an extra I strongly recommend.

Apart from the scratches, fiberglass in itself takes even less maintenance than plain aluminum, which in time will corrode. A few high-priced fiberglass canoes have wood trim, which will have to be varnished from time to time; most use anodized aluminum instead.

Vinyl-plastic-foam, mentioned earlier as a fourth type of canoe material, is similar in its general characteristics to fiberglass. It will be discussed later in this chapter under the builder that pioneered the use of this material, Old Town.*

Costs. The prices of canoes, like everything else, go up, not down, so we'll have to be approximate. For a standard, out-of-the-catalogue canoe, built to the maker's specifications (not yours), you'll pay anything from about two hundred dollars to close to one thousand dollars. You can buy a good aluminum canoe for around three hundred dollars or a little less. A typical fiberglass canoe will be about the same or a touch more, though some models run to about six hundred dollars. (The makers are remarkably reticent about explaining what you get for the extra three hundred dollars, but a couple of things are finely detailed hardwood trim and cane seats, as in the older wood-and-canvas canoes— both nice to look at and handle but requiring care.) For wood-and-canvas, with its dependence on thinning ranks of really skilled craftsmen, the range is from over six hundred dollars up, from the leading U.S. maker. While the top prices for a canoe begin to sound like a pretty good secondhand car, I wouldn't let the cost be the main consideration. Any canoe you buy is likely to be with you the rest of your life—you won't need to trade it in —and that's a lot of years over which to spread the initial investment. Look first for the canoe that's going to be right for you and what you want to do with it.

For an aluminum canoe, expect to pay closer to three hundred dollars than two hundred dollars, the lowest price I know of in aluminum. The cheaper makes may use an aluminum that's not heat-tempered or have fewer rivets to hold them together; or they may not be made with flush rivets, meaning more drag in the water, harder paddling, and some chance of popping out under stress. Sight along the keel; it should be straight and smooth. Feel under the gunwales and thwarts for sharp edges that can cut. Except for something for an occasional paddle around a summer pond, the one-hundred-dollar saving isn't worth it.

In fiberglass canoes, we've already noted excess weight and chopped fabric as possible clues to inferior quality. Another is surface bulges or indentations, which create drag in the water, make the canoe heavier to paddle, and may interfere with

---

* Things keep happening! As this book goes to press, several makers (Mad River, Old Town, and Sawyer among them) are experimenting with a fifth material, a new Du Pont fiber called *Kevlar 49*. Use in construction seems to be about as fiberglass but with a weight reduction of up to 25 per cent and far greater strength and abrasion resistance (also, so far, a price jump of one third or more).

I have not yet had a chance to try a Kevlar-built canoe, but the first reports are good, particularly for racing, and the material should be generally available by the time you read this. At the same time, if the high price holds, most of us will probably stick with the traditional materials and continue to be a little careful in how we use them.

handling. Again, sight along the bottom from bow to stern. *Feel* the surface. It should be smooth, all curves.

Design. Every canoe hull design is a combination of three sets of curves. Just how they're combined and the degree of curve in each dimension determines how the canoe will handle, both in general and under various conditions. The differences in handling that you'll actually feel are as subtle as the curves involved, as infinite as the possible combinations, but the more experienced you are as a canoeist, the more you'll feel—and appreciate—the differences. Each emphasis in design offers a particular advantage—and a corresponding disadvantage—depending on the circumstances. It's in that sense that there's no "perfect" canoe for all conditions: Every design is to some extent a compromise.

You can study a canoe hull *from below, from head on,* or *from the side.* In each of these positions, you'll see a different set of curves, each of which has its own importance. For the purpose of this discussion, we'll consider only the double-ended canoe, nearly always identical in its lines at bow and stern; a square-stern canoe won't be first choice if travel under your own power is your primary aim.

Looking at the canoe *from below* (or turned on its side), what you see is the bow line. If it's relatively sharp and long ("fine" is the designers' term), curving gently back to a comparatively narrow beam, the canoe will cut through the water better, be easier (and faster) to paddle. Conversely, a blunter, fuller, more steeply curving bow line, broader in the beam, will be a little heavier to paddle but also more buoyant, with a greater carrying capacity—because of the greater volume enclosed by the hull. Other things being equal, the full bow line is probably more apt to ride *over* waves than *through* them, hence will be drier in rough water.

When you look at the canoe *head on,* what you're seeing is the bottom curve, in effect a cross section. Here again, a continuous curve from gunwale to gunwale means speed and maneuverability—but a reduced load capacity. A flat-bottom canoe, on the other hand, will carry more (and not ride quite so deep with the same load) but feel a little heavier in the water. There's a difference in stability, too. In flat water, from calm to lightly wavy, a curved-bottom canoe is going to feel tippier than one with a flat bottom: it will sway a lit-

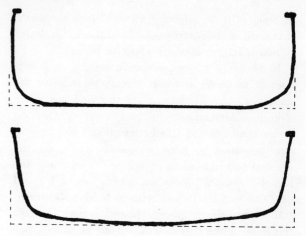

Bottom:
Canoe hull design: comparatively rounded cross section, fast, but somewhat deep draft; will feel somewhat unstable to the inexperienced canoer.
Top:
Canoe hull design: comparatively flat-bottomed cross section, shallower draft for the same capacity than a rounded bottom, but slower; will feel more stable.

tle from side to side with each paddle stroke (though with experience you compensate for that movement). In bigger waves, on the other hand—violent rapids or a storm—it's possible for a wave to grab the broad plane of a flat-bottom canoe and shove the canoe on over, where one with a curving bottom, affording less leverage, will recover and pop upright again like a cork. If you're a first-time canoer, you'll probably do best under most conditions with a flat-bottom canoe, and if you're renting, as I've suggested, that's exactly what you'll get: the aluminum-canoe builders don't make them any other way.

Viewed *from the side,* in profile, a canoe presents its third set of curves (and also an important difference in depth between bow and center, which we'll come back to in a moment). Here, too, the choice is between a flat bottom and a continuous curve from bow to bottom and up again at the stern (called a "rocker bottom"). The curving profile will turn a little faster, important in rapids, but, other things being equal, sit deeper in the water and carry less. There's not, in my experience, any difference in stability.

Three dimensions are important variables in canoe design: bow and stern depth (usually the same), center depth, and beam. Bow/stern and

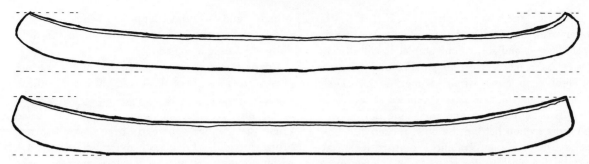

center depths are generally in rough proportion to over-all length: the longer canoes will be a little deeper at both ends. In the 17-foot canoe, the range in bow depths (measured, with the canoe flat on the ground, from its lowest point to the peak of the bow) is from about sixteen to twenty-six inches; twenty or twenty-two inches is typical. The higher the bow, the less likely you are to take on water as you slice through waves or the swirling turbulence of a rapid—but you'll also be more vulnerable to the cross winds you'll meet in lake canoeing, which can make it tough work trying to hold a course. After a day of that, you may feel too tired for dinner before crawling into your sleeping bag for the night! A canoe cut low in the bow to minimize this cross-wind effect will have to compensate in some other direction—with a rocker bottom that helps the canoe ride over the waves, perhaps with longer decks, or end caps, which of course reduce somewhat the usable space inside the canoe.

Again in the matter of center depth, canoe design has two opposite desirables to reconcile. You want it low enough so that the canoe won't be excessively affected by wind, high enough for adequate carrying capacity and safe freeboard with a load. In a 17-foot canoe, a 13-inch center depth is typical, with a range from eleven to fifteen inches. The 4-inch difference may not sound like much, but it can mean a lot if you find yourself in the middle of a lake with a storm coming up and the waves beginning to build. A rocker bottom will compensate to some extent for a low center depth. Another answer is to stretch the canoe out by a foot or more, increasing its capacity and general buoyancy.

The final dimension that matters is the canoe's beam, measured at the center from outside to outside at the gunwale level. A beam of thirty-six or thirty-seven inches is usual for a 17-footer, though in the Canadian Far North, where canoes are still

Bottom:
Canoe hull design: a flat-bottom canoe, providing great load capacity with comparatively shallow draft, probably easier than a rocker-bottom to hold on course.
Top:
Canoe hull design: a rocker-bottom canoe (continuously rounded from bow to stern), somewhat reducing load capacity and increasing draft but appreciably more maneuverable than a flat-bottom canoe.

the work horses of a frontier society, they're built up to forty-five inches and will carry a correspondingly huge load, sixteen hundred pounds! A narrower beam, down to thirty-three or thirty-four inches, makes for easier paddling, but with some sacrifice in capacity.

Before we leave the general question of canoe design, let's run through the practical effects of the basic options. For speed (which is also to say easy paddling even when you're not in a hurry), look for a fine entry line at the bow, a continuous curve in the cross section, a narrow beam, and a low profile at bow and stern and amidships; other things being equal, a long hull is always faster than a short one. These are the characteristics found in canoes designed for racing, with exact dimensions and proportions controlled by a complex formula devised by the American Canoe Association. The disadvantages of such a canoe in ordinary use are that it tends to plow through waves rather than ride over them, so that it will take water in conditions where a blunter, deeper canoe would stay dry; it's also less maneuverable and will feel less stable to an inexperienced canoer—the two paddlers need to be quite sensitive to subtle changes in balance; and, finally, it will carry less. The opposite extreme is a canoe that's comparatively blunt in the bow line, broad-beamed, flat-bottomed both in cross section and in bow-to-stern profile, and high at bow and stern and amidships.

It will ride the waves better, ride higher in the water with the same load (providing extra margin in shallows), and seem more stable; it will also be slower, take more effort to paddle, and be more vulnerable to cross winds. Some of the classic canoe designs of the past combined features of these two extremes: a fine entry line flaring to a full cross section behind the bow, rockered at bow and stern for maneuverability, comparatively flat-bottomed amidships for stability and capacity. A few modern builders make a hull with similar characteristics, and it probably comes the closest of any to being the best design for all purposes, but the prices are high.

There's one other matter of canoe design, much debated among canoers and canoe builders: the keel. As we noted earlier, a keel of some kind is a structural necessity in an aluminum canoe, but in wood-and-canvas or fiberglass there's a choice— and room for argument about how a keel or the lack of one affects handling. A narrow bar centered on the bottom of the canoe and running its length below the water line, a keel improves "tracking"—makes it easier to hold your course when you've wind to contend with—and also protects the bottom from rock damage. From that standpoint, the deeper the better, and five eights or one inch is standard, depending on the maker. In shallow water, though, a keel means just that much greater draft, and the extra inch can make the difference between sliding over a rock and getting stuck—or dumped. What's more, just because it does tend to hold its own straight line, a keel of any kind impedes the kind of fast turns and sideways maneuvers that are essential for getting through rapids. The aluminum-canoe builders' answer to that problem is what's called a *shoe keel,* flattened down to three eighths inch to reduce the drag in turning. Conversely, the keel-less fiberglass canoes favored for white-water use get their tracking characteristics from the complex combinations of curves discussed earlier. If most of your canoeing is likely to be on the lake systems of southern Canada and the upper Midwest, with those big stretches of windy water to get across, a keel's your best bet. And if fast rivers or a mixture of flat water and fast water is what you have in mind, you'll find the going a little better with a keel-less model.

One final point about keels: if you're buying (or renting) an aluminum canoe, turn it over and sight along the keel—it should be absolutely straight and without dents or bends. Any irregularities in the keel can add a lot to the difficulty of holding a course.

Adaptations of canoe design for motor use are outside the purview of this book, but if you want to combine paddling with a small kicker for getting across big stretches of water, avoid the usual square-stern canoe—the extra drag makes it a real brute to paddle. Look instead for what's called a wishbone stern—a narrow transom entirely above the water line. This design (available from Chestnut and from Sawyer among the builders listed below) accommodates a motor comfortably and for paddling is not much inferior to a double-end canoe of similar length and hull, though it will be appreciably heavier.

Canoe Makers

I've listed below, with brief characterizations, the leading canoe builders of the United States and Canada (for addresses and a few other details, see the Appendixes). The canoes of these manufacturers are, in my judgment, representative of the best available in the various materials and design types. I have *not* listed any makes that I consider inferior, but the fact that a particular make is not included here doesn't necessarily mean I think it's no good. If you have a chance to buy some other canoe, look it over carefully, judge it by the standards we've been discussing in this chapter, and, if at all possible, try it out—on your shoulders for portaging weight and balance, and in the water. Another simple test can be made on the dealer's rack or by placing the canoe upright on a pair of sawhorses. Check its lateral balance by sighting along the gunwales from one end or, if you're not sure, with a spirit level on a thwart. The canoe should balance exactly level. If not, it's asymmetrical, heavier on one side than the other, and will be off balance in the water as well, a nuisance at all times, which in bad weather could be dangerous. Because of the way they're made, the fault is more likely in fiberglass canoes than in other types.

In making my recommendations, I've considered the companies' general reliability as well as the quality of their products. Particularly in the fiberglass-canoe business, with its comparatively low start-up costs, small builders come and go with astonishing frequency, and their products may be available only in a limited area. All the builders listed are well established, with the reliability that implies: consistent control of quality, wide availability through dealers or directly, prompt service, meaningful guarantees, and, in most cases, a good line of accessories. All these manufacturers produce canoes that are excellent of their kind so that in making your selection you can concentrate on the main issue, matching the right design and size to your particular needs. Conversely, I've omitted a number of minor canoe builders whose designs I like, either because their products are available only in a limited area or because I felt they couldn't be relied on for prompt and effective service and consistent quality of finish.

Where to buy? If there's a dealer in your area with a good line of canoe makes and sizes, that's clearly your best bet, and if the dealer is a canoer himself you can profit from his advice. If not, you can usually order direct from the manufacturer; all the makers listed here are, in my experience, courteous and efficient in handling inquiries and retail orders. If you live near the factory, you can pick the canoe up yourself and carry it home on top of your car; otherwise, charges for crating and motor freight will add forty to fifty dollars to the retail price, depending on distance. Either way, write the makers of the canoes you're interested in, get the catalogues, and study them with care; it's a basic decision.

I've indicated approximate price ranges for the various makes with some trepidation. Canoe prices were fairly stable for about ten years prior to the mid-seventies, then went haywire along with most other prices. Those I've given may be out of date again by the time you read this, but at least they'll give you an idea of the comparative costs of different canoes.

Alumacraft Boat Co. *Aluminum.* The only canoe, other than Grumman, used in quantity by canoe-country outfitters. The basic hull design is hard to tell from Grumman's, though Alumacraft's appears a touch higher at bow and stern, a little finer in its entry line; prices (around $300 for the larger sizes) and general finish are comparable. Three superficial differences distinguish the Alumacraft product. Lightweight models (17 and 18½ feet) use a heavier gauge of aluminum (.040″) than Grumman's, making for slightly greater strength without adding much to the weight (about 5 pounds). The metal is anodized to cut glare and stain. And the company offers a choice of three

keels—standard (1 inch), cruising (⅝ inch, tapered at both ends, my preference for general use), and shoe (⅜ inch, for white-water use). In addition, Alumacraft has its own system for assembling its canoes, which may not be apparent on casual inspection: the two halves overlap along the keel line, and the joint is welded, with a limited number of rivets. The Grumman joint is butted and held together by riveted inner and outer keels. I have a slight preference for the Alumacraft method, but functionally I doubt that there's much to choose between the two. Sizes: 15 feet, 17 feet, eighteen feet five inches, with two 17-foot square-stern models.

Chestnut Canoe Co., Ltd. *Wood-and-canvas, aluminum, fiberglass.* The leading Canadian builder and the oldest (1897). The few aluminum and fiberglass models are a sideline. The firm remains intensely committed to wood-and-canvas, in which it offers by far the greatest range of hull designs and construction variants (number and size of ribs, weight of canvas, etc.)—and, in its catalogue, the most explicit and detailed run-down on construction details of any maker. Prices—$400+ to $500+ for sizes from 16 to 18 feet—are substantially lower than Old Town's (below), apparently, to judge from the ones I've seen, because the Chestnuts lack the superb finish in every detail that distinguishes the Old Town canoes. For potential U.S. customers, there are almost no American dealers, and getting a canoe through customs can be a major nuisance (import duty, however, currently 4 per cent of the wholesale valuation, is modest)—nevertheless worth investigating if wood-and-canvas is what you want. Sizes, in wood-and-canvas: 14–26 feet (the big ones designed for Arctic freight use and correspondingly heavy and expensive), plus two small, one-man models.

The Chicagoland Canoe Base, Inc. *Fiberglass.* Primarily a dealer, with an extensive stock of half a dozen makes and a good range of accessories—well worth a visit if you're anywhere in the area. The company also offers, in limited production, its own make, the Canadien, with a fine, V-shaped cross section at the bow, long decks, wide outwales (the outsides of the gunwales), extra depth at bow, stern, and amidships—design features intended for fast, dry paddling in rough waters. Keel-less, with hardwood trim. A bit heavier than many other fiberglass canoes, partly because of the extra depth

A 17-foot Grumman aluminum canoe under
way, here on a mountain-circled Colorado lake.
(Credit: Grumman Boats)

and fiberglass reinforcements at key points. Because I consider the Canadien design among the very best available in the United States for all-around canoeing, I've made an exception to my rule of general availability, but this is essentially custom building (delivery may take up to a year) and correspondingly expensive ($600, plus or minus, depending on size). Sizes: 14 feet 6 inches, 16 feet, 17 feet 3 inches, 18 feet 6 inches, 20 feet. The same builder also makes fiberglass replicas of the big birch-bark canoes used by the fur traders, and several of these have featured in re-enactments of their transcontinental voyages.

Great World, Inc. *Wood-and-canvas.* This Connecticut canoe outfitter, the best I know of in the Northeast, markets a number of useful canoe-oriented products specially made under its Allagash trade name: in particular, the least expensive wood-and-canvas canoe available in the United States (around $400, depending on size). The canoe, made by Indians in Quebec, has the traditional Canadian hull lines, in this case a little deeper in the bow than in the stern. With a double bottom and extra half-ribs to strengthen it further, it's heavier than I like (78 pounds in the 17-foot version) and lacks the fine detail of Old Town's wood-and-canvas canoes (see below), but, at the price, it's very much worth a serious look. It's built keel-less but can be ordered with keel ($15 extra). The company has a few dealers (and is itself one of the few U.S. dealers for Chestnut as well as for several top-rank U.S. builders) but offers good service on direct orders. Sizes: 15–18 feet in one-foot increments.

Grumman Boats. *Aluminum.* Think of them as the General Motors and Volkswagen of the canoe business, though, in the Midwest, Alumacraft may be more widely distributed. All double-end sizes are built to the same conservative design, with a ⅝-inch keel standard (a ⅜-inch shoe keel is available on the standard—heavier—models only). The company offers a good range of equipment—paddles, sailing rigs, car-top carriers, etc. The lightweight models use a thinner aluminum (.032″ gauge) than Alumacraft (above), but it's adequate for normal conditions, in my opinion, and at 60 pounds for a 17-footer it makes for painless portaging. Booklets listing the very numerous Grumman dealers and rental agencies are available on request; the company's policy opposes direct-to-customer sales if there's a dealer anywhere within reach. Sizes: 13–18 feet (double-end, lightweight or standard), plus a 20-foot canoe (standard weight only—115 pounds) and three square-stern models.

Mad River Canoe. *Fiberglass* and *ABS.* Like the Chicagoland Canadien (above), limited production, with a number of refinements in design and details of finishing. The Malecite (16½ feet, 65 pounds) and T-W Special (18½ feet, 80 pounds) are similar in design to the Canadiens of comparable size, but narrower in the beam. Endurall, the ABS model (for the curious, that means sheets of vinyl and acrylonitrile-butadiene-styrene laminated over a foam core), is a 16-footer, comparatively narrow in beam, high in bow and stern, intended for white-water competition; the Malecite, a fiberglass design, is now offered in ABS as well. Fairly expensive (pushing $600 for the T-W Special, close to $400 for the two others mentioned). Sizes: 16 feet, 16½ feet, 18½ feet, plus three shorties.

Old Town Canoe Company. *Wood-and-canvas, fiberglass,* and *ABS.* The oldest American maker still in business and probably the earliest builder of wood-and-canvas canoes—the Cadillac, if you like, of the canoe world. The company offers a great range of models in all three materials, though its canoe designs are generally on the conservative side. The six wood-and-canvas models are all distinctive but differ most obviously in weight (from 46 pounds for the 15-foot Featherweight to 85 pounds for the 18-foot Guide) and are available with a plastic reinforcing sheet over the canvas as an optional extra which I'd recommend. Keels are standard, but most can be ordered without. (Prices: from about $650 to about $850.) Unlike most other makes, Old Town's two fiberglass lines (Carleton and F.G.) are built over a balsa core, which increases buoyancy and, probably, strength; they're also appreciably heavier (88 pounds for the 17-foot Carleton), though in this case extra weight doesn't imply inferior construction. The F.G. has decks, gunwales, and seats molded in a single piece (with flotation foam under the gunwales), rigid enough to dispense with thwarts. Both fiberglass lines may be ordered with or without keel. Prices are a little higher than for other fiberglass canoes: $300+ for the Carleton, just over $400 for the F.G. Old Town's keel-less ABS line (Chipewyan)—vinyl and ABS laminated over a foam core, hence as naturally buoyant as wood-and-

Old Town's deep-hulled 17-foot Chipewyan Tripper, heavily loaded but still with ample freeboard (the author's canoe, here in the Mackenzie Delta, north of the Arctic Circle).

canvas—is priced about like the F.G. and is my personal first choice among the three (the deep-hulled Chipewyan Tripper, 17 feet 2 inches, weighs 74 pounds). The Chipewyan Tripper was the canoe I settled on, after much thought and experiment, for an eighteen-hundred-mile trip to the Canadian Arctic, and I never regretted the choice. The vinyl-ABS material abrades appreciably less than fiberglass and withstands impact somewhat better than aluminum. In design, the canoe is moderately full in the bow, exceptionally deep (25 inches at bow, 15 inches amidships), so that, while not as fast as some canoes, it will ride over waves of up to four or five feet without shipping a serious amount of water even when heavily loaded. The hull is rockered from end to end (and curved in cross section), a feature usually associated with white-water maneuverability but valuable in storms that call for a zigzag course (see Chapter 3). While this design requires more continuous steering than a flat-bottomed canoe with keel (rather as a nimble sports car does), the quick, short turns it's capable of more than make up for the extra effort in most conditions; it will spoil you for less responsive canoes.

Besides its conventional canoes, Old Town produces two hybrids primarily for white-water use, with limited possibilities for cruising: the Ojibway and the Berrigan. Both are fiberglass, short (16 feet or less), low, light, with long decks and sharply tapered bow and stern and narrow beam—highly maneuverable but lacking the space and capacity for much of a load. The Ojibway is open, the Berrigan decked all over, with oval cockpits for the two paddlers and a central hatch that

will hold a passenger or a small amount of gear. Each sells for around $500, and if you're using the Berrigan in the rough waters for which it's designed, you'll add another $70 or so for elasticized spray skirts and a hatch cover to seal the three openings. Besides canoes, Old Town offers the most complete line of equipment and accessories of any maker (nicely made, not inexpensive) and a large number of films and other informative materials about canoeing that are available to canoe clubs and other groups. Sizes: generally 14–18 feet in most lines (one 20-foot wood-and-canvas design), and several one-man models (11–12 feet) in fiberglass, ABS, and wood-and-canvas.

Sawyer Canoe Company. *Fiberglass.* This builder's designs reflect its founder's interest in competitive canoe racing: generally sharply tapered, narrow-beamed, cut low at bow, stern, and amidships, with an intricately curving hull cross section. The seats, set low to enhance stability, are contoured, molded fiberglass, which I find comfortable. The Super, which I've used a lot, is representative: 18½ feet long, with a sharp bow line and narrow beam (33 inches), low profile (16 inches at bow and stern, 11¼ inches amidships). It's the fastest canoe I've paddled—more conventional designs simply don't keep up—but the characteristics that make it fast also make it vulnerable to moderate waves. I like it for downriver travel (long enough, with its slender proportions, for adequate capacity) and have found it sufficiently maneuverable to be satisfactory even in narrow, rocky streams replete with rapids. Prices for most Sawyer models will be around $300 with end caps and portage yoke. Sizes: 15 feet 9 inches, 16 feet, 17 feet 9 inches, 18 feet (flat-bottomed, with a 36-inch beam and a considerable load capacity—around 1,000 pounds), 18½ feet (two different designs).

Voyageur Canoe Company, Ltd. *Fiberglass.* In Canada, a well-established, limited-production maker of high quality, using a classic Canadian hull form comparable to the one Ralph Frese has evolved at his Chicagoland Canoe Base. The Nor'Wester is a new, deep-hulled 17-foot model designed, like the Old Town Tripper, for the heavy loads (1,300 pounds) and long distances on big and rough waters of the Far North (on the heavy side at 78 pounds and not cheap—about $500). There are a few dealers in Canada, but if you live anywhere near on either side of the

The Sawyer Super, an 18½-foot fiberglass canoe designed for speed (two of the author's sons on the Schuylkill, in Pennsylvania).

border, you'll go to the factory and try the canoes out in a neighboring stream before deciding (avoid July and August, when the owner, Glenn Fallis, is generally off canoeing). Sizes: 12 (two versions), 14, 16, 17, and 18 feet; also, on special order, replicas of the old fur-trade canoes in lengths up to 36 feet.

Choosing the Right Paddle

There was a time when a paddle, like a canoe, was pretty much standard in its design and the only real question was getting the right length. That, too, has changed, and again it's the specialized demands of the racers and white-water enthusiasts that have led to new designs and the use of new materials—from which the rest of us can benefit. Today, besides the traditional, one-piece, solid-wood paddle in spruce or a hardwood such as ash or maple, you can choose among laminated wood, fiberglass, or plastic, with shafts of alumi-

num or wood, and several different styles of grip. Before we turn to the various materials—which make possible rather wide variations in design and hence in paddling techniques—let's think about the real basics: over-all length and blade width.

The old rule of thumb for length is that with the tip of the blade resting on the ground, the top of the grip should come about to your nose when you're standing up straight. Another way of accomplishing the same measurement is to take the grip in your right hand as if for paddling and reach your arm straight out from the shoulder; then, with your left arm fully extended in the opposite direction, you should be able to wrap your fingers around the tip of the blade. Either way, you won't go far wrong. The result, if you're 5 feet 8 inches (as I happen to be) will be a paddle of 63–65 inches. In practice, I like it a couple of inches shorter than that in the bow, a little longer in the stern, where steering strokes are longer and deeper.

The object here is to get a paddle long enough to ·give you maximum leverage for your reach when you're actually paddling. Since modern paddle blades vary quite a bit in length—from 17 to 27 inches or more—what we're really concerned with, then, is the length of the shaft (including 1 to 3 inches of grip) plus the blade, whatever its length. To go at the question from that angle, try a paddle out sitting down in a chair, as if paddling. Toward the end of a stroke, with your upper hand wrapped over the grip and your lower hand around or just above the throat of the paddle, both arms should be fully extended with a paddle of the right length—the upper arm straight out in front of the opposite shoulder and raised at an angle of about 45 degrees, the lower pointing down and back, a little behind your body. The distance between your two hands in that position plus the length of the blade yields the right paddle length for you. (With my arms and height, that comes out to about 42 inches for grip and shaft, which with a blade of, say, 22 inches gives a total of about 64 inches—about right for me at the stern; with a longer blade, the whole paddle would naturally be longer too; for use in the bow, I'd shave off two or three inches.) As you see, it comes out about the same as the old rule of thumb.

By whatever route you reach it, this standard for length is about right for general travel in a canoe of conventional design—lakes, rivers, some fast water. Up to a point, the longer the paddle, the

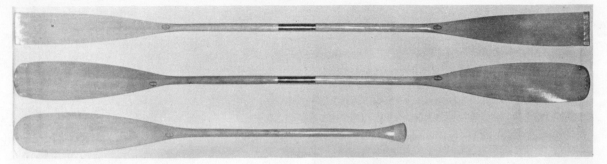

A solid, hardwood paddle of traditional design (below), with beavertail blade and pear grip; double-bladed, jointed kayak paddles by the same maker, which can also be used for solo canoeing—beavertail blades (center) and square-ended, "spooned" blades (top), both with metal tips. (Credit: Old Town Canoe Company)

more leverage you'll have (if your arms are long enough), hence the stronger your strokes—particularly the pries and draws (defined in Chapter 3) you need for quick maneuvering in rapids. For this reason, the white-water people tend to use paddles that are longer by 5–6 inches than is normal in general canoeing. The limiting factor is that the long paddle gets in the way in shallows and is more likely to be cut up on rocks or broken off at the shaft—especially if what you're prying against is a submerged boulder. Conversely, in some of the fiberglass canoes designed for flat-water racing (my Sawyer Super, for instance), which have a low profile and seats set comparatively far down, you can do with a shorter paddle—say 60 inches or less (you don't have as far to reach to the water). Even here, though, my own preference is still for a longer paddle—but perhaps that's no more than early training and habit.

How wide should your paddle blade be? If you make the dealers' rounds or study the manufacturers' catalogues, you'll find some as narrow as 6 inches, others, designed for racing, up to 12 inches (they look like wooden snow shovels). These are maximum widths—the blade is always tapered at the top, often at the bottom as well. The length of the blade is equally important: what matters is not width (though that's what the makers advertise) but area—the greater the area, the stronger your thrust through the water. Or, to put it the other way around, with a big paddle you'll paddle somewhat slower for the same forward speed than with a narrower one. (The voyageurs used paddles only 3–4 inches wide and paddled correspondingly fast —a stroke a second, which is the tempo of paddling

songs like "Alouette.") A one-piece, solid-wood paddle in the traditional teardrop, or beavertail, shape—the blade long and tapered at both ends for strength—will be from about 6 inches wide to a maximum of $7\frac{1}{2}$– 8 inches. A typical blade in this design is $6\frac{1}{2} \times 27$ inches, with the widest point (and hence the center of power) about a third of the way up from the tip. That gives you a total effective blade area of just over 100 square inches, provided you get the whole blade in the water at each stroke. That's standard for cruising and makes for a steady thirty or thirty-five strokes a minute, which you should be able to keep up all day without tiring.

Laminated-wood or fiberglass paddles don't have to be tapered at the tip for strength, and the blades can therefore be built quite a lot broader and shorter than the traditional style. A typical design suitable for general canoeing will have a blade $8\frac{3}{4} \times 22$ inches, squared off at the tip, with sides that run straight half or two thirds of the length before tapering in to the shaft: an area of around 150 square inches. Bigger paddles (9×25 inches, say, with an area of about 175 square inches) are used for racing and for white water. The boiling turbulence of deep, difficult rapids produces an effect rather like a partial vacuum, and it takes a big paddle to get enough purchase on such water to pull through it and control one's course. The big blades, indeed, make for fast, precise steering in all conditions—the zigzag course, for instance, that you'll follow to get through the chop of a gathering storm without swamping.

Apart from the advantage in steering, a big blade doesn't seem to provide a proportionate saving in effort in normal cruising. With a 140-square-inch blade, a paddling rate of 30 strokes per minute feels about right to me, but using a smaller, 100-square-inch paddle I have to up the tempo only to about 32–33 to maintain the same speed. I'll leave it to the engineers to explain why!

Whatever length and design of paddle you choose, you should have the same size blade at bow and stern. A difference at either end will make accurate steering a lot harder.

The traditional paddle grip is pear-shaped, 2–3 inches long and flaring out from the shaft (about 1¼ inches in diameter) to a width of 3–4 inches. That's the style I'm used to, but the newer, T-shaped grips available on laminated or fiberglass paddles—either straight or curved at both ends—give you something to wrap your fingers and thumb around and hence a little more control. The T-grip is favored for white water, but it's a little more fragile, I think, when it comes to poling in rocky shallows (remember, to save the blade, always turn the paddle upside down when faced with that kind of situation).

Paddle weight is worth thinking about. The range is from just over a pound to nearly 3 pounds; 2 pounds is typical. Spruce and some plas-

tic or fiberglass paddles tend to be rather light, ash or maple a little heavier. A lighter paddle will probably seem less tiring if you're paddling long distances—a statistician has calculated that an extra pound means lifting seven additional *tons* in the course of a day's canoeing—but the practical effect isn't as great as the difference in weight may suggest.

All four paddle materials have their good and bad points. A good solid-wood paddle is cut from the heart of the tree, and its elegant, traditional lines make it remarkably strong. The blade itself will abrade, perhaps split, as it slides over rocks in shallow rapids. The shaft tends to rub against the gunwale as you paddle and will in time wear to weakness—that's the point, just above the throat, where a wooden paddle's likely to break, though it's never happened to me. With a lot of use, the varnish on the grip will wear through, the wood get rough enough to cause a blister if it's not sanded and revarnished. Any wooden paddle, solid or laminated, will have to be revarnished periodically, perhaps once a year if you're doing much canoeing. A laminated paddle, made from many strips of wood glued together, is theoretically stronger than solid wood, particularly if the blade is reinforced at the center and tip; but a gouge in the right place can let water in and cause the laminations to come apart. The chief advantage of a laminated paddle is that the blade can be made much wider (up to 12 inches) than solid wood.

A fiberglass or plastic blade is generally more durable than wood (and never has to be varnished). The tubular aluminum shaft used on most such paddles is very nearly unbreakable, and if it's covered with vinyl (usual) it won't wear against the gunwale (or vice versa). The vinyl sleeve covering an aluminum shaft is important in other ways. The bare aluminum leaves its annyoing black residue on hands and clothes and will glare and be uncomfortably hot on a bright day; in cold water, aluminum's efficient heat transfer makes such a shaft feel quite painfully frigid. Stay away from a paddle with an unprotected aluminum shaft, but if you're stuck with one, taping it will help.

The weak point in all fiberglass and plastic paddles is the place where the shaft has to flatten down to connect with the thin blade—in rocky conditions it's not too difficult to split the blade at that point. (An emergency repair can be made with tape, a permanent patch with a fresh piece of

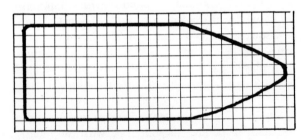

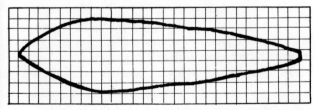

Top, white-water or racing paddle blade, fiberglass or laminated wood: 9 × 25 inches, total area of about 176 square inches (each square equals one square inch).
Bottom, beavertail paddle blade, solid or laminated wood: 6¾ (maximum) × 27 inches, total area about 107 square inches (each square equals one square inch).

glass cloth and resin, or with epoxy squeezed inside the split.)

If I'm doing much canoeing in rocky conditions I've found it's prudent to protect the tip of my paddle blades with tape. The better makers of paddles of all types will furnish their paddles with the tips reinforced with metal—copper or brass was the old standby, aluminum or stainless steel today. Fiberglass and resin are also used to reinforce the tips of wooden paddle blades, an improvement you can easily make yourself.

Prices? Solid-wood paddles run from about $7.00 to just under $20. Laminated paddles start higher and run to a few dollars more than the best in solid wood. The plastic paddles (flexible and fairly tough Cycolac or ABS) are in the wood price range. Fiberglass paddles start near the top of that range and can run as high as $40–50 for a deluxe, small-production make. All things considered, I'd stick to one of the better wood paddles with a pear-shaped grip for general canoe travel. For travel in rivers with a few rapids mixed in, I incline toward fiberglass for the sake of the bigger blade and some advantage in wear. Some form of T-grip helps with the precise and subtle steering you need in fast water.

There's one other type of paddle you may sometime be glad to know of: the double blade. It's primarily for getting around in a kayak, but if you want to travel any distance by yourself in a 16- or 17-foot canoe, you'll find the going a lot easier with a double blade than with a single paddle. Normal lengths are 8–9 feet, prices roughly double those for a comparable single-bladed paddle in laminated wood or fiberglass. Those who use them usually prefer to have the two blades set at right angles to each other, and most are jointed in the middle so they can be taken apart for carrying, portaging, or storage. Designs and materials vary even more than in single-blade canoe paddles, but I'd stick with those of the canoe builders in preference to the more extreme (and expensive) makes that are really meant solely for kayak use.

Several of the leading canoe builders make their own paddles, and a few manufacturers specialize in paddles. Here's a run-down of what's available (see Appendixes for addresses).

Cannon Products, Inc. A fairly good, low-priced paddle (about $7–8.00) with an ABS blade, pear-shaped grip, and shafts in bare, anodized aluminum (Featherlite, about 2 pounds) or wood (Wild-

wood, a few ounces heavier); these are good prices, but the aluminum shafts should be taped for serious use. The standard, 8-inch-wide blade has an area well over 100 square inches, the 9-inch blade (Magnum) an area of 140 square inches. Lengths 4½, 5, 5½ feet. Also, double-bladed paddles (7, 8, 9 feet) at about $15.

Clement Paddles. Laminated spruce blades and shafts with hickory reinforcement and cedar grips, weights under 2 pounds for most sizes. Paddles with blades of traditional shape but squared tips, with pear-shaped grips, are available with 6×26 and 7×26-inch blades (area over 100 square inches) in lengths 54–68 inches in one-inch increments (about $13); a bigger paddle of the same design (8×26-inch blade) is offered in lengths 58–72 inches (about $16). There are also two Clement T-grip paddles (blades 8×26 and 9×22 inches) in lengths 54–72 inches (about $18); and three extra-wide, heavily reinforced racing paddles with pear grips (about $20+, 8×22, 9×22, 10×22 inches, lengths 48–62 inches). Double-bladed paddles, too.

Grumman Boats. Hardwood (white-ash) paddles with a 6-inch-wide blade of traditional shape and pear-shaped grip, in lengths 4½–6 feet; and an inexpensive ABS-bladed paddle with aluminum shaft and pear-shaped grip (7¼×20-inch blade, 115 square inches), similar to the Cannon but a little smaller (about $7.00). I dislike the Grumman plastic paddles I've used: the grip is molded with a sharp ridge that will blister your thumbs.

Iliad, Inc. The best of the fiberglass paddles, also the most expensive (about $45 with shipping). Vinyl-covered shaft, modified T-grip. Most suitable for general canoeing: the 8¾×22-inch blade (area about 140 square inches), but there are two bigger sizes designed primarily for white water. Lengths 51–72 inches, and special lengths can be ordered; aluminum or stainless-steel tips (an optional extra the maker says is not strictly necessary, but I'd get it). In the past, Iliad paddles have been a bit heavy (over 2 pounds), but in current production a lighter alloy in the shaft has shaved off several ounces with, apparently, no reduction in strength.

Old Town Canoe Company. Spruce (under 2 pounds) and stronger ash (2¼ pounds) of tradi-

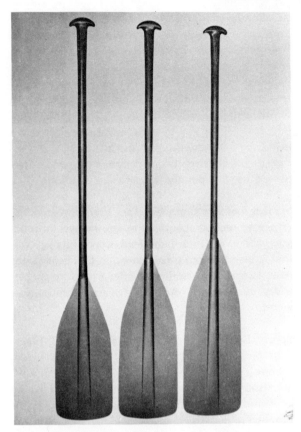

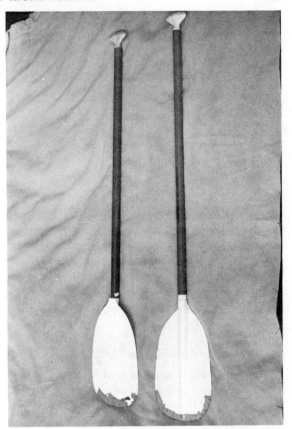

Iliad fiberglass paddles in three blade sizes, all with T grip: (left to right) 8¾ × 22 inches, 8¾ × 25 inches, 8¾ × 28 inches. This expensive, heavily built paddle features two useful refinements: the entire shaft is vinyl-covered and, above the throat, is oval in cross section for a firm and comfortable grip. (Credit: Iliad, Inc., John T. Urban)

The Sawyer Kruger Perma-Paddle, with modified T-grip and blade 9½ × 16½ inches, the lightest fiberglass paddle currently available. Note that in this design the shaft is attached to one side of the blade; the flat surface is the power side in paddling. (Both paddles, the author's, have been reinforced with tape at the blade tips for protection against abrasion by rocks.)

tional design, with pear-shaped grips, in blade widths of 6½ and 7¾ inches (actually, I measured the smaller blade at 6¾×27 inches, area 104 square inches). Lengths from 48 to 72 inches, in 3-inch increments. Not cheap ($15–20) but reliable and well finished. Also what they call a white-water paddle: fiberglass blade, aluminum shaft, T-grip, blade about 7½×22 inches, lengths 56–68 inches in 2-inch increments ($28). Also, double-bladed paddles in wood and fiberglass.

Sawyer Canoe Company. Unusual design, strong and quite light (about 1½ pounds), beautiful to look at and nice to use: ash shaft, laminated-cedar grip and blade (fiberglass-covered, with solid fiber-

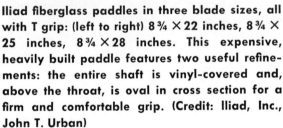

glass tip as a $5.00 optional extra). Blades 8, 10, and 12 inches wide by about 22 inches long ($15, $16, and $17, respectively), lengths 50–60 inches (O.K. in the low-cut, Sawyer canoes, but a little short, in my view, in a canoe with higher sides). Pear-shaped grips are standard, but T-grips can be ordered at the same prices. This company also makes the Kruger Perma-Paddle—an exceptionally light (just over a pound) fiberglass paddle (9½×17-inch blade, 100 square inches) with a pear-shaped grip and vinyl-covered aluminum shaft, same lengths as the others (about $20). I find the light weight and comparatively small blade particularly advantageous against waves, wind, or current, conditions that call for a fast

Moderate-priced fiberglass paddles (blades 8 X 22 inches) made by Sports Industries, with pear-shaped grip (l.) and T-grip (r.); these are the paddle lengths the author prefers at bow and stern, respectively, for a canoe of average depth.

stroke; the thin, flexible blade is fragile—carry tape and epoxy or resin for repairs if you're taking this paddle on a trip—but the light construction is worth the extra care it requires. The paddle was designed by Verne Kruger for a trip from Montreal to the mouth of the Yukon River, about eight thousand miles, one of the longest canoe distances ever traveled in a single season; I used the paddle myself on a substantial part of the same route. Although unconventional in design, this paddle has proved itself under the most varied conditions.

Smoker Lumber Company, Inc. Traditional design (6½ X 27 inches, about 107 square inches) in solid ash (about $15) or laminated wood (about half that); lengths from 6 feet down, in half-foot steps. Also, two racing paddles (blades 8 and 10 inches wide, about $20). All prices vary with paddle length.

Sports Equipment, Inc. A medium-priced fiberglass paddle (about $16) with 8 X 22-inch blade (about 150 square inches), vinyl-covered aluminum shaft, pear-shaped or T-grip. Very heavily built and seemingly indestructible, but the weight (about 2.4 pounds) and the thick shaft of heavy-gauge aluminum get tiring toward the end of a hard day of paddling. Lengths 48–66 inches.

Chapter 3

HANDLING YOUR CANOE

Back in the days when I was learning to ski, the *Schilehrer,* in his Germanic English, was constantly barking at his charges, "Ski in control!" Signs dotted around the warming hut underscored the point. Much the same idea applies to canoeing, too: *Canoe in control.* Learn to handle your canoe in all the conditions you're likely to encounter, so that it does what *you* want it to do, with ease and safety—not the other way around. That's the goal that will engage us in this chapter.

The chances are that sometime or other, perhaps at a summer camp, you learned something about paddling a canoe, if only to pass one of those water-safety tests. Perhaps you made a canoe trip or two, back then or since, or you've tried levering a rented hulk around a pond in a city park. If so, you can skim any of the following basics that you already know. Remember, though, that the technique of canoeing does keep evolving and, we hope, improving, along with the canoes and paddles it's done with. Personally, I like hearing and reading others on matters I think I know, on the chance of picking up something new or seeing a familiar aspect from a fresh viewpoint. I hope you will, too.

We'll start at the beginning: getting your canoe into the water and yourself into it—and out again.

Getting In and Out

Both the canoe and the paddle are made up of parts, which have names. So that we can talk about handling them, we need to be clear about what these terms mean (see the diagram below.)

Like any other boat, a canoe has a *bow* (front) and a *stern* (back). Bow and stern are each usually covered by a short *deck,* which may be extended in canoes designed for white-water use; some recent designs are fully decked (see Chapter 2), with small cockpits for the two paddlers. *Gunwales* ("gunnels") run from bow to stern along the tops of the sides and are braced by one to three *thwarts* placed laterally between the gunwales—the longer the canoe, the more thwarts it will have. If you have to portage the canoe, you'll use a *yoke,* either mounted on the center thwart or positioned just in front of it and attached to the gunwales. Wood-and-canvas and aluminum canoes are built up symmetrically from a shallow *keel,* running along the bottom from just behind the bow to just in front of the stern; while the function of the keel is primarily structural, it has some effect on handling and stability, though just how much is a much debated matter among the various builders (see Chapter 2). Such keeled canoes are usually strengthened with internal *ribs* running from the keel up the sides to the thwarts. Nearly all canoes have *seats* of some kind mounted between the thwarts at bow and stern, though some purists prefer to paddle from a kneeling position and most canoers will take to their knees in difficult white water—not necessarily to say their prayers but to lower the center of gravity.

The paddle has a *handle,* or *grip,* at the top, and a wide, thin *blade* at the business end. Between the two is the *shaft.* The reinforced place where the blade narrows into the shaft is called the *throat.*

The easiest way to get a canoe into the water is for two persons to take it between them. With the canoe right side up and pointing toward the water, you stand on opposite sides at the center, facing each other, and lift the canoe by the gunwales, with your hands on either side of the center thwart or yoke so that it balances. Then walk toward the

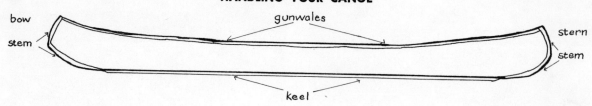

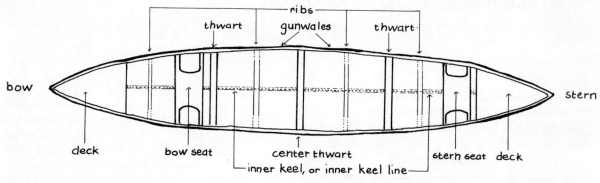

The parts of a canoe: above, side view; below, view from above.

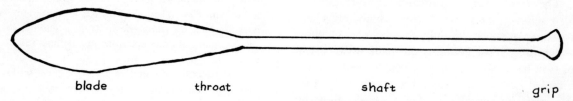

The parts of a paddle: traditional solid-wood design, with beavertail blade and pear-shaped grip, or handle.

water, lower the bow into the water so that it floats, and work your way hand over hand along the gunwales toward the stern until almost the whole length of the canoe is in or over the water. One person then places one hand under the stern for support and with the other takes hold of a thwart or the near gunwale and swings the bow in until the canoe is parallel to the bank, when he sets the stern in the water. One person can do this, too. Standing at the middle of the canoe, lift it by the near gunwale and center thwart so that the bottom of the canoe rests on your knees and you're balanced in a half-sitting position, leaning back. Then side-step toward the water, lower the bow into the water, and work your way back toward the stern,

as before. Either way, have your paddles where you can reach them as you hold onto the canoe, so that you won't have to run back to get them while your canoe drifts gently into the sunset.

The canoe can be launched sideways, saving a little time, if there are no shrubs, trees, or big rocks in the way—on a beach, for instance. Two people align the canoe with the shore, then lift at bow and stern. One person will balance the canoe on his knees the same as for an end launch, walk it to the water's edge, then lower the far side till it floats, while gently easing the near side off his knees, holding it by the near gunwale.

Ideally, for loading the canoe and getting in you'll have a soft bank with enough water to float

One-man end launch: lift the canoe onto the knees, and side-step toward the water . . .

Lower one end of the canoe into the water so it floats . . .

Then pass the canoe along by the near gunwale until it's fully afloat.

Two-man end launch: lift the canoe on either side from the middle, lower one end till it floats, then pass the canoe, along the gunwales, into the water.

One-man side launch: lift the canoe onto the knees parallel with the bank, walk it to the water's edge, and slide it down broadside into the water.

Two-man side launch: holding the canoe at either end, lower it gently into the water—quicker and more convenient for loading if the bank is clear enough to permit this method.

Loading: one partner holds and steadies the canoe while the other loads, lifting pack by the top flap and sliding it gently down the gunwale; the load should be distributed so the canoe is trim at bow and stern.

Boarding: the bowman usually boards first, holding his paddle, keeping low and grasping the gunwales for balance while his partner holds and steadies the canoe.

the canoe and no rocks or logs to put scratches or worse on the bottom of the canoe. Then, while one paddler squats in the middle to hold and steady the canoe, the other loads. Being symmetrical, the canoe will float exactly level, when it's empty, and that's about how you want it when loaded; distribute your gear or passengers from bow to stern and side to side so they'll balance. The bow seat is a little farther from the bow than the stern seat is from the stern, with the result that if both paddlers are the same weight the canoe will be a little higher in the bow. That's fine for flat water if there are no waves or wind to contend with. If you're going to be mostly in fast or white water, the canoe will handle more easily if it's exactly balanced—compensate by moving some of your load forward or back.

With the canoe loaded, you're ready to get in—bowman first while his partner steadies the canoe. Paddle in hand, step to the far side of the canoe, keeping low, with your other foot on the bank and grip the outside gunwale to help your balance; or steady yourself and the canoe by bracing the paddle blade on the lake or river bottom, on the far side of the canoe. Then take hold of the near gunwale with your other hand, lift your other foot into the canoe, and take your seat. You can then use your paddle to hold the canoe in place while your partner gets in, moving in the same style, and shoving off as he lifts his foot into the canoe.

Not all landings are open and easy, of course.

With obstructions in the form of rocks or fallen trees, you may have to stick the canoe out into the water at an angle from the shore and load from the stern. In that case, rest the tip of the stern on the bank while the sternman braces it between his knees. Have your packs within reach. Then the bowman steps in, lays his paddle in the bow, and the sternman passes him the packs. The man in the canoe keeps low, feet wide. To minimize movement, I generally set one pack at a time on the stern seat, where the bowman can reach it; he then shifts it forward into position, resting it on the thwarts along the way. By the time all the packs are in and he's in his seat, the stern should lift free of the bank. Then, if you're the sternman, you can lift it gently forward, stepping over the stern and shoving off as you do so. Don't forget your paddle!

In getting into or out of a canoe or moving around in it once you're out on the water, you're making use of a couple of basic physical facts: the canoe's symmetry and your own—which is what balance is all about. When you move, balance a foot on one side against a foot on the other, a hand steadying you on one gunwale against a hand on the other; that way, you'll keep your head and torso in balance and where they belong, low and directly over the keel. Once in and on your way, avoid sudden, excitable movement. Perhaps a sudden gust wafts your hat or drinking cup into the water—don't lunge for it! Your partner in the stern can pick it up as it floats past or circle gently back to retrieve it before it sinks. While caution

Shoving off: with the bowman in place, his paddle at the ready, the sternman shoves the bow out from the shore, then steps in, holding his paddle, and pushes off with the other foot.

Changing position in the canoe: keep low, with hands on both gunwales for balance.

and control are in order, you needn't be afraid of the canoe. It will probably feel, if you're not used to it, tippier than it really is: it moves with your movement, like a living creature, leans with you as you lean over the side to get a drink or study a water flower—and then pops upright again. In a lifetime of canoeing, I've never managed to upset a canoe—except once, on purpose, at a summer camp, and then it proved to be surprisingly difficult.

Landing the canoe and getting out are, as you'd expect, pretty much the reverse of getting in and shoving off. To avoid the scrapes of a fast and hard landing, the bowman stops paddling ten or fifteen feet from the shore and holds his paddle ready to fend off rocks or logs and bring the canoe to a gentle stop. Generally, the paddle should be inverted when used in this way, since a rock concealed beneath a rippling surface might break the blade: for this final landing maneuver, use the grip end, *not* the blade. From the stern, I like to take the canoe in on a smooth arc so that it comes up broadside to the landing place. Steadying himself on his paddle, the bowman can then get out and hold the canoe for his partner. Unless you're landing on a soft, gently sloping bank or a sandy beach, you'll do best to load and unload while the canoe is fully afloat, to avoid possible damage. Don't walk in the canoe when it's drawn up on land. It's not that it isn't tough, but you may add some needless dents that will mean weak spots and trouble later on.

Landing: the bowman stops paddling and up-ends his paddle to pole with the grip while the sternman steers the canoe in to the bank.

Seats and Stability

Seated in the canoe, brace your feet and legs so that your knees won't stick up in the way of your paddle strokes and you won't slide around on the seat as you paddle, wasting energy. In a canoe of normal dimensions, I mostly tuck my feet under the seat, crossed at the ankles, toes firm against the bottom of the canoe. If you tire of that position, you can extend one leg (the one opposite the side you're paddling on), bracing with your foot against a pack or the side of the canoe. Beginners tend to slide over to the side they're paddling on, lean out with each stroke. Don't. The movement makes it harder for your partner to paddle and sets up a side-to-side tipping of the canoe that could be dangerous. With a little practice, you become astonishingly sensitive to the canoe's lateral balance. If your partner leans to one side, you lean a little to the other to compensate. As you reach forward to stow a paddle or get out a camera for a picture, you grip the gunwale with your other hand, maintaining equilibrium. All these little movements soon become automatic, very much as in the complex balancing act that a child masters as it learns to walk. Indeed, the two processes are much alike, with the difference that a canoe is a simpler, more

elegantly symmetrical body than the human one—its shape is naturally in balance and will stay that way if you let it.

In a modern canoe, the seated position is the norm for both comfort and stability, and that's the assumption behind most of what I have to say about paddling later in this chapter. In rough water, though, you can reduce the chances of spilling by shifting to a kneeling position, lowering your center of gravity slightly. Given the purpose, a low kneeling position is best: leaning back on your heels, back and buttocks braced against the seat.

On a canoe trip, most of your travel will be in a loaded canoe—another assumption underlying my views on canoeing technique. An empty or lightly loaded canoe—as it will be if you take off for a day's fishing and exploration or a weekend of downriver paddling—is a different proposition, appreciably less stable. In that case, one or another kneeling position is very much in order. The low kneeling position is the most comfortable, but your strokes will be stronger from an upright kneeling position. Even better is the one-knee position favored by canoe racers: you kneel on the side you're paddling on, the other knee up and braced well forward, the torso erect; your whole body should

Leg and foot positions for paddling: both feet tucked under seat, knees down and out of the way.

Leg and foot positions for paddling: a change, one foot under the seat, the other forward, braced against the bottom of the canoe.

Low kneeling position, which may be advisable in rough water but is not the norm in modern canoes designed for seated paddling.

One-knee position: best for balance and a strong stroke in an empty canoe; both paddlers are positioned near the middle and pivoted slightly toward their paddle sides.

be rotated slightly toward the paddle side, and the two paddlers will be balanced toward opposite gunwales. The purpose of kneeling in a lightly loaded canoe is not only to lower the center of gravity but to shift the two paddlers forward or back to suit various wind and water conditions. Generally, and particularly in rough water, the canoe will handle best if both paddlers kneel within a foot or two of the center thwart. If you canoe much by yourself, the one-knee position near the center thwart will be best for balance and efficiency.

If you paddle any distance on your knees, you'll want to pad them—with a small pack, a spare life jacket. For more permanent kneeling pads, see the suggestions in Chapter 4.

Basic Paddling Strokes

When it's moving forward, a canoe turns from the back as if on a pivot directly under the sternman. This fact defines the quite different roles of the two paddlers. The bowman has comparatively little control over the direction in which the canoe moves. His job in essence is to supply motor power—and serve as lookout. From where the sternman sits, he often can't see obstructions directly ahead, especially on a bright day, with the sun glittering on the water. The bowman needs to keep his eyes open and call out any dangers he sees coming up—or shove off with his paddle from the big rock that suddenly looms just below the sur-

face, before the canoe comes to a grinding straddle on top of it. The sternman, in contrast, picks the course and has, or should have, full control over the direction of movement. These differences mean that the two canoers use a different repertory of strokes. If you're new to canoeing, you'll study these strokes and master them—in smooth water— separately, but in practice they're not so distinct: as you travel by canoe, you see every movement with your eyes, feel it with your body. Your progress through water is a matter of constant subtle adjustment to the motion of your canoe, and as you make those adjustments one stroke shades into another.

Paddling Bow. If you're paddling on the left side, place your right hand over the end of the grip— *not* around the shaft below the grip—and take the shaft in your left hand just above the throat so that your left arm is about at a right angle to the blade. Paddling on the right, you reverse the grip— left hand on the grip, right hand on the shaft. From either side, you reach and lean forward as you take the stroke so that the paddle blade enters the water at or in front of the bow and at a right angle to the surface of the water and the keel of the canoe. Then pull back with both arms in a strong, smooth movement—the resistance you feel is the canoe pulling forward through the water. As you make the stroke, the paddle will naturally pivot on your lower hand until the blade is pointing back and down, a little behind you. Then bring the blade out in a sharp swing forward for the next

Bow stroke: leaning forward just before start of stroke, lower arm straight, hand gripping the paddle at the throat.

Bow stroke: start, leaning forward, arms straight, lower hand gripping the throat loosely to adjust to changing angle throughout the stroke.

stroke. As you do this, rotate the paddle forward with your upper hand so that the blade travels parallel to the water. This is called *feathering* and saves resistance when you're traveling against the wind—enough to be worth making it a habit even on calm days.

Which side you paddle best doesn't seem to be affected by whether you're right- or left-handed, but you do need to practice this basic stroke until you can do it equally well, with equal strength, on either side. There will be water situations in which you *have* to be able to paddle on one side or the other, and if your upper arm and shoulder tire over a long stretch of paddling, a switch to the other side comes as a welcome relief. When you change sides, you'll also be changing the position of your hands: as you bring the paddle out at the end of the stroke, swing the blade up and forward with the lower hand so as to clear the bow; at the same time, grasp the paddle throat with the other hand and slide what was the lower hand up the shaft to the grip. You should be able to change sides gracefully, without missing a stroke.

After much thought and experiment, I find that the strongest, least tiring stroke is made with both arms straight, or nearly so, throughout the stroke (the upper elbow may bend slightly). It helps, too, to keep the shoulders straight, not hunched, the torso erect, so that your lungs fill freely with every breath. The grasp of the upper hand should be firm, fingers over the grip, thumb around the shaft, to control the angle of the paddle blade through the water; the lower hand should be loose and

relaxed, since the angle of the paddle at that pivotal point above the throat changes constantly throughout the stroke. "Long and strong" is a good bowman's motto: with the hands as far apart as possible for maximum leverage, reach as far forward as you can, pull hard against the water, and bring the blade back as far as you can reach while keeping the arms straight.

As bowman, you set the pace—you can't see what your partner's doing, but he can see you and will try to match his rhythm to yours. How fast? It depends somewhat on the size of the paddle blade and the kind of water you're in. For normal flatwater canoeing, I favor a long, steady, strong pull, about one stroke every two seconds (which probably sounds faster than it is). Against wind or strong current—sometimes it seems that, like Alice, you need all the paddling you can do to stay in one place—you'll tend to paddle slower, adjusting to the greater resistance you feel, but *don't:* that's the time to raise the beat. Conversely, riding a downriver current, you can often slow down and let the water do your work for you.

To slow the canoe or back off from a danger spot or out from an awkward landing place, you need to be able to *back-paddle,* which is simply the reverse of the basic stroke. Reach the paddle backward and put it into the water about in line with your seat, then push it forward and bring it out. This back stroke will also tend to turn the bow of the canoe toward the side on which you're paddling, and you can use it, therefore, to help your sternman make a turn a little faster, if need be.

Bow stroke: near end, the blade well back, both arms straight.

Feathering the blade: the blade is turned flat to cut wind resistance as it returns for the next stroke.

While the bowman really needs only his two basic strokes, forward and back, there are a couple of others the canoe traveler can borrow from the technique of white water. They're called the *draw* and the *pry,* and are essentially bow turning strokes, used in fast currents when you need to get out of the way of trouble *fast* and the sternman can't see what's coming as well as you can from the bow. In such waters, in fact, you reverse the normal flat-water situation: the bowman may not set the basic course, but he does make the small quick adjustments, and when he swings the bow in one direction or the other, his partner must follow his lead.

To make the *draw,* reach the paddle out away from the canoe, keeping the blade parallel to the keel and, as you set it into the water, pull it toward you. This will swing the bow *toward* the side on which you're paddling.

You can think of the *pry* as the reverse of the draw—putting the blade into the water next to the canoe and pushing it away, keeping the paddle nearly vertical; or (as the name implies) as a levering movement, where the lower hand holds a nearly fixed position near the side of the canoe (or on the gunwale) and serves as a fulcrum while the upper hand moves toward you. The stroke is done both ways and serves to swing the bow *away from* the side you're paddling on.

As with your other basic strokes, you need to be able to do both the pry and the draw equally well on either side. Moreover, since the times you need them will be in fast-moving water where quick re-

Don'ts: the bent arms, short grip, and slumped back all make for a weak and tiring stroke.

actions can save you a ducking—or worse—it's worth learning to do them both with your hands reversed from the normal (right hand above, left hand below, when you're paddling on the *right* side—and vice versa). That way, in a pinch, you can switch sides without changing the position of your hands—saving a fraction of a second that might just be vital.

Paddling Stern. If you were paddling by yourself at the stern, using the basic bow stroke, each stroke would swing the bow ten or fifteen degrees away from the side you're paddling on. This is the effect

Back stroke, at bow: reach well back and draw the blade forward through the water, slowing the canoe and turning the bow toward the paddle side.

Pry stroke: one technique, here using the gunwale as a fulcrum to push the blade away from the canoe, turning the canoe (at the bow) away from the paddle side (or do the stroke as a draw in reverse, pushing the blade away from the canoe without touching the gunwale and keeping the shaft vertical).

Draw stroke: turn the blade parallel to the line of travel, reach out, and pull the blade through the water toward the side of the canoe, making for a fast turn (at the bow) toward the paddle side.

of the leverage mentioned earlier. You compensate for this by paddling on the opposite side from your bowman and timing your strokes to his, but that's usually not enough. Unless you correct for your extra leverage, the canoe will travel in circles, going nowhere. The solution is to combine the strong, forward-moving pull of the bow stroke with a subtle angling of the blade that compensates for

the off-side thrust: the *J stroke,* the basic steering stroke at the stern.

To make the J stroke, reach and lean forward and set the blade in the water vertically, at a right angle to both the water surface and the keel of the canoe. As you pull the paddle back, keep the shaft close to the gunwale, and at about the midpoint of the stroke rotate the near edge of the paddle blade toward the rear with your upper hand so that as you finish the stroke, with the blade reaching back behind the stern, the blade is turned inward at an angle of about 45 degrees to the keel line, which is also the natural direction for the canoe's forward movement. The first half of the stroke supplies the power to move the canoe forward; the second half, with its rotation of the blade (which, on the left side, if carried far enough, would make a figure like the hook of a J), balances the swing that follows from that power and holds the canoe on a straight course. In general, when the weather's reasonably calm, you want to hold as straight a course as possible—the shortest distance between two points, meaning a saving of time, effort, and paddle strokes. To do that, pick a distant landmark—a tree, a big rock at the water's edge, a point of land—and keep your eye on it and the bow of the canoe pointed toward it. Adjust each part of the J stroke so that you hold that course— extra power at the start, a little more angle at the finish, as needed. Make it a habit to feather the blade as you bring it out for the next stroke.

J stroke, at stern: start, with the blade at a right angle to the keel line of the canoe, for power.

J stroke: end, with the angle of the blade reversed as it is about to leave the water.

J stroke: midpoint, with the inner edge of the blade angled back about 45 degrees to offset the turning effect.

J stroke: recovery, the blade feathered to cut wind resistance.

Like other paddle strokes, you should practice the J stroke until you can do it equally well—and automatically—on either side. In normal conditions, you'll change sides only as often as necessary to give yourself or your bowman a rest, and when you do change, learn to do it quickly, without breaking the rhythm. When I'm paddling stern, I like to bring the paddle straight up, *over* my head,

so as not to wet a passenger or scatter drops of water on the packs in front of me in the canoe.

The double movement of the J stroke—the power pull at the start, the rotation of the blade during the second half—is not easy for a beginner. The foundation is mastery of the basic bow stroke, then hours of practice with the steering hook of the J stroke so that you can do the whole thing in

V stroke: near start, with the inner edge of the blade angled *forward*, the reverse of the J stroke.

V stroke: midpoint, blade still at same angle.

rhythm with your bowman, with maximum forward thrust and, at the same time, holding an efficient straight-line course. An alternative, which I think makes an inherently stronger stroke and which you may find easier to learn, is one I call the *V stroke.* You begin with the outside edge of the paddle blade angled back at about 45 degrees and hold that angle all through. Toward the end, check the blade momentarily and at the same time rotate the outside edge forward to slice up and out of the water for the recovery, making the second arm of the V.

Unless you're traveling in a dead calm, you may not need to steer on every stroke in order to hold your course. A head wind striking the bow at an angle opposite your paddle side, for example, will balance the turning effect of your strokes at the stern with little or no steering effort on your part. Indeed, it's likely to overcompensate, a problem we'll take up later in this chapter.

Turning Strokes. A more extreme version of the J stroke or V stroke will turn the canoe in a gradual arc toward the side you're paddling on. For a faster turn toward the paddle side, hold the blade at the end of the stroke at a right angle to the direction of travel and move it out, away from the canoe. For a gradual turn in the opposite direction—away from the side you're paddling on—use the *C stroke,* or *sweep.* Start it at the same point as

the J or V, but as you bring the paddle back, move it out from the canoe and back again toward the stern so that the paddle travels in a half-circle course through the water. For a quick swing toward the paddle side, use the paddle as a rudder, dragging it behind you with the blade at a right angle to the keel line—or bring the blade forward through the water in a *back stroke* like the one described earlier at the bow; if you have to turn fast in the opposite direction, switch sides and rudder or back stroke on the other side, a maneuver you should be able to make in emergencies without changing the position of your hands (in which case it would be called a *reverse rudder* or *reverse back stroke*).

For fast turns with less loss of forward movement, you can use the two bow turning strokes, the draw and the pry—but remember that they have the opposite effects at the stern. The draw will pull the stern *toward* the paddle—and hence swing the bow *away from* the paddle side. The pry will push the stern *away from* the paddle—and turn the canoe *toward* the side you're paddling on.

Lifting and Carrying

The basic strokes we've been reviewing are all you need to get from point to point as you travel by canoe. How about those points along the way

V stroke: end, with a momentary check to offset the turning effect of the stroke as the upper hand rotates the paddle for recovery and start of the next stroke.

Stern back stroke, or rudder: the blade is drawn forward through the water or held at a right angle to the direction of travel, slowing the canoe and turning it toward the paddle side.

where you're *not* paddling but carrying, or *portaging*—the old voyageurs' term—your canoe and packs, between two lakes or around rapids? Once the canoe's up on your shoulders, its natural balance makes it surprisingly easy to carry over distances of up to a mile—as long as you're likely to encounter. The effort—and the risk of dropping the canoe or falling—comes in getting it up there and setting it down again. There are several ways of minimizing that effort.

For a start, since the paddles are a nuisance to carry separately, wedge them into the front half of the canoe. How you do this will depend on the layout of the canoe, but in a typical 17-footer with a thwart right behind the front seat, the paddle blades fit neatly between seat and thwart, pressed together at the tips, with the grips angled back toward the gunwales, pressing against the carrying yoke from above. With other canoes you may have to reverse this, facing the blades toward the stern, or tie them in with quick-release elastic straps. However you arrange it, the object is to keep the paddles with the canoe so they'll be handy when needed and not have to be carried separately.

Since a yoke is almost indispensable for convenient one-man carrying, I wouldn't rent or buy a canoe without one. In a pinch, you can usually wedge the paddles to do the job—blades pointing toward the stern and positioned to rest on your

shoulders—but it's an uncomfortable makeshift for anything more than a short distance.

For the lifting process, let's assume that you're right-handed, hence approach the canoe from the left side (lefties can reverse the following description). Facing the canoe just in front of the yoke, lean over and grip the near gunwale with your right hand and reach across with your left to take the opposite gunwale a little farther forward (or the front thwart, if there is one and you can't reach the gunwale). Then, if you're big enough —six feet or more, say, with arms that are correspondingly long and strong—you'll swing the canoe up in one smooth motion and set the yoke pads down on your shoulders. If you're smaller, you'll do what I do: swing the canoe part-way up and over, with the stern down so that it's resting on the ground, then step backward, sliding your hands along the gunwales until you can lower the yoke onto your shoulders. Either way, once up, the canoe should balance with the stern a little down, the bow a little up, so you can see where you're going. If you have it balanced right, the canoe should stay put without your having to hold on, but it's well to reach forward to the gunwales or paddles with one or both hands to steady your load. If you haven't got the balance quite right, hunch your shoulders, lifting a little on the thwarts, to jump the canoe forward or back a frac-

Getting ready to portage the canoe: wedge the paddles into the canoe so they'll be out of the way and won't have to be carried separately.

One-man canoe lift: grip the gunwales.

Then swing the canoe up and over with the stern resting on the ground, and lower the yoke onto the shoulders.

With the yoke properly positioned, the canoe should balance on the shoulders, bow slightly up, hands used only to steady it, with a minimum of effort.

tion of an inch. Usually, once the canoe is unloaded, you and your partner will carry it between you up from the water to a reasonably level place where you can pick it up. If you're big and wearing waterproof boots, take the canoe halfway out of the water, step into the shallows, and lift as described —you'll save a little time and shorten the portage.

If you tire before you get to the end of the portage trail, avoid setting the canoe down—the effort of doing that and getting the canoe up again pretty much nullifies the rest. Instead, look for a natural canoe rest—a smooth branch growing horizontally seven or eight feet off the ground, or a pair of trees growing close together so as to form a V a little narrower than the canoe. You can then let the stern down to the ground and slide the bow of the canoe a foot or two over the branch or into the

crotch and take your rest without the work of setting the canoe down and lifting it up again.

When you reach the other end of the portage, look for a good loading place and step to within a foot or two of the water. Let the stern down to the ground, take a firm grip on the gunwales, and swing the canoe over your head to your right (if you're right-handed), lowering it gently onto your knees. You can then rock the canoe over your knees until the bow floats, and slide it on in from the stern; leave it half out till you're ready to load.

If you're using a car carrier to transport your canoe to your starting point, you can get it on and off the usual passenger car by yourself. To take it off the carrier, angle the canoe and slide it so that the stern half is sticking out to one side while the bow is still supported by the carrier—you can then

Setting the canoe down: lower the stern to the ground . . .

Then slide it gently down to the ground or side-step it into the water.

Loading the canoe onto a car-top carrier: lift the stern slightly and slide one gunwale onto the rear rack . . .

Then lift the bow onto the forward rack, grip the outer gunwale, step out from under the yoke, and slide the canoe onto the carrier.

get your shoulders under the yoke, lower the stern, and lift the bow clear. Reloading works in reverse: rest the inside stern gunwale on the carrier and slide the bow on, stepping out from under the yoke so that you can take hold of the outside gunwale and ease the canoe onto the rack. A van or camper, being higher than a passenger car, will have to be loaded over one end, resting the bow of the canoe on the roof rack, then sliding and lifting it into place, a job best done by two people.

Even a little guy like my third son can portage a canoe by himself, but, at least for a beginner, there's a certain knack to it that takes practice. Your partner can help you lift the canoe by standing a foot or two in front of you, facing you so as to see what you're doing, and reversing the movements already described (where you take the far

gunwale with your left hand, he uses his right, and so on—or vice versa if you're left-handed): grasping the gunwales, he lifts when you do, steadies the bow while you lower the stern to the ground for support, then holds the bow up till you're in position and ready to let the yoke down onto your shoulders. Setting the canoe down again at the other end can be managed the same way. (This two-man lift also works with the helper facing forward and duplicating your movements.)

Two or three persons can carry the canoe between them. Two people can take the canoe at either end, where the gunwales come together at bow and stern. You then lift the canoe and let it down so that the gunwales rest on your hands with your elbows braced against your ribs. Or, standing at bow and stern on opposite sides of the canoe,

Two-man canoe lift: the portager and his helper grip the gunwales with *opposite* hands and swing the canoe up . . .

And over, with the stern resting on the ground; the helper then supports the canoe while the portager steps backward so that the yoke can be lowered onto his shoulders.

you can carry the canoe *upright* on your shoulders, as the voyageurs often portaged their big, thirty- or thirty-five-foot freight canoes. With three people, one can take the yoke on his shoulders while the other two provide support and balance at either end. All these methods are tiring over any distance, compared with the normal one-man carry, but they may be preferable for children or small adults. On a very steep portage or one that's cluttered with big rocks and fallen trees, you may be glad of one of these forms of help no matter what your size.

The pads on your carrying yoke will be made of leather or vinyl and filled with foam rubber (soft) or horsehair (firm and durable but getting scarce). I find both kinds comfortable, but if your shoulders get tender you can use a sweater to provide extra padding. My father protected his knobby gymnast's shoulders with a cushion contrived from a pillow and an old pair of my football shoulder pads. Now that federal law requires life preservers in a canoe, you can use one in the same way.

Special Conditions and Techniques

The canoeing techniques we've discussed so far all assume that you're traveling flat water, with little in the way of wind, waves, or current to contend with. How do you handle these conditions? And what about rapids? Basically, you'll be adapting your standard techniques, but there are several little tricks that will help you do that. Let's consider.

Waves. On a good-sized lake—which in canoeing terms means two or three miles across and up—strong winds and big waves can build up in a hurry. (Big rivers can produce the same conditions.) Because of that, it's a good rule to stay within half a mile of shore so that you can get in fast if a storm blows up. In rough water, you'll generally find the going easier close to shore, where the water's shallower, the waves smaller (and the river current slower)—but keep your eyes peeled for big rocks that may be just below the surface and can overturn or smash your canoe. You can spot them by the circular ripples they make as the water rises and falls, perhaps flecked with foam. Weather as it affects canoeing is so complex and variable that it can be judged only from much experience, but a few pointers can be given. For one, beware of the black clouds and rising wind that portend a storm. If you're on the water, work in close to shore so that you can get out fast when the storm breaks; if you're on shore, better stay there till you can see what's coming—maybe it's time for making camp early and getting inside the tent, where you can stay dry. In general, on a windy day, don't judge a good-sized lake by what you can see from water level near shore: it may not look rough, but scattered whitecaps in the shallows probably mean that there are a lot, farther out where you can't see them—waves big enough so that it may be impossible to turn and head for shore once you're out there among them. If in doubt, look for a hill near shore that you can climb for a better view.

Most canoes will be safe, manageable, and dry in waves of a foot or two even when a full load leaves only six inches or so of freeboard amidships, twice that (or more, depending on the design—see Chapter 2) at bow and stern; some canoes built especially for rough water will stand waves twice that size. When properly loaded, a canoe headed into the waves lifts to ride up and over them and down the other side as if on a miniature toboggan run. On the other hand, if the waves are closely spaced from crest to crest, the canoe will slap down between them with a splash that, if they're big enough, will put water in amidships. *Any* water in the canoe is a nuisance, wetting you and your packs, but at a cupful a time it will accumulate until it can be dangerous—making the canoe heavy and hard to steer, altering balance and stability as it sloshes back and forth. It's well, therefore, when you're planning a trip, to find out in advance how much your canoe will stand. Take the canoe out near home with a load on a windy day and experiment. When you know what the canoe is capable of, you can adopt the right tactics in the rough weather you're almost certain to meet in the course of an extended trip.

With its sharp bow, a canoe tends to plow through waves that it meets head on; it gets its lift from the flaring out of the hull a foot or two back from the bow. In moderate to big waves, you can increase that natural buoyancy (and lessen the slope the canoe has to climb) by setting your course at an angle of twenty or thirty degrees to the waves. By doing that, you lessen your chances of taking on a dangerous amount of water even in very choppy weather, keeping the canoe nimble and responsive. When your intended course is down a lake against wind-blown waves (wind blowing against a strong river current can produce much the same effect), you'll have to tack, as in a sailboat, to keep your general course and avoid getting too far out: travel at an angle across the waves and away from the shore, then swing toward the shore so that you keep the same angle to the waves but on the other side of the canoe. The turn needs to be made quickly and with care; the waves will try to swing you on around, lengthwise in the trough, where you'll take on water, perhaps tip over. In rough water, the sternman must be doubly watchful—one eye on a landmark ahead for the general course, the other on the waves in front of the bow to gauge the right moment to zigzag. (Call out as you start the turn so your bowman can assist with a pry or draw.)

Heavy waves taken at an angle to the bow make it difficult to hold a course (hard work, too); the normal steering stroke may simply not be strong enough to compensate. It will help if you both paddle on the same side, opposite the one that's meeting the waves. Then, with you both using a straight bow stroke (or perhaps even the turning C stroke at the stern), you should be able to balance the wave pressure. Watch, too, for any point of land sticking out into the lake—there will be a lee, or patch of calmer water, on your side of it, and you can get into it for a rest—or put ashore to wait out the heavy weather.

Paddling with the waves behind you will be easier—and faster—but requires the same angling and tacking course as paddling into the waves. A big wave from straight behind can as easily come over the stern as one from the front over the bow.

It will sometimes happen that you'll hit a spell of weather rough enough to keep you ashore for several days. If you *have* to travel—because the vacation's near the end or you're running out of food—you can do so in early morning and again in late afternoon and early evening, and camp and rest in between. Even in the worst of weather, the wind will usually drop, the waters calm, at the beginning and end of the day. The sun, warming and stirring the air, is the factor, of course. To take advantage of the calm, you'll have to start well before dawn, when there's barely light enough to see, and by mid-morning in the aftermath of a storm the wind may be blowing hard again and keep up till nearly sunset.

Wind and Current. In lake travel, you may face fairly strong winds that don't necessarily build up into heavy waves. A following wind is a delight, carrying you along effortlessly—the bowman can raise his paddle like a sail and the sternman has little to do but rudder. Paddling into the wind, of course, is another matter. Course permitting, paddle as straight into the wind as you can—a cross wind tends to swing the canoe around and requires that much more effort at the stern to hold the course. If the wind's from the bow quarter and you're loaded a little heavy in the stern, the bow will tend to swing with the wind—and conversely if the wind's off the stern quarter and you're light back there. I've found also that with the canoe stern-heavy in a wind coming squarely from either side, it's the stern that tends to swing around, again making it tough to hold the course. The sternman will be most conscious of this and can help somewhat by sitting well forward on the seat (or by sitting as far back as possible if it's the bow that seems to be swinging); if he has a pack within reach that he can easily shift, that will do some good, too. However, since the wind keeps on changing direction, you're generally better off with the canoe as nearly balanced as you can manage. From the vantage point of a canoe, the whimsical changeableness and general orneriness of wind is the subject of an ancient joke in my canoeing family. To us, the wind is a very sensitive being who'll play tricks on you if he hears you talking about him. So we never refer to "the wind" when we're canoeing, we talk about a certain "Mr. Smith": "Mr. Smith is nice today" or "Mr. Smith seems a little touchy." After a day of paddling against the wind, you'll wish you could invent a charm of your own.

If you have "Mr. Smith" against you and are carrying a passenger, it will sometimes help to hand the passenger your spare paddle, which he can use sitting or kneeling in the middle of the canoe. It's awkward and tiring paddling from that position—the widest part of the canoe—for any length of time, but for a short spell it can make the difference between forward progress and standing still, like a squirrel on a treadmill. The same resort will also work if you're trying to get upstream against a strong current.

In paddling downriver, the general rule is to keep the canoe in line with the current. The shape of the bank and the bottom may well generate cross currents that feel very much like cross winds and are handled about the same way—it may help you hold your course, for example, to have a little more weight in the bow than in the stern. In general, you won't need to paddle hard, but make enough effort to keep moving a little faster than the current so that you, and not the river, control your direction. As with waves, the current will be easier in the shallows near the riverbank than out in the middle; and it will be slower on the inside of a bend than on the outside. Both these facts are worth remembering when you're paddling upstream—and sometimes down as well.

Rapids. Any time you're canoeing, but above all in wilderness travel, rapids are to be approached with caution and respect. A few writers have made shooting rapids sound like a lark, but you won't find that attitude among serious white-water canoers or racers. In going down rapids, a ducking, lost gear, or a damaged canoe is the least of your risks; if you're spilled into the turbulence that swirls around submerged rocks and ledges, you may come out badly skinned or with a head injury that's a prelude to drowning in the deep pools below. It happens.

Hence, when you're traveling a river, caution begins with an accurate, large-scale map that marks the rapids ahead. Study it. Have it handy in a pocket or spread open on the bottom between your feet. And keep your eyes peeled. If the wind's behind you, you may not hear the rapids till you've come too close for comfort. Remember, too, that rapids exist because there's a drop in the river bed at that point—you may see only the smooth, dark lip of the water, not the white water and spray. As you get close, keep to one bank or the other. Usually, rapids are fast not only because there's a drop but because the river narrows. As a result, the current will be slower near the bank just above the rapids, perhaps gently eddying, and you can land there with little risk.

If there's one invariable rule for canoeing rapids, it's this: never try to run them without landing first and walking along the bank to see what's ahead. Rapids that look easy from above may be impassable fifty yards down. Nor is past experience always a guide. A rapid that was easy in spring high water may be too choked in summer with deadwood and boulders to be taken. So *look it over first* and figure your route as you would at the top of a difficult ski run.

By the time I've done that advance scouting and planning, I'd just as soon portage—which is one reason white-water canoeing as such is beyond the scope of this book. Nevertheless, there is a certain excitement in going down rapids, and there will be times when the riverbanks are so high and steep that you have no alternative. In that case, in planning your course you need to "read" the water, and you'll be looking for the deeper channels where the current won't land you on a submerged rock an inch below the surface. Look for a V in the current with the base pointing downstream—it's made by a pair of upstream rocks, and if the space between them is wide enough, it's probably deep enough for you to get through. If the V points upstream, it indicates a single obstruction, and you'll need to steer to one side or the other. "Standing waves"—waves that seem confined to one patch of water—are another indication of a channel that's probably deep enough to be safe: the waves are made by the water piling up as it drops between obstructions. If the waves are not too high for your canoe to ride over without taking excessive water, that's the spot to head for: the choppiness may bounce the canoe like a car on a potholed road, but you'll soon be past it. Unlike standing waves, a smooth, dark hummock of water indicates a single big boulder just below the surface, and hitting it could be disastrous. White-water canoeists call such formations "pillows," but as someone has remarked, these pillows are stuffed with rocks—they're to be avoided.

If, in your advance inspection of a rapids, you see the turbulence of many small rocks below the surface so that there's no clear, deep channel, you may be able to let your canoe down in safety, half empty, from the bank by means of a rope, or line (the technique is known as *lining*). One person can maneuver the canoe with forty or fifty feet of rope tied at bow and stern and his partner in the canoe for more delicate guidance with a paddle; or the two of you can manage it with separate ropes twenty or twenty-five feet long. (For river travel, it's advisable to have bow and stern lines—painters —permanently attached; for ways of doing this, see Chapter 4.) But as I've already suggested, you may well decide that portaging is less trouble.

With caution as the watchword, the foregoing advice will get you safely down the kind of oc-casional fast water, riffles, or small rapids you're likely to meet in the course of normal distance canoeing. Don't, however, try anything more serious or prolonged without study, instruction, and careful practice with your partner in easy waters. In the Appendixes, I've listed some books that describe white-water technique in detail. Such reading needs to be filled out by the kind of guidance you can get from experts by joining a local canoe club (again, see the Appendixes). And there's no substitute for practice. Under any conditions, bow and stern need to work as a team, but in rapids their co-ordination becomes doubly important, and as I suggested a few pages back, their respective roles are rather different. The sternman sets the general course, but he can't see what's immediately in front of the canoe: he must rely on his partner at the bow for the minor course corrections needed to avoid obstacles he can't see from his position at the stern. Hence, the bowman must watch the water ahead—for the circle of ripples that signifies a rock just below the surface—and react fast with a draw or pry stroke, a quick shove with the paddle. The sternman must watch both his partner, assisting the changes of course, and the water farther ahead. Paddle just hard enough to keep ahead of the current, hence keep the canoe properly aligned. The keynote is concentration and the teamwork that can only be developed by careful practice *before* you need it.

It will happen from time to time that you'll have to get yourself *up* a rapids, an entirely different proposition from descending—for instance, a brief stretch at an approach to a portage. If the distance is short, the current not too strong, the water at least a foot or two deep, you'll probably manage with a spell of fierce paddling. Or invert your paddles and *pole* your way through the fast spot, pushing with the paddle grip against the stream bed. As I suggested earlier, you turn the paddle upside down to avoid cracking or breaking the blade, a point important enough to bear repeating: Whether pushing against fast water or holding the canoe steady at a landing, always use the grip, not the blade. You can use the same paddle-poling technique to get yourself through a shallow reedy stretch more effectively than by ordinary paddling, and again it's well to turn the paddle up in case there are rocks among the muck. Such half-swampy areas are part of the cycle by which nature, often assisted by beavers and their dams, endeavors to convert a lake back into solid land, and since they're likely to occur at one end of a lake, you will sometimes have to get through them to reach a portage.

For getting *up* or *down* a short stretch of fast, shallow water, the best method will often be for you and your partner to step out into the stream. The canoe, riding lighter and higher, is less likely to be damaged on the bottom, and you can make sure with a little judicious lifting over the shallowest spots. You can get out and wade a few steps with equanimity if you're wearing the kind of boots recommended in Chapter 5—high enough and reasonably waterproof. Remember to stow your paddles with care so as not to knock them out as you ease the canoe over the rocks. The only thing more disheartening than watching your paddle sail off down the current is losing the canoe itself. Hang on to both!

Poling, properly speaking, was a method the voyageurs often used to get up a lengthy stretch of rapids, perhaps to avoid a long or difficult portage. The technique is also used in the shallow, gentle, meandering streams of southern New Jersey and in swampy rivers on south to Florida. To do it, you'll need a straight, slender hardwood pole (such as ash) ten or twelve feet long, which in wild country you can cut on the bank. It should be carefully trimmed to save your hands; for permanent use, the lower end is tipped with a metal ferrule.

Poling is done from a standing position, your feet braced wide for balance, one ahead of the other so that your whole body is angled slightly toward the side on which you're poling. Two canoers may pole in unison, on opposite sides; more commonly, it's done from near the stern while the bowman keeps his paddle ready to change course or fend off snags. Poling is a stop-and-go movement. You lever the canoe forward until the pole's leaning at an angle, "walking" your hands up to the top; then lift, swing the pole forward, and let it slide straight down, brace against the river bottom, and lever forward again. Against a very strong current in a deep river, you may have to tow, or *track,* the canoe from the bank—the same general idea as the one described a few paragraphs back for letting a canoe down a rapids. (A pole can also be used for getting a canoe down a rapids that's fast, shallow, and not too heavy, digging the lower end in among the rocks and then slowly letting the canoe down to the next stopping point while you drag the pole along the bottom to keep the canoe from going too fast; old-timers call this *setting.*)

You're not likely to face most of these difficulties if you plan your canoe travel with care. Still, the unexpected *does* present itself sometimes, and it's good to know what to do if it does. Remember the canoer's motto? *Semper Paratus!* You're on your own, and that independence has its price as well as its rewards.

Emergencies

The sort of emergency you're likely to face on a canoe trip is losing or breaking a paddle or losing or seriously damaging your canoe. None of these is *very* likely if you exercise the kind of common sense outlined in this chapter. (*Lose a canoe?!*) Still, they can happen. What can you do?

As I suggested earlier in discussing rapids, when your mind's on something else you can knock a paddle out of the canoe and lose it that way—because of its shape and length, it will tend to stick out past the gunwales when you put it down to do something else. Be careful to lean it on a thwart (so you can retrieve it again quickly) with the handle well inside the canoe, whether you're lifting the canoe over a rock or a beaver dam or landing to investigate a portage or camp site.

Any time you have to pole the canoe with your paddle or hold it in position, save wear on the blade by turning the paddle upside down and pushing with the handle—as I've already said. In rapids, however, there's not always time to make the switch, and in a shallow, stony—but navigable—stream, you may be scraping the blade across jagged rocks at every stroke. Either situation will leave gouges in the blade, perhaps split it. In fast water, prying the canoe over or around a submerged rock may produce enough stress to break the paddle at the throat. For minor repairs of all kinds, I carry a role of cloth tape in my pack (Mystic tape or ordinary furnace tape), and it will probably hold a split paddle together well enough to finish your trip. Much poling with the canoe handle may roughen the grip enough to make it uncomfortable, a potential source of blisters. In that case, a little careful whittling with your knife will smooth it out again.

The obvious precaution against loss or damage to a paddle, of course, is simply to carry a spare. So that it will be out of the way and won't get forgotten on a portage, tie it to the back thwart and rear seat, blade wedged into the stern. Use light twine

A compact camp site, with the canoe turned over for the night and as far above the water line as there's room to move it (providing a back rest while dinner cooks), on a Mackenzie River beach.

and bow knots so that you can release the paddle quickly if you have to—or use an elastic shock cord of some kind. The weight of the paddle won't have much effect on the balance of the canoe when it comes to portaging. On a trip of up to two weeks, one spare paddle ought to be enough, though on a longer trip it would make sense to carry two, tied in at bow and stern. Be sure the spare has the same size blade as your regular paddles.

On the first night of nearly every canoe trip I've made in the past few years, while the lapping waters lull me to sleep in my tent, I have a sort of half-waking dream of water rising, floating the canoe, and carrying it away. Fresh waters are not tidal, of course, but the strong winds and high waves of an overnight storm can produce the same effect if you've left your canoe too near the water; a river with many tributaries can rise a foot or two after a heavy rain, and the release of water from an upstream dam will make an even greater difference. As a precaution, carry the canoe well up the bank for the night and turn it over; that will keep it from filling with water if it rains and make it less vulnerable to being knocked about by a sudden gust of wind. Leave your paddles under the canoe, where they're handy and less likely to be floated away in the downpour.

When you land to have lunch or look over a possible camp site, everyone wants to jump out and see for himself—with the result that no one remembers the canoe until it's drifting gently away from shore. Don't forget! Always lift the canoe half out of the water (or more), even if you're only

stopping for a few minutes. If it does get away from you and you're sure of your strength as a swimmer, strip quickly and swim for it—from the bow, you can fairly easily swim it back. Or climb into the canoe and use that spare paddle to come home in style. If worse comes to worst, don't panic. Wind and current will eventually lodge the canoe against the shore again like any other piece of flotsam, and you'll be able to retrieve it, though probably at the cost of some rough and time-wasting walking. Don't let it happen in the first place!

To the non-canoeist, the possibility of tipping over is probably the biggest single source of anxiety. It needn't be. As I suggested earlier, a canoe may *feel* tippy, but that's because it's responsive. Even in the trough of good-sized waves, it can heel far enough to take in several gallons of water and then pop upright again without going over. Still, not to tempt my luck, I wouldn't start out in a loaded canoe against waves of more than a foot or a foot and a half, and if they came up beyond that while I was out, I'd head for shore.

U.S. law now requires an approved life jacket or flotation pillow for everyone in a canoe. The law also specifies that your life jacket must be within easy reach (not put away in a pack) but doesn't say you have to wear it. You'll put life jackets on your children and wear one yourself in fast water (for representative types, see Chapter 4)—no matter how good a swimmer you are, clothing and boots make the going tough, and getting dumped in rapids can give you a bang on the head at the same time. Even without injury, water no colder than 50 degrees will rather quickly exhaust you.

If you do capsize in deep water, the fundamental rule for a canoe is the same as for any other small boat: *stay with it;* and hang onto your paddles. The canoe will right itself and, even full to the gunwales, will still support you in the water: the older, wood-and-canvas types have the buoyancy of their materials, while those built of fiberglass or aluminum achieve the same effect with sealed flotation tanks in the bow and stern. Holding on to the canoe, you and your partner can then—slowly!—swim it to shore. When you've reached a place shallow enough to stand, empty the remaining water, and carry the canoe on up—taking it out full could wreck it. After a ducking like this, a wood-and-canvas canoe will be heavy for days with the water it's soaked up, but the newer materials, of course, don't present this problem.

The rules for surviving a spill in rapids are

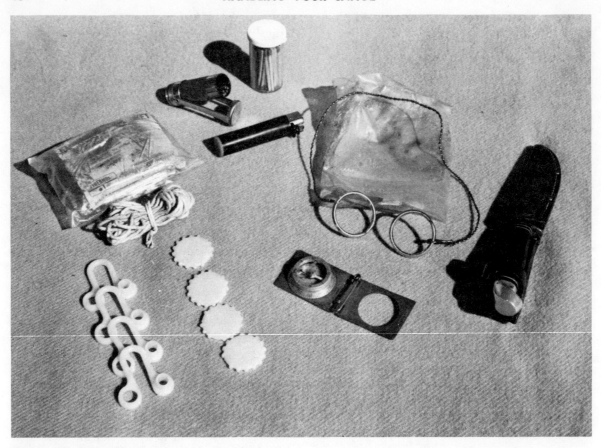

Some emergency items, most of which can be carried in pockets: (clockwise, from top) matches, in waterproof, screw-top match safe (or a plastic pillbox); disposable butane lighter; pocket **saw with plastic case; sheath knife; compass; Versa-Ties (see also Chapter 8); plastic rescue blanket (or a sheet of utility plastic, folded flat), with a length of twine.**

rather different from those that apply in the middle of a lake. The immediate threat is not gradual loss of strength from a prolonged float in cold water, but a sudden bang on the head, which may have the same effect. Get over on your back, feet pointed downstream to fend off rocks, head up so you can see where you're going; control your direction by sculling with your hands at your sides. It may be possible to grab the upstream end of the canoe as it goes past and ride it down, but on the whole it's best to keep an eye out for it and steer clear—with its weight and momentum, a canoe can be as dangerous to you as a rock, hit head on.

Unless the water's very cold or you're far from land, getting back into a capsized canoe from the water simply isn't worth the effort. Although tricky, it can be done, however. The first step is to get out as much of the water as possible. Treading water at either end, the two canoers rock the canoe back and forth, sideways, to slosh some of the water out

over the sides, then swing it completely over, as high as possible, to dump most of what remains. They then move to the middle of the canoe on opposite sides and one holds it steady while the other climbs in and then helps his partner over the side. To get in, you need a strong kick so that you can lunge for the opposite gunwale while at the same time flopping torso and legs over the near gunwale; even with help, not easy to do without taking in more water. A less athletic and perhaps easier method is to climb in over one end while your partner steadies the canoe from the other end. The canoe will be safe enough to paddle even if still half full of water, but slow—water's *heavy*. Even if you've lost your paddles, you should have the spare (one reason for tying it in). Failing that, it's possible to paddle with your hands, from a crouching position at bow and stern, where the canoe is narrowest; but most assuredly not my idea of fun!

Even if you manage to capsize, you're not likely to lose your canoe or your paddles, which are equally floatable. The more serious risk is dumping your gear into water too deep for retrieval by diving or dragging. One answer to that unpleasant possibility is to tie in your packs. My father did just that on our first canoe trip, forty years ago—for the first few portages—but never again. The nuisance is considerable, and in lake-and-river flat-water canoe travel, with reasonable canoe sense, it shouldn't be necessary. On the other hand, if you're traveling a fast river with a succession of rapids that you expect to run rather than portage, tying things in makes sense (for some methods, see Chapter 4). At the same time, your canoe can take on a fair amount of water without in fact being in danger, and your packs can get nearly as soaked that way as if they'd been spilled overboard. My personal compromise, therefore, is to use packs that shed water efficiently—and then double that precaution by sorting everything *in* the packs into sturdy plastic bags, tied shut. That way, the contents will be proof against prolonged wetting and probably buoyant enough for quick rescue in the event of an overturn. As a final precaution, I like to have a few indispensables on me, just in case—matches in a waterproof container, a compass, my knife in its sheath on my belt; also, lately I've taken to carrying a sheet of plastic (the space-blanket idea) that folds up to handkerchief size and in a pinch will make a tent, a screen against wind, or an oversize bucket for collecting and carrying water. With those few items—and your canoe and paddles—you can get yourself out of any wilderness you're likely to come up against.

If, in the course of grinding across a rock, you puncture your canoe, you can make a quick repair with the same waterproof cloth tape suggested for a cracked paddle (or for a torn tent or pair of pants or a broken boot). Put the tape over the hole on both sides and smooth it down tight—it will stick equally well on canvas, aluminum, or fiberglass. You might well add a roll of tape to your list of indispensables, tied to a thwart of the canoe. In the old days, with the wood-and-canvas canoes, we carried a little cloth bag of resin for the same purpose, as the voyageurs and Indians did before us—but never had occasion to open it. Indeed, that's the case with the other emergencies we've been thinking about. I've seen a good many broken paddles and canoes but have never lost or broken a paddle or capsized a canoe (except for fun).

Chances are, you won't either—especially if you're prepared for what *can* happen and know what to do about it.

Some Options

All the canoeing techniques we've discussed so far assume two paddlers who supply all their own power. There are alternatives.

In the quiet of early evening, you may feel like paddling out by yourself for a little fishing or simply to be alone. In a canoe of normal length (15 feet and up), the bow will be too high to steer easily from the stern. It will balance better if you sit in the bow seat *facing* the stern and paddle in that direction. Smaller canoes (12 or 13 feet) are designed primarily for one person (they'll carry two and a minimal amount of gear) and are usually paddled from near the middle. Although easy to handle because small and light, they're still slow for real travel: with a single paddle, half your effort goes into steering. One solution for one-man travel is a double-bladed, kayak-style paddle. Another, favored by some Maine canoeists seventy-five years ago, is light oars and a rowing seat, as in a single scull, and a few canoe makers still build such a rig (see Chapter 4).

If you have to paddle any distance by yourself, using a single-bladed paddle, and the water's not dead calm, you'll balance better and be more efficient in one of the kneeling positions described earlier in this chapter. The one-knee position is the strongest and least uncomfortable. In a two-man canoe, your position should be a little back of amidships (farther forward for paddling into the wind), your body angled toward the paddle side so that you can reach the stroke easily while counterbalancing with feet and legs toward the opposite side of the canoe. The J stroke is made a little differently in solo paddling: begin by reaching out with the inside edge of the blade angled forward, then bring the paddle diagonally back toward the gunwale and slide into the regular J stroke. The beginning of the stroke is a modified draw stroke, which swings the bow slightly toward the paddle side, helping, with the hook of the J, to balance your off-center paddling.

Sails? Historically, the fur traders carried sails and mounted them on masts cut on shore for an occasional run before the wind across such big lakes as Superior and Winnipeg. You can do the

Solo paddling: low kneeling position; or . . .

One-knee position, less comfortable for long distances but more efficient; in either case, the solo paddler should be near the middle of the canoe for balance.

same with a poncho tied to a pair of paddles, using the spare as a rudder, but the wind won't often be right—and when it is, a sudden gust can turn you over as abruptly as a tidal wave. Several canoe makers supply sailing rigs, some with outriggers for stability (see Chapter 4), but the cost comes close to that of a second canoe, and except for showing off in the pond in front of your summer cottage you're not likely to get your money's worth.

A motor may be worth a little more thought. It can get you fairly quickly through familiar waters to more remote areas and can be easily mounted on a bracket between the gunwales of a double-ended canoe. With that arrangement, a 1–2-horse-power motor is *plenty* from the standpoint of safety and speed (a little faster than paddling)— especially if you have to portage it; and the small

motor uses a minimum of gasoline, another problem in wilderness logistics. If you're going to use a motor much, a square-ended canoe, with a mount at the stern, may be the solution; it will carry a 3-horsepower motor safely. Such a canoe will paddle fairly well, though appreciably slower than the usual double-ended canoe, and, in addition, the square-end canoes I know of are rather heavily built, slow-moving without their motors and burdensome on portages. My father went through a motor-canoeing phase. Eventually, we decided that we preferred the silence, broken only by the plunk of our paddles, the water whispering against the sides of our canoe, and the sounds of our own voices and the loons', raised in conversation or song.

Chapter 4

EQUIPPING YOUR CANOE

Once you've settled on your canoe and acquired a set of paddles, you've got the essentials for successful canoeing. There are, however, several kinds of equipment that you'll find in the manufacturers' catalogues (or in some cases you can make for yourself without too much trouble) and may want to give some thought to. Some of these accessories are more or less necessary if you're going to be traveling much by canoe. Other items represent special adaptations of the canoe that in all likelihood you'll never try, and still others come under the heading of luxuries more encumbering than useful—like a transistor radio clipped to the handlebars of a bicycle.

Protection

Unlike most aluminum and wood-and-canvas canoes, the typical easy-paddling, low-profile fiberglass canoes, with their fine bow lines (Sawyer, for instance) are generally not decked at bow and stern—short thwarts provide structural support at those points and give you a handle to grab when taking the canoe in and out of the water as well as a convenient tie point for car-top carrying. The catch is that if you're canoeing in water the least bit choppy, with anything approaching a maximum load, you'll take water over the bow (and probably at the stern if the waves are behind you). It may be only a few drops at a time, but if you're crossing a mile or so of open water, that can add up to an inch or two sloshing around in the bottom of the canoe—not dangerous, probably, but it will gradually soak whatever's in your packs. The solution is to order the canoe with *end caps*—molded fiberglass decks about three feet long, riveted to the

White-water end cap: a long deck of molded fiberglass to keep waves from washing in at bow and stern; available for several makes of fiberglass canoe.

gunwales at bow and stern, with a raised lip on the in side to deflect water. They'll cut down slightly on usable space but will make the difference between canoeing dry and having to head for shore when the water's even a little rough (cost: under $10 each).

With end caps on a fiberglass canoe, you'll have to have some means of tying the canoe to front and rear bumpers when you're carrying it on top of your car. The handiest thing is a rope *loop* or a metal *painter ring* anchored in the bow and stern about six inches above the water line—specify it when you place your order. On aluminum canoes, such as Grumman, and Old Town's fully decked white-water canoes, such a ring or loop is standard; other makers use a *painter strap* bolted to the bow and stern decks or have a hole drilled through the decks to hold a knotted rope for the same purpose. If you don't find one of these items

Painter loop: one method, rope knotted through holes drilled in the hull, for attaching painters at bow and stern or tying the canoe down on a car-top carrier.

Painter ring: Old Town method, attached to plate bolted through bow and stern stems, same functions as painter loop.

in the maker's specifications, inquire and have it installed at both ends. If you're canoeing much in white water, you'll find other uses. Twenty or thirty feet of rope securely tied at both ends makes it fairly easy to let a canoe down through shallow rapids ("lining")—you and your partner can maneuver the half-loaded canoe from the bank—or to haul it up again ("tracking"). The same geology that creates rapids may also mean a shore line too steep to haul a canoe up when you want to take a rest, reconnoiter, or stop for lunch. In such conditions, those long bow and stern lines can be used to secure the canoe to a tree or a rock. White-water canoers and kayakers make it a point never to hit the rapids without such lines, not only for the functions indicated but for rescuing a boat that the force of water has jammed against a rock—a situation in which I hope you'll never find yourself.

If you use long lines at bow and stern, you can hold them coiled and firmly inside the canoe with rubber *tie-downs*—short lengths of rubber cord with hooks at either end (Old Town and several suppliers of camping equipment; Sports Equipment, Inc., a paddle and kayak maker, sells its own design of hooks and rubber cord in two diameters that you can make up for yourself). The same thing, wrapped around a thwart, will also serve to hold the spare paddle in the canoe and out of the way (or use heavy twine tied with a hitch that can be undone with one hand); a longer piece can be used to tie a pack into the canoe, if you find yourself unavoidably in the kind of rough water where capsizing (and losing your baggage) is a real possibility.

As I indicated earlier, I don't tie my packs into the canoe, primarily because I don't believe that, with reasonable canoe sense, one need ever get into a situation in which there's a serious risk of capsizing. Beyond that, I'm not sure that the obvious method, lashing the packs to the thwarts, would be effective; it's quite possible for the weight of the packs to tear the thwarts loose if the canoe does indeed turn over. Nevertheless, I know some very competent canoers who do tie their packs in, and if you're so minded, you might attach a couple of pairs of cleats or small eyebolts to the gunwales for the purpose, keeping them well away from interfering with paddling at bow and stern. With rubber rope of the right size (or ordinary rope), they should protect your gear in any emergency that could possibly arise.

For canoeing the rough waters of the remote North, you might think about an all-over *splash cover* to keep yourself and your cargo dry—a waterproof fabric fitted over the gunwales from bow to stern, with elasticized openings over the two seats. (One of the more harrowing forms of canoe racing was an annual marathon across Lake Michigan, inconceivable in an open canoe without a splash cover.) Old Town catalogues this piece of equipment (at the price of a spare canoe); Mad River is now making comparatively inexpensive splash covers (under $100) to fit its canoes. Unless you've acquired one of these canoes, you'll have to rely on your own ingenuity, which might include seeking help from a local convertible car-top maker.

Another bit of canoe protection worth knowing about is what's called a *stem band*. The stem is the rounded structure, above the water line at bow and stern, joining the two sides of the canoe: on an aluminum canoe, a narrow exterior strip of metal sealing the two halves; on others, generally internal (though some wood-and-canvas canoes are made or can be ordered with external stems). Since the bow stem takes the greatest impact in any encounter with a rock, a metal covering at that point will help avoid the need for serious repairs and generally lengthen the canoe's life—traditionally a brass plate attached with screws, though aluminum is now normal. A stem band may or may not be standard on a wood-and-canvas canoe; check, and specify if it's not (minor cost). Except for Sawyer, most fiberglass builders do *not* offer a stem band (the "bang strip" mentioned in Chapter 2), but I'd ask about it and get it if it can be supplied. The wood-and-canvas builders (and Sawyer in fiberglass) will also supply, as an optional extra, a similar protective strip running the length of the keel line—useful for the same reason as a stem band but less necessary. One advantage of an aluminum canoe is that it has no need for either of these extras: the metal keel and stems provide all the protection needed.

One other protective item is available from Grumman to fit its own canoes but from no other maker I know of: snap-on *gunwale covers* made of vinyl ($10–15). They're useful, not for looks or for the sake of the gunwales but to protect wooden paddles from wear. (With paddles of other materials, save your money.)

Unless you have a boathouse or a spare slot in your garage, you'll presumably store your canoe outdoors. Since I prefer to keep my canoe off the ground to avoid scratches and general banging around, I set it, bottom up, on a pair of saw horses made of two-by-fours. You can make a sturdier,

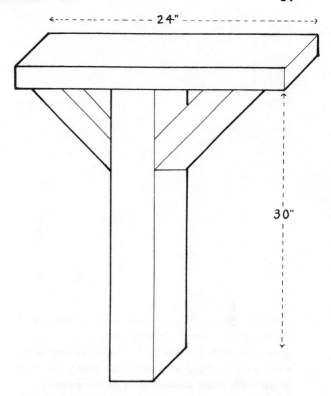

Canoe storage rack, using 2 × 4s for crosspiece and braces and a 4 × 4-inch post set in the ground; the 30-inch height is the minimum for conveniently setting the canoe down or picking it up by yourself. Two such racks are needed for stability, positioned 8–9 feet apart for a canoe of average length; the canoe should be tied or strapped down. For two canoes side by side, use crosspieces 7 feet long, with a post at either end, and omit the braces.

and more permanent *canoe rack* from a pair of four-by-four posts, set about three feet out of the ground and eight or nine feet apart, with two-by-four crosspieces about three and a half feet long (and braced against the posts to prevent warping). Either way, you'll have to tie the canoe down, using ropes or the straps from your car-top carrier—unless you enjoy watching it being lifted by every passing wind and dropped with a clunk. There's no need to cover an aluminum or fiberglass canoe. With wood-and-canvas stored outdoors for any length of time (or one of the deluxe fiberglass canoes trimmed with wood), use a large sheet of heavy plastic, carefully tied or taped around the canoe.

Paddles are best stored indoors. So that they won't be stepped on and broken if left standing in

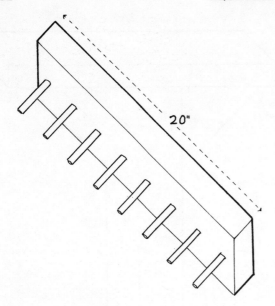

20"

Paddle storage rack, made with a 2×4-inch board and ½-inch dowels spaced 2½ inches apart on centers. The rack shown is the minimum size to hold four paddles hung by their grips, with some overlapping of the blades.

a corner (and wooden paddles have a tendency to warp), I'd suggest a rack that can be attached to a wall in the basement or the garage; make it with a 2×4-inch board, for example, with pairs of pegs cut from half-inch dowels to support the paddles by their grips.

For canoe repairs, as I've suggested in earlier chapters, cloth adhesive tape, inside and out, will do temporarily for cuts or small holes in any canoe material. For greater permanence, I use epoxy, molded in place with tape, which doesn't require clamps, warmth, or exposure to air in order to set. A small hole in aluminum can be fixed with aluminum paste applied like plastic wood and held in place with tape or fabric till it's hard, when it can be filed or sanded smooth; a big gash should be smoothed and flattened at the edges, then covered on the inside with an overlapping aluminum patch sealed with liquid rubber and riveted in place (*not* welded; the heat softens the metal). Small cuts in canvas (which will let water into the wood planking underneath) can be sealed with a waterproof cement; a hole is patched with a piece of muslin or light canvas slipped between the fabric and the planking and cemented.

The canoe manufacturers and their dealers sell cleaners and waxes suitable for aluminum and fiberglass. Unless your canoe has been exposed to one or another form of industrial discharge, hosing down with a sponge is enough to get rid of the inevitable mud and sand. Apart from looks, a coat of wax (as in the old Simoniz treatment for cars) may be slightly functional in helping a canoe slide off rocks and provide some protection against minor scratches. Nicks in wood trim (or paddles) should be touched up at the end of the season with marine varnish, preferably the same kind used by the manufacturer if you can get it. With hard use the wood may, after several years, have to be sanded down and revarnished. A major repair to a fiberglass canoe is probably best done by the manufacturer, but you can buy fiberglass cloth and resin from him and do the job yourself. (Liquid resin, which has a short shelf life, is not easy to find in retail outlets. Hardware stores may carry a resin-based waterproof cement, such as U.S. Plywood's Resourcenal, which must be mixed with a dry catalyst and takes several hours to harden—under pressure, at a temperature of at least 70 degrees.)

So far, we've been thinking only about protecting the canoe. What about the passengers? National law has now answered that question by requiring a *life jacket* (or equivalent flotation cushion) for everyone in the canoe. So far, you don't have to wear one, but you do have to keep it handy (not tucked away at the bottom of a pack). Personally, I obey the law, but I don't put on a life jacket myself or expect other adults to unless we're heading through rapids or crossing a big, stormy lake (but small children—of course). You can satisfy the law with a kapok-stuffed jacket for $6–7.00, all the flotation material packed into two compartments across the chest, like a pair of over-sized bosoms. That inexpensive type is adequate and will do the job if it ever has to, but it's a bit bulky and not too comfortable if you're wearing it much of the time. For more serious use—meaning that a lot of your canoeing will be in fast rivers and rapids—you'll do well to invest in what's called a *racing vest*, made with a less bulky flotation material (or sealed air cells) around the torso, usually with a zipper closure ($20–40+). Several canoe builders and many boat and sporting-goods dealers sell both types.

Most canoes are either naturally buoyant or are made so with built-in flotation tanks, but those that aren't need something equivalent to a life jacket: flotation bags, which are made of plastic

seat and the thwarts so that the blades point toward the stern and rest on your shoulders, but it's not comfortable for more than a short distance.) Most canoe builders have their own design of yoke in aluminum or wood, bolted or riveted to the gunwales or attached with wing nuts (hence movable); some supply a yoke in place of the center thwart, others in addition to it. Either way, it should be positioned a couple of inches ahead of the canoe's mid-point, so that the bow will balance up and you can see where you're going. The modern, foam-rubber shoulder pads are softer but less durable than the older horsehair, which has pretty well gone the way of the horses themselves. (The Canadians still seem to like an elegantly carved, unpadded yoke, which, though I've never tried one, looks more suitable to oxen than to humans.) Even so, if you have knobby shoulders you may

Kapok-filled life jacket, inexpensive and bulky but satisfies U.S. legal requirement.

and are inflated, sealed, and inserted under the bow and stern decks. Old Town offers fitted flotation bags for its decked canoes as well as for its fiberglass kayaks (about $20–30 per pair, depending on the model). Waterproof plastic cargo bags like those described in Chapter 5 will perform a similar function, but not so neatly.

Transportation

Moving your canoe from place to place begins on your shoulders. There's more than one way of doing this (see Chapter 3), but with a little practice, a satisfactory *yoke*, and perhaps an assist from your partner in lifting the canoe, you'll find it easiest on your own. Hence, even if the only portaging I did was from the car to the nearest stream bank, I wouldn't buy a canoe without a yoke; prices run from about $10 to $25, depending on the builder. (You can, as I suggested in Chapter 3, portage a canoe by wedging the paddles between the front

Old Town carrying yoke: hardwood with foam padding, clamps that screw down to gunwales so it can be adjusted or removed when not needed.

Sawyer carrying yoke: aluminum with foam padding, bolted to center thwart.

want some extra padding—a sweater or jacket wrapped around your neck, perhaps a life jacket, which otherwise would have to be carried separately.

Once you've finished your trip and gotten your canoe out of the water, you still have to get it home again on top of your car. You can make do with an old blanket or a sheet of foam rubber (to protect the canoe and the car's roof) and stout ropes carefully tied to the front and rear bumpers. A *roof rack* will do the job better and be easier on your nerves at highway speeds. Most of the canoe builders have their own versions of the basic type: a pair of crosspieces made of wood or plastic-padded aluminum that clamp to the rain gutters (or inside the window frames of gutterless cars), with straps, heavy-duty elastic shock cords, or clamps that screw down on the gunwales to hold the canoe in place. (With the belt-and-buckle type, pad the buckles with a bit of foam rubber so they won't scratch the sides of the canoe.) Car-top racks of this basic type are generally available in two sizes: 60 inches wide, for one canoe (about $25); and 76 inches wide, just enough for two canoes carefully positioned (about $35). Whatever the design, strapping or clamping the canoe to the rack isn't enough at high speeds; it should also be tied at bow and stern to the car's bumpers, and for that you can use a set of Grumman's tie-downs (about $7 per pair), with rubber-coated S hooks and metal brackets for tightening the nylon ropes. Or you can do the same job for less money with a couple of pieces of rubber rope and a set of utility

Car-top canoe carrier: attached to rain gutters with thumbscrews and metal plates, wide enough to hold two canoes; canoes must be strapped or tied to the carriers and to the front and rear bumpers.

hooks like those mentioned earlier made by Sports Industries, Inc. (and several other suppliers). Except in an emergency, *don't* rely on ordinary rope tied around the bumper or bumper guards; fraying gives it too short a life.

The car-top carriers designed for gutterless cars have a serious drawback: they're supported by metal posts mounted on rubber feet which, when the rack's strapped down into the window frames tight enough to be secure, press permanent dents into the roof. Short of trading your car for one equipped with rain gutters, you can adopt a newer idea in car-top carriers: a set of molded plastic units that snap onto the canoe's gunwales, padding them against the roof of the car (about $20 with tie-downs and lateral ties, from Crawford Industries—see Appendixes for address; several canoe makers now offer a similar carrier). They can be left on the canoe as extra flotation while you're on the water, and are short enough to be locked safely in any car trunk when you're elsewhere. The older type, however, has the advantage that the vertical support will clear a car's roof rack (if it has one) and still leave room for some topside baggage.

There's one other solution to the problem of transporting your canoe from waterway to waterway, and that's a *trailer*. That's not as extravagant as it may sound. Great World is one source for a canoe trailer that will carry several canoes, with or without a compartment for baggage (under $600, either model). Or, with a little ingenuity, you can build your own and save some money. You can start with a small, stock trailer (under $200 from Sears), though you may have to replace the hitch to get adequate clearance for a canoe; then build up from the trailer's four corners a well-braced framework to support a conventional canoe rack. The trailer itself will carry as much gear as you're likely to need. It's not that even a car as small as a Volkswagen Beetle is unsafe with a canoe or two on top, provided they're properly mounted. But if you do much canoeing with a lot of camping equipment, the trailer will carry everything and still leave plenty of space for comfort inside the car, and that's why some canoers use it.

Propulsion

Paddling is still the best way of traveling by canoe—quiet, efficient, inexpensive, and with a minimum of gear that has to be lugged around. But there are alternatives.

If you're going to be using an *outboard motor* much, you'll start with a square-end canoe. There are a number of variant designs (Chestnut offers the best choice), but, as we noted earlier, none paddles quite as well as the same canoe would with a double end. Still, with a small motor they'll move well, better than an aluminum or fiberglass rowboat with a considerably bigger motor. On the other hand, if paddling will be your primary means of travel, with occasional use of a motor—for getting across big, uninteresting water or going upstream—start with a double-end canoe and add a *motor bracket*, which most canoe builders can supply (about $20). Or, with a couple of pieces of 2×2-inch wood, some 4-inch bolts, and wing nuts, you can make your own. The bracket is mounted on the gunwales just ahead of the stern deck, sticking out to one side. Most canoe makers indicate in their catalogues (or will tell you) what size motor a particular canoe is good for, but 3–5 horsepower is about tops, and I'd prefer, myself, a smaller motor; it will still do the job a bit faster than paddling, will be a lot less painful to portage, and will consume less gasoline. There *are* gas cans that really are leakproof, but they're all a nuisance to carry, take up space in the canoe, and can't be put in a pack with anything else (unless you like the smell of gasoline in your clothes, sleeping bags, and food).

Rowing is another possibility, with a more respectable history in the canoe world than you might suppose. In fact, the first book about canoeing I ever read was a story published in the nineties about a group of boys on a canoe trip in Maine, each with a different type of canoe, and one was fully decked, solid wood, with a rowing seat and oars. Grumman and some other makers can supply a simple rowing rig at a price ranging from about $50 to $100. Old Town, in addition, sells (for the price of another canoe) an assembly with movable seat that, as they say, converts a humble canoe to a glamorous single shell. Both ideas are at least worth thinking about if you do much canoeing on your own.

Sailing is yet another possibility, though the mast has to be positioned about where the front seat is and thus excludes paddling from that position or travel with both a passenger and a sizable amount of gear. Several leading canoe builders (Old Town, Grumman, Sawyer) sell sailing rigs

adapted to their own designs—sail, mast, braces, leeboards (with the function of a deep keel or centerboard—essential for stability and direction), rudder, and necessary rigging (you *can* use a paddle instead of a rudder); Sawyer's outfit substitutes outriggers for leeboards. The prices range from about $200 to $500, depending on the maker and the size of sail. Old Town also makes a special, 16-foot sailing canoe with built-in slots for the leeboards (called dagger boards in this case). It sells for $850 and with the sailing rig removed can still be paddled.

Somewhat analogous to leeboards are pontoons, which can be mounted at the water line outside the canoe's mid-point (Grumman, about $50). Unless you have small children who are going to paddle around a summer lake on their own, however, I see no point to this particular piece of equipment.

Earlier (Chapter 3), we discussed the technique of *poling*. Assuming that's something you'll do only rarely, when getting up or down a tricky set of rapids, you can, as I suggested, cut the necessary pole on the bank as the need arises. In some shallow, meandering streams—in southern New Jersey and on south—poling may, however, be less tedious than paddling, and if you're doing it much you can get a suitable hardwood pole, with a protective metal pick at one end, from Old Town (about $16) or Great World (about $10–15, depending on length). One is enough—the bowman uses his paddle to ward off obstructions and help steer—but two-man poling is also feasible.

Comforts

The only canoe comfort that's at all necessary is a kneeling pad of some kind—if you're canoeing much in rapids, where the kneeling position is a real safety factor—and even that's hardly an essential. For short stretches, I use whatever's handy in the canoe: a tightly rolled tent or sleeping bag in a waterproof sack, perhaps a life jacket (unless I feel nervous enough to wear it). The sort of foam-rubber pad that hardware stores still sell for those who scrub floors on hands and knees is also adequate; if you use it a lot, you can cement it to the floor of the canoe, in position, with rubber cement. Or use an old cushion and cover it with a sheet of tough plastic, taped, to keep water out; or an old hot-water bottle or section of inner tube (seal the end), filled with chips of rubber or plastic foam. Old Town sells knee pads along with most other kinds of canoe equipment (about $6–8.00), and Great World has its own, less expensive versions (under $4). They strap around the knees, one each; mostly for kayakers—and an uncomfortable nuisance, in my view, any time you're off your knees and on a portage—but useful if you canoe a lot in rapids.

There are a couple of other extras you might consider, but only if you never (or almost never) have to portage. Slatted, removable flooring ("duckboards") will keep your packs out of as much water as you're likely to take on. On rainy days I sometimes lay three or four small logs (about 2-inch diameter) in the bottom of the canoe to keep my packs above the wash, but there are a few situations in which a permanent floor is functional—a trip along the shore of one of the Great Lakes, for example, or down the Yukon River in Alaska, where you'd never portage but would have rain and storm-driven waves to contend with in plenty. I would not carry *any* piece of equipment that might inhibit portaging when prudence called for it, as at a borderline-dangerous rapids. For old and creaky backs and all-day fishing sessions—or to prove to your wife that a canoe really can be comfortable—there are several kinds of back-rest chairs that you can get. Most are designed to sit on the floor of the canoe, leaning against a thwart, though some can be attached to the bow seat.

A moderately handy carpenter can make a suitable floor or back rest at the basement workbench, if he must have one. Or Old Town or Grumman can usually be counted on for some version of either one.

And that's it! The list of canoe extras is a short one and, as we noted at the outset, a comfortable yoke and a car-top carrier are the only essentials.

Chapter 5

GEAR

Clothing the Canoer

There's really no article of clothing that I'd call essential to canoeing. If you've done other kinds of camping, you'll use what you have; or make do with the tired old garments you wear for working around the yard or house. If you stick with canoe camping, you'll evolve your own preferences in clothes, depending on where and when you travel. There are, however, a few general principles to bear in mind.

Bulk, in the first place, is important. In buying clothes or packing for a two-person canoe trip, don't take more than you can fit in a single pack, and preferably less than that. Avoid non-essentials that you may never wear: you don't need two sweaters unless you know it's going to be cold enough so that you'll have to wear both a fair amount of time (and that's *cold!*). Don't take a windbreaker when a poncho or rain shirt will do the same job, probably more effectively.

In line with that advice, my canoe clothing list works out as follows for a two-week trip: boots, trousers, shirt, hat, a knee-length rain shirt, and a light sweater for the cool nights and mornings that are likely in most canoe country even in mid-summer; and a somewhat Spartan maximum of four sets of socks, underwear, and handkerchiefs or bandannas. For a shorter trip, you can cut down on the latter; for a longer one, soap the dirty socks and underwear occasionally, then tie them behind the canoe to rinse while they drag through the water (they'll dry stretched across your packs or the bottom of your upturned canoe when you stop for lunch). I also take a spare shirt and pair of trousers to have something dry to change into after a rainy day; and a pair of cotton work gloves—not for paddling but for handling hot pots over the cook fire.

That basic list, well chosen, will do for all seasons except the depth of winter, when you're probably not going to be canoeing anyway. In really cold weather, I add a second, heavier sweater and a suit of long underwear. (I've tried the fishnet style of long underwear, by the way, and found it not as effective as claimed; if the weather's chilly enough to require long johns, the traditional style is what you need, with some wool content.) I've never used the sort of down quilted jackets or parkas that are currently popular among skiers (I don't use them for skiing either, for that matter); the bulk and restrictiveness would rule them out even if the high prices didn't. In cold weather, from the freezing point on down, several thin layers, topped by a light, windproof jacket or parka, will always be more effective than one thick one. As you warm up with exercise, you can shed a layer or two and stay comfortable—and safe; over-dressed, you'll sweat, even in extreme cold, and your own sweat will have a dangerously chilling effect.

There's one other factor to bear in mind any time between about the first of May and the end of September: the billions of insects who share this planet and its waterways with us. In some parts of the continent, there are flies—deer flies, horseflies, little bulldog flies, other local names and types—that will bite ferociously if they get the chance, but mosquitoes, in my view, are worse for sheer numbers. There's nothing quite so unnerving as walking into an apparently peaceful meadow and being greeted by swarms of the little devils streaming up from the ground, covering your body black while they strain to make a meal of you. Hence, any time you're canoeing in the mosquito season, wear long trousers and a long-sleeved shirt, both of material tough and thick enough to ward off insects—*not* shorts and a T shirt; and they'll also protect you against sunburn, which on a bright day on the water can sear even the toughest human hide.

Detailed lists of canoe-oriented clothing and camping equipment are included in Chapter 8, with sources for all of these items in the Appendixes. Although we're concerned here with the principles behind these recommendations, a few items are important enough to bear special comment.

Both for loading and unloading the canoe and for support on a rough portage trail, you'll need a pair of boots high enough and waterproof enough to protect your feet and ankles. A nine- or ten-inch boot (mid-calf) is about right; a smooth sole (not lugged) won't track dirt into the tent. Dunham's in Canada and several American makers produce silicone-tanned leather boots of this type that are guaranteed waterproof, if periodically treated with silicone in liquid or paste form. Or, for less money, you can start with an ordinary work or hunting boot of the right height and make it adequately waterproof with one of the waterproofing grease or wax compounds available from most outfitters. (Rubber boots are waterproof, of course, but provide less support than leather, and I find them sweaty.) In all seasons, I like thick wool socks inside my boots (such as the Norwegian Ragg type) —they're comfortable and, unlike cotton, continue to insulate even when wet.

Except perhaps on the very hottest days, a thick, soft wool shirt (what's known in the trade as a jacket-weight material, a twenty-ounce fabric) has the recommendation of being bugproof, and it will take a good deal of wetting without the chilling effect of cotton; it also provides some insulation against heat. A good wool shirt shouldn't *feel* scratchy, though if you can't stand wool you might try one of the thick cotton flannels (chamois cloth) —mosquitoproof and fairly warm on a cool day but not so good as wool when wet.

Whatever trousers you settle on should be loose-cut for easy movement: most blue jeans are too stiff and tight for comfort; a knit cuff that can be tucked into your boots and stay there keeps mosquitoes and flies from getting up your legs. I like a tightly woven cotton twill (it dries quickly), with long underwear underneath in cold weather, either net or, preferably, wool. In choosing shirts and trousers, look for ample pockets, with button flaps that will hold whatever odds and ends of survival equipment you carry on you.

A good sheath knife with a four- or five-inch blade is useful in so many ways on a canoe trip that I think of it as an article of clothing. Most pocket knives big enough to do the job are risky to use. Buck, however, makes a couple with good blades that lock in position and can be carried in a case on the belt (more expensive than a comparable sheath knife but less in the way when you're paddling).

Since much of the canoe country is also rainy country, you'll travel often enough in wet weather to need adequate rain wear. For cost and convenience, a calf-length rain shirt of rubberized nylon is preferable to a rain suit (short shirt with trousers that go over your pants); any form of poncho, open at the sides, is just about worthless. A crushable waterproof hat with a two- or three-inch brim keeps sun as well as rain out of your eyes and is handy for anything from carrying water to fanning a reluctant fire.

Tents

As with canoes, you can rent tents and sleeping bags from outfitters in the vicinity of the leading canoeing areas. Prices are likely to come out to three to four dollars per day for a good-sized tent, half that for each sleeping bag. If you're trying the sport for the first time, it's a good way of postponing an investment till you're sure you want to make it, and it's a means, too, of finding out for yourself the desirable properties before you make the commitment of purchase. Except for outfitters for whom the rental business is a front-line sales technique (Eastern Mountain Sports in Boston, for instance), the rental equipment will probably be on the heavy and bulky side, chosen for harder and more careless use than you'd give your own gear.

Canoers at the moment are not terribly well served by the tentmakers. Tents designed for hiking emphasize minimum weight and bulk and with few exceptions are correspondingly cramped; most have the low profile that will withstand the gales you'll sometimes have to face above timberline. Unless you're canoeing above the Arctic Circle, you'll always be able to pitch your tent in the shelter of trees (even so, I always stake my tent out and anchor it to trees at front and back as if I ex-

Baker tent: a classic design now available in lightweight, waterproof nylon, with awning and zippered storm door that can be opened out to form side walls shielding the interior on a rainy day (also, sewn-in floor and mosquito-netting door, with zipper, both essential). (Credit: L. L. Bean, Inc.)

pected a howler to come up in the night—"ready for anything"). Conversely, tents made for car camping, while spacious, are likely, at forty or fifty pounds, to be excessively heavy and too bulky to fit in a pack or be carried on top of one—a serious impediment on every portage. You can get by with what you have, but if you're buying a tent primarily for canoeing, the right choice will make a big difference both in the ease with which you travel and your comfort in camp. You're looking, then, for something between the backpacker's nylon upper berth and the car camper's Taj Mahal.

The best size for canoe camping is what most tentmakers call a four-man tent, meaning a floor area of at least sixty-five or seventy square feet. It's still small enough to fit into a compact space—level tent sites aren't always easy to find—and will be luxuriously unconfining for two people, with plenty of room for bringing your packs in at night and storing a little dry kindling for the morning fire in case it rains. A tent that size allows you to snuggle a couple of children in with you, in com-

fort, and is feasible for four adults provided they don't walk in their sleep; a bigger party will need a second tent. For myself, I likewise prefer a tent high enough—say six feet at the peak—to stand up in for dressing and undressing, making life a little easier at the start and end of the day; but, as I said, I'm careful to stake it tight against overnight storms, particularly if I have to pitch it in an exposed spot.

Regardless of size or type, several features are virtually indispensable. One, certainly, is a sewn-in floor, heavy and waterproof enough so that in a downpour water can flow under it, if need be, without coming through. Another is attached mosquito netting at the door and any windows and a waterproof storm door that can be zipped up or tied down when it rains. There are still some cheap tents on the market (under one hundred dollars) that are made without a floor (they use a separate ground cloth instead) and without netting, but regardless of the price you'll be wasting your money if you buy one.

A few other features are desirable but not essen-

Draw-Tite tent: another traditional design, in the four-man Ranger size; waterproof poplin entirely supported by an external aluminum frame so that it can be set up (as here) on bare rock. (Credit: Eureka Tent, Inc.)

tial. A ventilation window, covered with mosquito netting and hooded against rain (or with a curtain that can be drawn down from the inside), will help keep down moisture from condensation in the tent. For mosquito netting and doors, the newer nylon zippers are less likely than metal to corrode and jam. And although it's not easy to find any more, I like a tent with an awning in front; it helps keep rain out, provides extra support when tied to a couple of trees, and gives you a dry spot for cooking on a rainy day.

On the whole, your best bet when it comes to picking out a tent is a retailer with a good representation of types and makes, either a sporting-goods store or one of the big mail-order camping equipment operations that produces its own catalogue; *not* the manufacturer.

Gerry Fortnight tent: a four-man nylon tent ("breathable"), with all-over waterproof fly, light and compact for its size.

Sleeping Bags

As with a tent, you don't have to start by *buying* a sleeping bag; you can rent—from the same kinds of places that rent tents and other camping equipment. Or you can take a couple of blankets off your bed, double them over, and pin them together with blanket pins to form a double-walled, rectangular envelope that will be about as effective as a medium-grade sleeping bag. This old-fashioned al-ternative is more of a nuisance and rather less comfortable than a sleeping bag, but it's a lot less expensive.

When you do decide to buy your own sleeping bag, your first consideration will be the minimum temperature for which it's rated. Most manufacturers and dealers provide such an indication—good for a minimum of 30° above zero, 20°, 10°, and so on. Bear in mind that most such ratings assume that the bag will be used inside a tent, protected against the chilling effects of direct wind. Also, I think that even the most forthright of sleeping-bag makers tend to rate their products on the

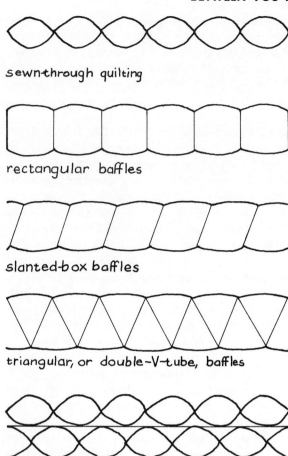

sewn-through quilting

rectangular baffles

slanted-box baffles

triangular, or double-V-tube, baffles

double quilting

Sleeping-bag quilting in cross section (sewing or baffles generally run from side to side). The five styles are shown (top to bottom) in order of efficiency, cost, weight—sewn-through quilting is the lightest and least expensive but also the least efficient even when covered with a one-piece outer shell. (Materials used for the baffle walls and the names for the different designs vary from maker to maker.)

optimistic side, but comfort is, of course, a fairly subjective matter as well. My young and frisky sons will sleep as if hypnotized in the same temperatures and the same type of sleeping bags in which I lie awake debating whether to get up and put on a union suit and a sweater; my wife likes a temperature inside her sleeping bag that for me would be equatorial. These family differences of ours seem to be typical of adult men and women and the healthy young.

For general use, I'd recommend a bag rated in the 10–20° range. It will be fine from spring

through fall—on the hot nights of midsummer, you needn't zip it up; in cold weather (down to zero or so), I put the regular bag inside a cheap summer bag and find the result just as effective and a lot less expensive than a separate low-temperature model. (In *really* cold weather—minus 30° or lower—you can't do without a proper double bag designed for Arctic conditions; costly, of course, but life-preserving.)

A sleeping bag's effectiveness in keeping you warm depends on the kind and amount of material—"fill" in the trade—with which it's stuffed. Prime-quality *goose down* is best from nearly every standpoint. It has the greatest "loft"—volume per weight—of any natural or synthetic fiber and therefore the most effective insulating properties. It's also luxuriously soft to sleep on, highly compressible (a bag filled with goose down can be packed small and will spring back into shape when unrolled), and will dry out again fairly readily when damp. The catch is that while demand for good goose down has risen steeply, production, mostly from Europe, has declined in both quantity and quality. The result is that the prices for goose-down sleeping bags are stiff, and even reputable manufacturers are tempted to mix their fill with cheaper and less effective materials, such as goose or duck feathers.

Most of the synthetic fills that have been tried in cheap sleeping bags are to be avoided, but one new one, a Du Pont Dacron known as Fiberfill II, bears serious comparison with goose down. It's not quite as effective; to achieve the same temperature rating, a Fiberfill bag will be somewhat heavier and bulkier than one made with goose down but the difference is of less moment to canoers than to backpackers. In loft and resiliency, it comes close to down, doesn't absorb moisture (wet down mats), dries quickly, and is a lot easier to wash. The great advantage, however, is in the price. Prime goose down is becoming scarce through overuse and declining production. A good Fiberfill bag will cost about a third or a half of what you'll pay for a comparable bag stuffed with down.

Between You and the Ground

As a young sprout wrapped in my Hudson's Bay blanket stretched out on a quarter-inch layer of fallen pine needles that felt as soft as a bed at the Waldorf, I rather scorned anyone who needed a mattress to lull him to sleep. Now that my bones have grown middle-aged and creaky, though, I wouldn't venture forth on a camping trip without that luxury.

There are two basic alternatives: a plastic-foam pad and an air mattress. A pad is more an insulator than a mattress. If the weather's at all cool, you need one under you to retain heat. In summer, though, you may well find a pad sweatily overwarm (like a foam-rubber mattress) and generally uncomfortable to sleep on unless you're used to a board-firm mattress at home. In addition, if the pad's thick enough to be useful it makes a bulky roll that's awkward in any pack. For these reasons, I prefer an air mattress about half inflated (too much air and it's uncomfortably firm). Apart from comfort in sleeping, the air mattress, when empty, folds flat, is easy to stow, and in a Duluth pack makes an effective pad between your back and any hard lumps of equipment inside. For a child, the air mattress he'll sleep on at night makes a dandy raft for paddling around the shallows while you're cooking dinner. There are a couple of drawbacks, though. *Someone* has to blow the thing up every night, a 5–10-minute job I try to get the kids to do (there *are* pumps for the purpose, but blowing up the mattresses is easy enough, and for the cost—and the weight and bulk in the pack—I wouldn't bother with a pump). And on a cool night an air mattress is definitely *not* warm: the air cells act like the coils of a refrigerator, drawing off your warmth. One answer to that problem, admittedly a nuisance, is a thin sheet of plastic foam (cheap, easy to pack, obtainable at most hardware stores) between you and the mattress. Luxury indeed!

Food and Cooking

The canoe-country outfitters are generally prepared to rent basic cooking and eating equipment (pots, grill, plates and cups, cutlery, etc.) at reasonable rates (a dollar or less per person per day). They'll also put together a food supply for a trip of a specified length at a flat rate per person (four to five dollars per day)—always, it seems, on the assumption that canoers are equipped with Paul Bunyan appetites; and they will, of course, fill specific food orders from whatever lines they carry, usually assisting the process with checklists you can go over well in advance. Even if you take one of these easy routes, though, you need a general idea

of what's essential, and why. That's what we'll be considering in this chapter, in the broadest terms. Later (Chapter 8), we'll get down to the specifics you'll want to keep in mind when doing your own planning, with checklists that I hope you'll find helpful.

Pots, Pans, and Other Vital Matters. All things considered, I prefer open-fire cooking to using any stove compact enough to be practical for a canoe trip. The fire provides enough cooking space for several pots at a time—a main dish, vegetable, dessert, coffee, even the after-dinner dishwater—and if the fire's properly made it will give a range of heats, from barely warm to blazing, depending on where you set your pots. Besides, it's cheery and warming at the end of the day, it smells good, and by the side of a wilderness lake its gray-blue column of smoke, rising to heaven like an offering of incense, is your signal to God and the world that another party of humans has taken up residence. At any rate, the equipment suggested here assumes you'll do most of your cooking over a fire, but it can be adapted to even the smallest of stoves, which you may want to carry in any case (for suggestions, see below).

For a start, you'll need a set of pots—a big one of, say, 8–10-quart capacity and two or three smaller ones that nest inside; a frying pan, preferably with a handle that folds out of the way for packing; and a set of plates, mugs, and bowls (for desserts or morning fruit or cereal) made to nest inside each other and fit in the pots. I use metal plates and mugs—they'll dent, where plastic will break—but they can be touchy to handle with hot

The author's cooking pack, an Alpine frame type with side pockets and expandable top.

The author's cooking kit, all of which fits into the pack: (rear to front, from left) the empty pack, fire lighters, fuel bottles, stove, funnel for fuel, wash rags and scouring pad, gloves, dish towels, soap and scouring bar in aluminum cases; canvas bag for pots, first-aid kit, water-proof salt shaker, toilet paper, tableware and spatula in roll-up caddy; frying pan with folding handle, aluminum plates, pot lids; three sizes of bucket-style nesting aluminum pots (in paper bags for protection against mutual soot), coffee pot, bowls, cups, folding grill in cloth bag.

food in them. I still carry a small coffeepot that fits inside the smallest cooking pot, but I've long since lazily abandoned real coffee—boiled, perked, dripped—in favor of instant. For all pots, I prefer *firmly attached*, semicircular (bucket style) handles that lie flat, out of the way, for packing; the removable kind tend to get lost or give way at the critical moment if carelessly put on. Tight-fitting lids are essential for keeping out ashes and whatnot. The big pot does fine for carrying water to your cooking area, and when you're traveling by canoe the water supply's always at hand; I don't, therefore, bother with a separate water container, though there are inexpensive, collapsible plastic jugs (two and a half or five gallons) that are light and fairly durable. On the other hand, if the water can't be trusted—an unfortunate possibility even in some quite remote areas—a large container is es-sential, so that you can fill it from any safe springs along the way or, failing that, purify water in quantity.

Even when most of your cooking is on a stove, the pots will collect soot and dirt on the outside, so a canvas carrying bag with a draw-string top is a must for packing. Particularly when cooking over a wood fire, I don't do much more than rinse the outsides of the pots—scouring them after every meal is a dirty and time-consuming job that can just as well be saved till you get back home, when you'll want to clean all your equipment anyway before putting it away.* Instead, I pack each pot in

* You may have heard or read that sooty pots will clean up readily if coated with soap or liquid detergent before each use. I've tried it and found it only moderately effective—a wasteful nuisance. I don't, myself, use liquid detergent anyway on most trips; soap is enough.

a paper bag cut to fit, so that the soot on the outside of one isn't transferred to the inside of the one it's packed in.

As I suggested earlier, a pair of cotton work gloves belongs in the bag with the pots and plates, partly to keep soot off your hands but chiefly because the pots will be hot to handle in the course of cooking.

A set of aluminum pots adequate for half a dozen people, with plastic or aluminum plates and mugs, will run fifteen to twenty dollars. You can get a comparable outfit in stainless steel, but the price will be more like fifty dollars, one reason I prefer aluminum (weight is another).

Inexpensive and nearly indestructible eating utensils, in chrome plate or stainless steel, are available at the nearest hardware or dime store. You'll need a knife and fork and small and large spoons for each member of your family or party, with a couple of spares all around; and a spatula, long-handled fork, can opener, and at least one really sharp, all-purpose knife, with a small Carborundum or sharpening steel to touch up the blade (sharpen it well before the trip). Unless you make it yourself, a *caddy* to hold all this—a roll-up bag with slots for each kind of implement—is harder to come by. L. L. Bean seems to be the only outfitter that sells one, along with a set of tableware for six and the other utensils mentioned except the Carborundum (about fifteen dollars complete).

For cooking over a fire, a grill of some kind is a great convenience. I prefer a light wire grill with legs that fold flat and a canvas bag to pack it in (L. L. Bean again, about ten dollars, with a fire pan that adds to the weight and price and had best be left behind). There are a couple of less expensive, small backpackers' grills without legs—they have to be set up between two rocks, and it takes a certain amount of ingenuity to get them both level and stable, at the right height for cooking. In a pinch, you can do without a grill. For example, a pair of crotched saplings stuck in the ground on either side of the fire and braced with rocks will support a cross bar from which you can hang your pots. Any such arrangement takes time to set up, though, and risks spilling your dinner into the fire if someone stumbles against it in the twilight.

One of the natural laws of camp cookery is that dishwashing follows eating as night follows day. As we sit down to eat, I fill the biggest pot with fresh water and set it on the grill so that it will be hot when the meal's over. Then, while we sip the after-dinner cup of coffee, we toss coins or play cards for the privilege of washing the dishes (the dishwasher gets his hands *really* clean). The hot water is mixed with cold to a bearable temperature and divided into two pots, one for washing, the other for rinsing. A bar of Ivory, which you can also use for washing yourself, does as well as any, assisted by a wash rag and a scouring pad and a bar of Bon Ami,† for tough spots inside the pots (save the outsides till you get home). You *can* leave the utensils to dry by the fire, but drying them is an important final step in the cleaning process, particularly for the knives, forks, and spoons. I carry a couple of cloth dish towels for the purpose—you don't mind losing or throwing out the pressed paper-cloth kind you can buy at the supermarket, but they're less absorbent.

After the evening meal, you can save time by stacking the dried plates and cups around the fireplace, bottoms up and weighted with rocks in case of an overnight wind. Make a point of tidying away all your food and equipment, ready for the night, as soon as the dishes are finished, so you won't have to do it while stumbling around in the dark (suggestions later in this chapter for protecting food). Then you're ready for the evening, whether that means an hour or two of sunset fishing, reading, singing, playing cards, or simply sitting around the fire and talking. And so to bed!

Fires and Fire Making. A number of writers on camping and wilderness survival (see Appendixes) describe methods of starting a fire with everything from the Indian fire bow and drill to a bit of plastic that can be used as a burning glass, but, for all practical purposes, cooking over a campfire begins with an adequate supply of dry matches. Indeed, the prospect of *not* being able to get the fire started when you need it is so depressing that several precautions are in order, a series of increasingly sure defenses against cold and hunger, if you like, to fall back on.

For ordinary use in camping, I rely on wooden

---

† Molded like a bar of soap, Bon Ami is preferable to a scouring powder because easy to carry without spilling, but in the United States it's now vanished from the marketplace and is obtainable only from L. L. Bean. Sand, if you can find it, will do the job but is tougher on hands and utensils. Horsetail—a low, bright-green plant that looks like a cross between a reed and ordinary grass, common in wet areas in the North—is also effective; its stalk is a natural source of silica.

safety matches, allowing about a box per day. Although you have to have the box to strike them on, I think that in damp weather they're less prone than the big, non-safety wooden kitchen matches to soak up moisture and become useless. (Paper matches are no good at all.) The match supply should be kept in a plastic bag, tightly tied, well inside a pack, where rain's not likely to penetrate. For emergencies, most outfitters sell a small, waterproof metal match safe with a hinged screw top **that holds ten or twenty kitchen matches; get one** and carry it in a breast pocket. As a further precaution, you can waterproof a small supply of kitchen matches by dipping them in paraffin or lacquer. A few outfitters sell waterproof matches. Finally, I've taken to carrying a throw-away butane lighter in case all else fails. Although it's not much good in a wind, with careful shielding it's a sure source of fire, with a fuel supply that should last a month or two even with constant use; more to the point, if you're a smoker, the lighter will reserve your matches for more serious purposes. Acquire a supply of fire lighters (small, compressed blocks of sawdust, impregnated with resin and kerosene, that can be lighted with a match even in the rain) and resolve always to carry them with your cooking kit. A little dry newspaper, sealed in a plastic bag, is also useful in wet weather, though not so sure as a fire lighter.

For cutting the wood that goes into your fire and for a good many other camp-site jobs, you'll need an ax. A full-size, single-blade head with a short handle (about twenty-four inches) is best, since it will fit in a pack, where the longer handle will stick out and leave an opening for rain to come in; a hatchet is too light for serious work. Whatever you use, be sure to get a stout leather case for the head to protect whatever's next to the ax in the pack. (Ax sheaths are not easy to come by in these decadent times, but can be made fairly easily from leather, heavy vinyl, or oilcloth.) Sharpen the ax well, before you set out on your trip, and it should see you through; though, with patience, you can touch up the edge with the same Carborundum you use for your knives (or carry a small file for the purpose).

From the safety standpoint—an ax, carelessly used, *is* dangerous—a few canoeists prefer a folding saw, of which there are several makes available. It will do to cut down a small tree or saw it into fireplace lengths (slow going, though), but it's no use for trimming branches, splitting wood, or sharpen-ing tent stakes, and it won't pound your stakes into the ground, either. (When driving stakes with an ax, by the way, use the flat of the blade butt, not the butt itself.) As a compromise, you might use, with your ax, an inexpensive Varco pocket saw, an 18-inch strand of saw-tooth wire with a ring at either end (holding the rings with your thumbs, you can cut down a fair-sized tree; strung over a lithe sapling, it makes a small bucksaw). In its protective plastic case, the pocket saw belongs in your pocket along with the waterproof match case, a tool for survival in the unlikely event you lose your entire outfit.

One of the first making-camp chores, along with setting up the tent, is collecting a firewood supply. Look for dead trees an inch or two in diameter that are still standing (wood that's been on the ground for a year or two is likely to be rotten, but it too will burn on a good fire, though smokily). The small trees can be broken off at the base and broken up by hand into fire lengths. On a river, you can count on plenty of well-dried driftwood along the high-water line, already, if you're selective, broken up to the right size; being impregnated with minerals from the water, though, it makes a smelly fire much inferior to the aromatic sweetness of seasoned pine. In beaver country, you can collect incomparable wood from the top of this industrious animal's lodges or dams. He and his family will already have eaten the bark from these discards, so you're not depriving him.

Whatever your wood source, it's handy to sort the supply into two piles, on either side of the fireplace: big pieces for burning, the trimmed branches and twigs for kindling. Avoid big logs, which are a lot of work to split with an ax; in general, use your ax no more than absolutely necessary. There are a few precautions you probably learned long ago in summer camp. One certainly is deliberation. Don't be in a hurry when you're using an ax. In cutting a tree down, take time to look around and make sure there's no undergrowth that will catch your back swing or stand in the way of a strong, accurate cut; clear anything that may interfere before you start chopping, and when you begin, stand with your legs braced wide apart and as far from the cut as you can get them. In trimming branches, stand on one side of the fallen tree and cut the branches along the other, letting your arm and the ax handle swing like a pendulum, working up from tree butt to top—the weight of the head will do the work. In cutting up the wood, use a good-sized fallen log as a chopping block, wedged with rocks if need be to hold it firm. Make sure there's no spectator looking over your shoulder before you take the first stroke, and, again, brace your legs solidly and keep them as far as possible from the cutting point. You're less likely to be hit by a flying piece of wood if you cut your tree from the middle, cutting each piece successively into halves until they're short enough for the fire.

Since prebreakfast woodcutting consumes some of the pleasantest moments of the day, avoid it by saving enough wood over from the night before. Cover the woodpile with a poncho or rain shirt weighted with rocks, in case it rains. Or take enough wood and kindling to start the morning fire under the tent awning or into the tent itself; or leave some under the upturned canoe. As a matter of woodsmen's courtesy, before breaking camp, collect some spare wood for the next guy, who may well arrive when it's dark, cold, or rainy—or all three at once.

A good many national, state, and provincial parks in the canoe country now require you to use established camp sites along the water routes, where permanent fireplaces and grills are provided. Elsewhere, the chances are that any appealing site will have been used before by someone who will have bequeathed you a fireplace. If you do have to start from scratch, look for an open, level spot downwind from your tent site, preferably with a boulder to serve as a fireback. Clear twigs and pine needles, which might spread the fire, down to bare earth or rock. Build the fireplace sideways to the prevailing wind, using rocks, say a foot long by six inches wide and high, overlapping them and wedging them with pebbles, rather as with a child's building blocks. A foot or a foot and a half high is adequate for containing the fire and sheltering it from wind, and is also enough to support whatever type of grill you're using.

In making a fire, I start with a few of the smallest, driest twigs I can find, broken into lengths of a couple of inches (if they don't break with a snap, they're green and no good). Pine is best for the purpose. Other woods, such as birch or willow, may seem dry but retain enough moisture to be hard to light. Arranged tepee-fashion, the twigs should light with a single match, and as the fire catches I feed it from all sides with successively larger twigs until it's going well and ready for the bigger pieces. I then put a pair of logs on either side of the fireplace and lay several across them to

Cooking dinner: the fireplace, hastily made from rocks picked up on the beach, braces the grill, provides a shield against wind, and keeps the fire from spreading. (Credit: Jim Mead.)

catch from the kindling; then a second layer of wood at right angles to the first, loose enough for a good draft. If wood is abundant, I put in as much as I can fit in this manner at the start; it makes a fast, roaring fire that will burn down to hot, steady coals by the time you're ready to cook. My father, however, whenever he made a fire, invariably repeated an old Indian saying: "White man build big fire, stand far away. Indian build little fire, stand close." For saving both wood and work, it's a good principle.

Contrary to what you may have heard, the bark of the white birch is not necessarily an ideal natural tinder. The flaky, paper-thin outer bark of a dead, standing birch, which you can remove with your fingers, does fairly well when torn into strips. The inner bark, dead or alive, standing or fallen, is more likely to smother the match (birch seems to rot from the inside out). *Don't* use your knife on a live birch; you'll go too deep, and the girdled tree will die.

A two-burner Coleman stove, folded up for carrying, with a one-gallon fuel container (ordinary white gasoline can also be used but burns a little smokier than Coleman fuel).

A two-burner Coleman stove, ready to use: note windscreen, folding legs, fuel tank which fits inside when not in use (since the fuel vaporizes under pressure, the tank must be pumped up periodically).

If it's well sited in an adequate fireplace, the fire you cook dinner on will probably have burned down safely by bedtime; except in unusually dry weather, you really don't need to put it out with water. In breaking camp, however, pour a pail of dishwater all over the breakfast fire until it's really dead, no longer giving off smoke (the hot rocks may still steam a bit, but that's harmless). In our American mania for self-accusation, we've made it sound as if all forest fires are caused by careless campers. That's nonsense. In my observation, lightning is the more common offender, and it's probable that a periodic burning over is an essential stage in the natural cycle of a living forest. Nevertheless, fire, like other powerful natural forces, *is* dangerous and it can be immensely destructive, not least of the country where canoeing and camping are best. Treat it, always, with caution and respect. Too much dousing before you shove off is obviously better than not enough.

Stoves. Although an open fire is generally the most convenient means of camp cookery, there are times and places in which it's not possible or practical. In some of the best canoe country, fires may be restricted or forbidden because of a midsummer dry spell. In heavily used areas, firewood can get too scarce to be relied on. In such circumstances, for a family-size canoeing party you'll find it difficult to do without one of the big camp stoves. The Paulin stove uses propane gas and is available with two burners (twenty-five dollars plus) or with three

(about thirty-five dollars). I prefer the old reliable two-burner Coleman stove (comparable prices, also now in a three-burner model), because the fuel, similar to white gasoline but more refined, less smoky, is easier to come by. Both are efficient for cooking but bulky, require substantial quantities of fuel in heavyweight containers, and are as awkward to fit into any pack as they are cumbersome to carry separately. Except by necessity, I wouldn't use either for canoeing.

The alternative is one of the tiny, single-burner stoves designed primarily for hiking, where every ounce must, shall we say, be seriously weighed. Some of these burn alcohol (Optimus), others one or another compressed gas in a specially designed container (Gerry, Bleuet, Paulin, Prolite, Grasshopper). The Swedish Svea burns white gasoline, which you can buy at many gas stations, and ingeniously uses it own heat to pressurize the fuel, producing a blowtorch-like flame; I've found mine simple to use and reliable. The Primus, another European make and a name nearly synonymous with camp cooking, also uses white gasoline, but in a tank that has to be pumped up periodically, as with the Coleman stove (Phoebus and another Optimus work on the same system). All these small stoves sell in the ten-to-thirty-dollar range; cartridges for the various compressed gases cost a bit over one dollar, while for the two gasoline stoves you'll need one or two quart-size aluminum fuel bottles (about four dollars each, leakproof and virtually unbreakable). With any of the liquid fuels,

Svea stove, model 123: a light, compact, back-packers' type, fueled with white gasoline and self-pressurizing, good for a quick hot lunch or wet-weather emergencies; the key controls the gas jet; the tool at lower left holds a needle used to clear the jet of soot.

Two types of one-liter fuel container: sheet-metal (l.), with airtight, gasketed pouring and filling spouts; cast aluminum (r.), a stronger design.

don't forget to take a small funnel to minimize spillage when you fill the stove.

Of the three fuels (there are also stoves that burn kerosene, but except in backwoods areas it's becoming hard to get), white gasoline burns hottest, is most readily available, and is cheap for what it does, even in these inflated times. Compressed gas, besides being quite expensive and obtainable only in specialty stores, becomes less efficient as you climb above sea level. Such a stove as the Svea, which is primed by lighting a little of its fuel in the vicinity of the pipe connecting the tank with the burner, has the recommendation of simplicity (pumps, relying on airtight seals and valves, are not altogether reliable) and is safer than it sounds. It may, however, be hard to get going in cold weather or high, thin air. All the little stoves will have trouble if its windy, as it often is. A folding metal windscreen helps (about five dollars), or you can improvise. In stormy weather, you'll have to take the stove and your cooking inside the tent, where caution is in order. In that confined space, it's well to provide a flat rock as a base, both to reduce the risk of knocking the stove over and to insulate the tent floor from heat, which can melt nylon and scorch canvas.

Although the small stoves are designed for one or two persons, it's possible, with a little holding of the breath, to cook enough stew, say, for five or six on one of them, the catch being that it will handle only one thing at a time and is rather slow with a big potful. As insurance against a wet day, though, or for a quick pot of lunch-time coffee, it's worth having one in your cooking kit, even if you rely on a fire the rest of the time.

And a Few of the Comforts

One person's luxury is another's necessity—like the little goose-down pillow my mother considered indispensable to a good night's sleep on a camping trip. Strictly speaking, none of the items of equipment and supplies that we'll consider in this section is advisable if you're intent on traveling fast and unencumbered. All, however, add to the comfort of a camping trip, and some you'll probably think essential, depending on your particular tastes and inclinations. Think about them, anyway, when you plan your own trip, striking a balance between what you're actually likely to use and enjoy and what will merely weigh you down and never come out of the pack.

Above, traditional type of folding candle lantern, which can stand or hang.

Above right, cylindrical lantern, collapsed, for packing (*l.*) and extended (*r.*); it must be hung.

Right, one type of 6-volt lantern suitable for camping: this one, with a webbing shoulder strap (Nichols Brothers Co.), is made of high-impact plastic, is waterproof and buoyant, and has a red emergency flasher light in addition to the powerful main beam.

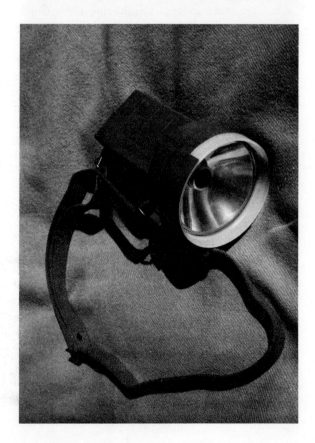

Lighting the Night. On a camping trip, you soon adopt, almost unconsciously, the natural rhythm of the day: get up when it's light, go to bed when it gets dark. You don't really need anything very elaborate in the way of lighting, therefore. If you feel like sitting around after dinner (and the insects co-operate), simply build up the fire a little. For undressing in the tent, a folding candle lantern provides adequate light. One rectangular design, elegantly brass-plated, with isinglass windows, seems to have been around since the Civil War (L. L. Bean and a few others, about six dollars). Backpackers favor a newer, cylindrical type that originated in France and telescopes down to under five inches for packing (EMS and other hiking specialists, about the same price); note however, that this French lantern *doesn't stand;* it must be hung from one of the tapes usually sewn into the tent peak, but it seems not to produce enough heat to be dangerous even for nylon (the older, rectangular lantern can stand *or* hang). Half a dozen 4-inch candles should see you through a two-week trip, but the supermarket variety tend to soften into surrealist curves and loops in hot weather; sticklers can use, instead, a harder candle designed especially for the purpose (EMS, about ten cents apiece). Considering the vulnerability of tent floors, especially nylon, put something solid and fireproof under any candle lantern: a flat rock or a metal tackle box; if the candle burns down or the lantern tips over, it could make a hole in a tent floor in seconds.

Since time immemorial in our family, the last camping activity of the day has generally been a word game played in the darkened tent while the players, one by one, drop off to sleep (game's end, rarely more than fifteen minutes). Books all around are just as sleep-inducing, and the candle lantern provides enough light for those few minutes before drowsiness triumphs (a relief from cards, too, on a rainy day when you're stuck in the tent). Even paperbacks I don't mind losing I pack in plastic bags to be sure they last the trip. For the after-lights-out trip out of the tent for a final cup of water or whatever, a flashlight is handy, and I keep one within reach. The dime-store variety is good enough; roll it up in a sleeping bag when you're traveling, to protect it from damp, and that way it will wind up in the tent, where it belongs. For more light in such situations (and an effective night-time signal in emergencies), you might consider one of the sealed, plastic, 6-volt models that promise both to stay dry and to float, if they have to, and are not too heavy (Eveready, L. L. Bean, and others, about two pounds, under eight dollars). If you'll remember to check or replace bulbs and batteries before setting out, you needn't bother to carry spares on a two-week trip.

If you must have the sort of brilliant lamp that will illuminate a whole camp site when hung from a tree branch, several of the stove makers will provide it (Bleuet and Coleman, for instance, about fifteen dollars). It's a matter of taste, but that's more light than I want. A more serious objection is that they're bulky, unyielding objects that don't fit into a pack very well: in daylight, you can identify the users because they're carrying their lanterns along the portage trails in their hands, generally with several other bits of gear they haven't yet managed to lose. And the big lamps mean just that much more fuel that has to be carried, a further nuisance. Leave the lamp at home and use the dark for sleeping, I'd say.

First Aid, Repairs, and Personal Care. On a canoe trip, first aid begins with prevention. You don't have to be a bred-in-the-bone woodsman to handle your canoe, in and out of the water, with care and caution, treating rapids, falls, and sudden storms with common-sense respect. The same unhurried carefulness applies to the few other possible canoe-camping hazards—ax or saw, fire, unknown plants that may or may not be edible, animals. You have a double motive for taking care of yourself. Apart from your own discomfort, if you hurt yourself you may spoil the trip for the others you're traveling with, perhaps even, in remote country, endanger them.

For minor, day-to-day scrapes, your first-aid kit should include the following items: adhesive bandages in several sizes; gauze pads; a roll of gauze bandage and another of elastic bandage (useful for sprains); iodine rather than mercurochrome (stronger when needed, doubling as a water purifier), perhaps also some zinc-oxide powder (mild, good for open abrasions, bad burns); Unguentine (an old-time burn ointment, still more effective than the newer sprays); tweezers and possibly a small pair of scissors (but your sheath knife will do); aspirin; and a compact laxative of some kind (Ex-Lax or Carter's Pills, for instance) if you're slow in adjusting to camp cookery. You can buy these ingredients and a few others in a variety of kit forms from most outfitters, saving you the trouble of assembling them and providing a compact case to carry them in (Cutter Laboratories puts up three sizes of first-aid kit, at prices from about five dollars to ten dollars plus). For canoeing in places like the Everglades and some other parts of the South, where poisonous snakes are common, you should probably add a snake-bite kit (Cutter again; I've always carried one but have never had to use it). Remember, though, that most snakes are *not* poisonous and, like other wild animals, are as nervous of you as you probably are of them; resist the implse to smash anything that slithers across your path—it's simply in a hurry to escape. Let it!

The old-fashioned bandanna handkerchief is big enough to bind a wound, tie a splint, or make a sling, and has many other uses. (L. L. Bean and a few other outfitters still sell them, about sixty cents each.)

No matter how tough you think your skin is, on a bright day on the water a periodic application of sun-tan lotion is in order. (For myself, the object is preventing sun tan/burn—one reason for long pants and sleeves plus an anti-sun lotion on the few exposed places.)

In summer in areas where the mosquitoes are thick, the first line of defense is a breezy camp site, on a point or island (as I suggested earlier). The smoke from your campfire will repel the few hardier insects that can cope with the wind. Out on the water, the breeze from your movement will carry off any mosquitoes that try to follow. As a further protection, once the tent is up make a point of keeping the mosquito netting zipped shut and go in and out as little as possible. When everyone's in for the night, use your flashlight or lantern to find any mosquitoes that have come in with you and knock them off with a judicious use of an aerosol spray. *Don't* try to use the same stuff to clear the whole camp site; apart from the huge quantities of insecticide it would take and the possible health hazards to you, it really doesn't work. Bear in mind, too, that mosquitoes and flies have their own insect predators: the mosquito hawk, which looks like a treble-size mosquito; a black wasp (name unknown to me) that bears a striking resemblance to an oversize house fly and lives by eating them; and dragonflies, which relish mosquitoes and all kinds of flies and can do wonders in making a swampy camp site tolerable to humans. Keep your spray off these insects. They're on your side.

Wet, shady portages will probably be the one place where normal precautions against mosquitoes won't work. Properly chosen clothes help, but for such occasions you'll want a good insect repellent as well. In solid form, like a Chap Stick, 6–12 does a good job; Cutter's liquid cream repellent is even better—longer-lasting and more obnoxious, apparently, to the bugs (to *people* it smells good!). Both of these are available as aerosol sprays, but the solid or liquid form is better because small enough to carry in a pocket. In the Far North, you may have to resort to a head net, perhaps even gloves.

The secret of finding a particular article in any of the several packs you're likely to carry is *association*. That's why I carry in my tackle box one tool whose real purpose is first aid: a pair of alligator-jaw pliers with a wire-cutting edge. While the pliers serve mainly to extract a deep-swallowed hook from a fish's mouth, you'll need them if you ever have the misfortune to hook yourself. The problem is a hook that's gone in barb deep. In that case, don't try to pull it out again; that will make the wound worse. Instead, push the hook on through on it's own curve until the barb comes out on the other side; then use the pliers to cut it off. And of course, after pulling out what's left of the hook, sterilize and bandage the double wound.

Again working by association, I stow everything that seems like a toiletry in a cloth, drawstring bag ("ditty bag" is the old-fashioned term) and keep it with the cooking kit: toothbrush and toothpaste, hand soap, medicines that have to be taken regularly, comb and brush, nail clippers, nail brush, and so on. That's the place, too, for whatever you use as shaving equipment, if you feel like bothering (guides, the real pros in the canoers' world, do)—including, in that case, an unbreakable steel mirror (no bad luck). Those with a not-too-heavy beard and strong feelings about frequent shaving can use one of the light, battery-powered shavers, such as Mallory or Panasonic, the latter with a pop-up trimmer (around fifteen dollars). If you're a stickler about washing your hands before lunch, you might want in a pocket a small tube of one of the new concentrated liquid soaps made for the purpose, with a spare in the ditty bag; Pocket and Trak are among the brands available from outfitters (one dollar and three dollars, respectively), claiming fifty to sixty washings per tube and other benefits. (I've tried these and found them so effective in cold water for grease, soot, and general grime that I now regard them as more needful than luxurious.) And don't, finally, forget the toilet paper, squeezed flat to save space, in a plastic bag to stay dry, and packed where it's easy to find—in the cooking kit, let us say (association again!). If you run out, you can imitate our forefathers by substituting a non-hairy leaf, such as maple.

To repeat what I've suggested in earlier chapters, waterproof cloth tape is good for so many kinds of quick repairs—the canoe, paddles, all fabrics, even your boots—that a roll belongs somewhere in your kit. (The same kind of nylon used in tents is also available in the form of adhesive tape, but it's harder to come by and relatively a lot more expensive than the hardware-store variety.) In addition to the bow and stern lines on the canoe, a 50-foot length of medium nylon rope is useful for such things as tying down the tent against a storm, drying wet clothes, and hanging the food pack out of bears' reach; you might carry it with the tape. Twine will do some of the same jobs and can be used for resewing a ripped pack or tying shut plastic food bags; it will also replace a broken bootlace, if you forgot to bring an extra pair. Elastic tie-downs with hooks at either end are inexpensive and do well for battening the tent or tying into the canoe anything meant to stay there—Tingley Flex-Stas (L. L. Bean, lengths up to thirty-one inches) or rubber rope (made up, in any length requested, by the paddle maker Sports Equipment, Inc.; see Appendixes).

Living Off the Land. Canoeing and hunting rarely combine, if only because, for the most part, they belong to different seasons. In the fall, though, in the lake country of the north-central Midwest, there are those who set out after the ducks, geese, deer, and moose, and, until the freeze comes, do so by canoe. In that watery country, it's the most practical way of getting where the game is. If you're a hunter and can go there yourself, you might try combining that sport with canoeing.

Fishing is another matter. I've never thought of my canoe trips as primarily fishing trips, in the sense that that was their chief purpose. But fishing for me is a part of the whole that canoeing is, and one I wouldn't willingly leave out.

Fishing gear is so much a matter of personal preference—and of what you're fishing for and where—that I can't offer much in the way of specific advice. There are, however, some general pointers to keep in mind. As with every other kind of equipment, your tackle can easily balloon to un-

wieldy proportions unless you limit it to essentials. Keep the lures down to a few you like and are sure of, so you can fit them (along with a spare line, a few extra leaders, perhaps a reserve reel) into a flat, light tackle box. If you choose the box and what goes in it with care, you can tie it under a canoe seat with webbing straps and it will always be handy when you're ready to go fishing. A big tackle box, on the other hand, with several trays, is awkward to fit into a pack, can't be tied into the canoe without spoiling the balance on portages, and will make a general nuisance of itself.

Although live bait usually makes for a surer catch than a plug, I've rarely used it even where it's allowed: it means carrying a minnow seine and a pail to keep the bait in once it's caught. Nor are you likely to have enough need for a landing net to include one in your outfit.

Packs and Packing

If you're a hiker planning your first canoe trip, you probably have one or more of the rigid, rectangular aluminum pack frames, with separate, fitted nylon pack bag, that are generally favored for hiking. You *can* use a pack of that type for canoeing, but it won't be satisfactory. It's designed for carrying a fairly light, compact load (up to forty or fifty pounds) over long distances. As a canoer on a trip of a week or two, your requirements are the opposite: a comparatively heavy, bulky load on the short distances of a typical portage (as much as a mile is exceptional). Moreover, because the hiking pack is designed to carry the weight high up on the back, centered at shoulder level, it won't stand up in the canoe but has to be laid flat, taking up undue space for the weight and awkward to get in and out. Although hiking packs are now the most widely available type from outfitters and sporting-goods stores in all parts of the country, *don't buy one* if canoeing is your primary purpose. What you need is a Duluth pack, which will cost you about half what a good pack frame and bag currently sell for. Or outfitters in the U.S. and Canadian canoe country will rent you the packs you need, at modest rates.

The Duluth Pack. This is the type of pack nearly all canoers use. Essentially, it's a big canvas bag shaped something like a Manila mailing envelope, usually with flat seams at the sides and bottom,

Oversize Duluth pack (Paul Bunyan Special, rear): 28 × 30 inches, with 6-inch set-out at sides and bottom, side flaps and straps; with a pack of normal size for comparison (front)— good for bulky items such as clothes and sleeping bags but likely to be excessively heavy when full.

Duluth packs: back and front views of two packs of the most usual size (24 × 28 inches), one empty and opened out, the other full; both these antiques (the author's) have tump straps, leather shoulder and closure straps, and have served a lifetime without wearing out.

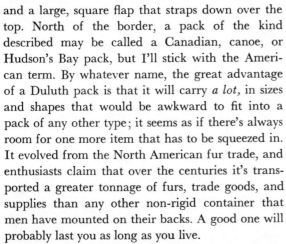

and a large, square flap that straps down over the top. North of the border, a pack of the kind described may be called a Canadian, canoe, or Hudson's Bay pack, but I'll stick with the American term. By whatever name, the great advantage of a Duluth pack is that it will carry *a lot,* in sizes and shapes that would be awkward to fit into a pack of any other type; it seems as if there's always room for one more item that has to be squeezed in. It evolved from the North American fur trade, and enthusiasts claim that over the centuries it's transported a greater tonnage of furs, trade goods, and supplies than any other non-rigid container that men have mounted on their backs. A good one will probably last you as long as you live.

The most usual dimensions for a Duluth pack are twenty-four inches wide by twenty-eight inches high. In that size, there will be three straps on the flap closed with buckles on the front so that the pack can be tied down tight whether it's half full or loaded to capacity. Wide (2¼-inch) leather or webbing shoulder straps on the other side also attach to buckles so that their length can be adjusted to fit big or small people. The bigger Duluth packs are also provided with what's called a *tump strap* (or *head strap*), an American Indian idea for making big loads easier to carry: the canvas strap goes over the forehead and transfers some of the weight from back and shoulders to neck. (Great World makes an elegant leather tump strap—at about fourteen dollars, it *should* be!—that can be

lashed to any pack not already equipped with one.) For my own use, I prefer a pack with leather shoulder straps, because they're more durable and more comfortable (you can get or make foam-rubber pads for the straps if you have tender shoulders, but you don't really need them). In heavy duty canvas (18-ounce), a 24 × 28-inch pack with tump strap and hand-riveted shoulder straps will cost you around thirty-two dollars. A pack the same size in 15-ounce canvas, with machine-riveted webbing shoulder straps, costs about half that, and smaller sizes are proportionally less (suitable for children or for carrying the cooking kit). With a 6-inch set-out at sides and bottom, the Duluth pack offers a rectangular interior space and an even greater carrying capacity than the usual envelope-flat design, but that's probably more than you'll need (or want to carry) for any but a very long canoe trip. The biggest Duluth pack now available, appropriately called a Paul Bunyan Special (twenty-eight inches wide by thirty inches high with a 6-inch set-out), has plenty of room for all the sleeping bags, air mattresses, pajamas, the tent, lamp or lantern, and other night-time conveniences. It's a handful, though, and if packed with anything heavy (food, for instance) it's just too weighty for convenient handling. In the 18-ounce canvas appropriate for a pack of this size, with tump strap and leather shoulder straps, it's priced at about fifty dollars.

In the north-midwestern canoe country on both

sides of the border, you can buy Duluth packs from just about any canoe outfitter. Waters, Inc., in Ely, Minnesota, has an unusually complete line with several exclusives, goes in for mail order, and produces an excellent catalogue. Or you can order direct from the leading manufacturer, the Duluth Tent and Awning Company. Elsewhere, though, packs of this type are harder to come by, though canoe outfitters that handle them can be found in the Adirondacks, New England, and some other eastern states (see Appendixes for sources, with addresses).

Although the Duluth pack is the one most generally used by canoers, two other systems have their proponents. One is the *Adirondack pack basket*, still used quite a lot in Maine and a little elsewhere; the other is the *tote box*.

Adirondack pack basket: made in three sizes, with rigid bottom, padded-webbing shoulder straps, leather strap at center rear for lifting in and out of canoe; can be fitted with tump strap; available from L. L. Bean with zippered water-repellent cover, which is recommended. (Credit: L. L. Bean, Inc.)

A pack basket is just what the name implies: woven basketry on a flexible hardwood frame, open at the top, with a harness to which shoulder straps are attached (sometimes, Indian-style, with a tump strap as well). With typical dimensions of about eighteen inches high by eighteen inches wide by fifteen inches deep, its capacity is rather less than that of a Duluth pack. Its advantages are that it costs less than a good Duluth pack and is comparatively rigid, so that breakables will travel in it with somewhat less wear and tear; and, with its flat, wood bottom, it will stand upright for packing and unpacking or for loading into the canoe. The obvious disadvantage is that it's not waterproof—it will have to be protected with a waterproof cover, or else whatever's in it must be wrapped up in plastic bags. Further, given the sort of knocking around that any pack endures in camping, I doubt that a pack basket will give the many years of wear that you can expect from a canvas pack.

Outside New England, pack baskets are scarcer than Duluth packs, but if you want to give them a try you can order from L. L. Bean, which sells three sizes, each with padded shoulder straps and a fitted, water-repellent cover (about fifteen to twenty-five dollars, including cover, depending on size); Great World is another source but doesn't have the water-repellent covers.

The tote box has an even smaller circle of admirers, but they're no less devoted. (You may hear it called a *wangun*—several variant spellings—an Indian word for the box in which some fur traders carried their beads, bolts of cloth, and other trade goods.) It's a pack-size box of wood or fiberboard (generally with metal reinforcements at the corners, like a camp trunk), made to strap onto a pack frame; it's generally designed so that the front forms the cover, attached with hooks or straps. It's rigid, should be waterproof, and needn't be much heavier than a pack or a pack basket; the rigidity protects fragile contents of any kind and is particularly good for food (flour, say) packed in cloth or plastic bags. Since you can take the whole front off, you can find things inside easily (with a pack of any kind, it always seems that whatever you're looking for is on the bottom). If heavily built and well reinforced, a tote box should also be proof against most animals, including bears. Unfortunately, despite some experiments in making tote boxes out of fiberglass and other exotic materials, there is nothing of the kind available commercially now, so far as I know. If you want one, you'll have to make it yourself; or you can assemble a serviceable wangun from a stock pack frame and an army-surplus ammunition case of appropriate size.

Two comparatively new pack ideas deserve mention as specially designed for canoeing. On the West Coast, Canoe California makes frameless nylon packs in several sizes, of which the Big Foot (zipper opening down the front, making the contents easy to get at, about $35) and the Klamath (tie closure at top, like a sack, under $20) look to me the best bets. Both are somewhat smaller than the usual size of Duluth pack and should be ordered with heavy-duty plastic liners since they're no more waterproof than most other nylon packs; or put anything that can't stand wetting in smaller plastic bags inside the pack (Gerry's three sizes of bags, stocked by some outfitters—the supermarket variety just isn't tough enough to stand up). That's a good idea with a canvas pack, too: it will shed rain indefinitely, but if it has to stand in water for any time, the water will soak through from the bottom. One solution to the moisture problem is the big cargo bags made of reinforced sheet plastic by Voyageur Enterprises and sold by some of the canoe makers and outfitters. They're really waterproof and seem to be fairly durable. The catch is that they're not packs; they have to be carried in the hands, like suitcases. They're suitable, therefore, for straight canoeing on a big river but no good on any route where portaging is likely.

Finally, as a special-purpose pack, I like the new polyethylene Rec-Pac when I want to carry a lot of photographic equipment, because it's tough and *really* waterproof. Except that it's on the small side and opens from the top, it's much the same idea as a tote box. Perhaps if enough people like it, the manufacturer will offer other sizes and variations on the present design.

Segregate your cooking equipment in a pack of its own. For myself, I use a canvas Norwegian mountain pack with a European-style attached aluminum frame (Bergans, a well-known make available from selected North American outfitters). The canvas is waterproof, there are a couple of big side pockets that hold a liter each of fuel for the stove, and the frame is made so that the pack will stand by itself for loading and unloading, but the main reason I use it is size. The dimensions (about twenty inches high by fourteen inches wide by ten inches deep—expandable, with a drawstring top) are right for my particular set of cooking equip-

ment, with room over for such small items as the first-aid kit. A small Duluth pack would, however, do about as well, particularly the type with the set-out (the smallest of these, twenty inches high by seventeen inches wide, sells for about seventeen dollars). If you're traveling with a child, the cooking kit is a good one for giving him the feeling that he's useful on portages: his size and not too heavy.

In and Out of the Canoe. In loading the canoe, the object is to get the trim as even as possible—the same depth at bow as at stern. If both paddlers are about the same weight and there's no passenger, you can accomplish that by leaning the two heavier packs against the center thwart, or the yoke, with the cooking pack in front of them and balanced by the tent toward the stern (if you carry it separately) or by the tackle box, spare paddle, rod case, or whatever else you have tied into the canoe. Remember that anything tied should be

Rec-Pac, a waterproof pack made of rigid polyethylene, with gasketed lid closed by snap buckles, back and waist bands, padded shoulder straps; useful for any equipment that is fragile or vulnerable to moisture.

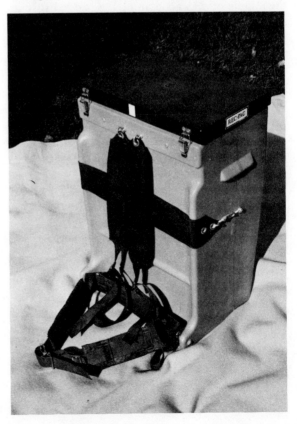

Canoe fully loaded, with cooking pack, two Duluth packs, tent, life jackets, spare paddle—enough equipment for two people on a two-week trip; here, packs stand upright, leaning against the center thwart, fast and easy to get in and out.

Canoe fully loaded, same as in preceding picture but with packs laid flat—advisable in rough water to increase stability by lowering the center of gravity.

positioned so that the canoe will balance *just a little* down in the stern in portaging; it should still ride easily on your shoulders, but angled slightly up at the bow to let you see where you're going.

The most comfortable place for a passenger (and the best from the balance standpoint) is in the middle of the canoe, using the padded yoke as a back rest. To give him room and trim the canoe properly, you'll have to move the packs forward and back, again compensating for one weight with another. The same principle applies if the two paddlers are of different weights, as they probably will be with a husband-and-wife team (move a pack forward or back, toward the lighter partner).

Occasionally, you'll meet conditions in which there's some advantage to trimming the canoe to bow or stern. For example, if the wind's coming at an angle off the stern, it will help you hold the course if you have a little more weight back there; and vice versa. But wind is so variable that it's hardly worth trying to keep up with: by the time you've shifted the load around, the wind will have changed. You'll just have to fight it out! In getting through swift water with a pole, it will be easier to hold the canoe straight, in alignment with the current, if you trim it a little heavy at the downstream end. In other words, in poling upstream, you want the canoe high at the bow, slightly down at the stern. When you use a pole to let yourself down rapids (*setting* is the canoer's term), the canoe should be loaded heavy in the bow so that it rides up somewhat at the stern (the person handling the

pole can accomplish this by moving forward, toward the center thwart).

As we noted earlier, the canoe should be fully afloat before being loaded, and if the water is shallow and rocky near the loading place, it's advisable to hold the canoe out from shore and step into the water to set the packs in; teetering on a submerged rock may damage the canoe bottom, and it will certainly add an ugly gash or scratch. For the same reasons, I prefer to position the packs upright in the canoe, leaning against a thwart; it's easier to get them in and out, and there's less chance, therefore, of damaging the canoe in the process (or of dropping a pack). Even though the tops of the packs are above the gunwale line, the center of gravity will still be low if you've been careful to put heavy items well down in the packs—meaning that the canoe will be stable-riding, won't tip from side to side in wind or waves. In stormy weather or in descending a rough, difficult rapids with a course requiring a sequence of sharp turns, you might want to increase the canoe's stability still further by laying the packs down flat so that they're below the gunwales. But I'd say that if you're that close to the limits of what you and the canoe are capable of, shifting the packs won't give you much extra margin. It's the sort of wild water you'd inspect first from the bank, then run with an empty canoe—or not at all.

With everything loaded into the canoe, I take a last look around the camp site before shoving off.

Partly it's simply a traveler's instinct for checking the dresser drawers for a forgotten shirt before locking the hotel-room door: have we left some wood by the fireplace for the next guy, whenever he comes? any telltale bits of foil or glass or plastic that we could just as well take away again? a wisp of smoke curling up from a fire that's not quite dead? That final inspection has a more general function, of course. All that carefully chosen equipment and food has the purpose of allowing you to travel freely, dependent only on yourself, and that freedom is diminished in some degree by whatever you leave behind or lose. Beyond that, it's a moment of farewell to the spot of earth, water, rock, and trees where you've spent a night or two, where you've eaten, slept, swum, fished—*lived*. It's a moment of anticipation as well: of the day's travel about to begin, of whatever new and fresh the remainder of the trip holds for you. Of all these feelings of departure and arrival, your loaded canoe, waiting for you at the water's edge, is the exact and concrete symbol. So, satisfied, you go back to it, help your partner in, grab your paddle, and shove off to another day. And *bon voyage!*

Chapter 6

TRAVELING FREE

When I was still quite small and the laws were a lot less protective than they have since become, the Fourth of July began early in January, when the catalogues came through the mail from the fireworks companies. For what now seems like weeks, my father and I studied them with the utmost seriousness, discussing choices, quantities, costs, making lists and revising them. When at length we settled on our order, and the carton of fireworks in due course arrived, every day I'd get it out, take everything out and look at it, study it, imagine what it would be like, and then carefully pack it back. The Fourth of July, when it finally came, was an all-day festival of sound and light that began with strings of explosions at dawn, reached a raucous climax sometime in the afternoon, and wound down in darkness to rockets, the glowing pastels of Roman candles, and the cool light of sparklers whirled and tossed. All those weeks of planning and anticipation were part of the final day and made it all the grander when it came.

A canoe trip is much like those boyhood Independence Days of mine, particularly if it's your first and you're doing some or all of the outfitting for yourself: weeks of pleasurable thinking, planning, and imagining, the results of which will all be compacted in the week or two of the trip. That, in effect, is what we've been doing so far in this book—planning a canoe trip—but the first steps are, of course, where to go and when, for how long, and with whom.

Planning a Canoe Trip

In the final chapter of this book, we'll be looking at some of the major U.S. and Canadian canoe areas that are especially good for distance canoeing—the *where* of the planning equation—but there are traveled canoe trails in every state and province. Information about the possibilities is available, often without charge, from a great variety of government agencies (see Appendixes for sources), and there are also books to be had about much of the canoe country, from historical or broadly descriptive works to detailed itineraries (again, see Appendixes for recommendations). Once you've decided, in general, where you're going, you'll want to provide yourself with some of this material and get detailed, large-scale maps of the area. The U.S. and Canadian governments publish excellent maps based on aerial surveys that cover their respective countries (the most complete series are at scales of two or four miles per inch), and for the major areas there are maps geared specifically to canoeing, obtainable from private or state and provincial government sources (see Chapter 8 and Appendixes).

With accurate maps, you can figure your route to fit the available time and do so as closely as your inclinations demand. In the flat-water midwestern lake and river country, you can expect to travel ten or fifteen miles per day without pushing, and going down a good-sized river with a moderate current will be about the same. Either way, you'll have time for hearty, leisurely breakfasts, exploring, picture taking, and perhaps a little fishing along the route and still be able to make camp at the end of the day with plenty of time to set up, cook dinner, swim, and fish. A lot of portages may slow you down somewhat. Even quite modest rapids take up time, too: the whole route should be inspected and worked out from the bank before you attempt it, and I like to study the entrance point from the water as well, back-paddling and holding off till I'm sure. The suggested average daily distances can, however, be doubled, if you have to, without undue exertion. Conversely, in planning the route, it's well to build in some leeway for the day you're windbound on a big lake or a strong head wind holds you to five or six miles instead of the ten or fifteen you expected; and if an all-day rain sets in, I'd rather stay in camp than travel in it. In addition, if there are children in your party, they'll be grateful for a day or two when there's nothing to do but laze around camp, try a little casting from the shore, perhaps go off by themselves to explore the stretch of lake or river that, for the moment, is theirs—and yours.

In general, you'll enjoy the trip more if you don't lock it into an ironclad schedule. Allow for serendipity—finding what you didn't know you were looking for. Let yourself go off in a different direction if it looks inviting. More than in most other forms of travel, you're *free* when you travel by canoe: you can go wherever inclination leads.

If the canoe trip is your summer vacation, you'll probably be taking it in the traditional month of July or August. Even in the far South, heat's not likely to be a real problem, though in the smaller rivers low water levels may be if the weather's dry; farther north, you'll be escaping from midsummer city heat to springlike sunny days and cool nights. In the leading canoeing areas July and August are also, of course, the peak travel months—meaning that in wilderness country on any given day you may be sharing the lake or river with two or three other parties. They're also the months when flies are most numerous, though by late July the mosquitoes should be past their peak. If you crave solitude and the best fishing, you might try to go as early as mid-May, ahead of the crowd; in lake country, the big muskies and lake trout, which by midsummer will have retired to the cool depths, will still be up near the surface, where you can take them by casting. Since the water levels are generally higher, the rivers faster, spring canoeing is for the more experienced canoeist—and the mosquitoes will be at their fiercest. Finally, if you can manage it, there's much to be said for a September or early-October trip in Maine or Minnesota. The insects will have vanished with the first frost, the leaves on the hardwoods will be starting to turn, and solitude, if you want it, will be real, not relative. As in the northland spring, the days will be

sunny and brisk but at night you'll want warm pajamas and a better-than-summer-weight sleeping bag, and it will help to pitch the tent near the fire and leave a well-built blaze before you go to bed—though, as always, with care for the possibility of wind-driven sparks.

Travel in any form with other people is an intimate kind of experience: like marriage, it can bring out frictions and personal oddities that in the ordinary course of things would never reveal themselves—and a canoe trip is particularly so. As a group, you're free of the world, but precisely because of that you're dependent on each other. That's one reason canoeing is so fine for families: you're used to living at close range with each other and know or can imagine what to expect in a great range of situations. Other kinds of groups should be considered with care; physical stamina is less important than how you'll get along together in the day-to-day intimacy of canoeing and camping. Particularly for canoers of limited experience, a party of two or three canoes (four to seven or eight people) is a common-sense safety precaution: if emergencies *do* come up, you'll be able to help each other, but the larger group also means more variety, more fun. I'd avoid a much bigger group, however. With too many people, you'll find it hard to fit into most camp sites, and the more there are, the greater the chance that some will be constantly lagging behind, on portages or in the canoes— gnawingly tedious for everyone else—or discover after you start out that a canoe trip isn't what they wanted to be doing after all.

If you're planning a canoe trip for a youth group —Scouts, Y, church—the size of the party may be a problem: you don't want to leave anyone out. You'll find it more satisfactory for all concerned if you break it down into groups of eight or ten, each with an adult leader, that can travel more or less independently, even if they're following roughly the same route at the same time. (That's the rule in some areas, such as the Boundary Waters country in northern Minnesota, where a no-charge permit is now required: parties no larger than ten, each with an adult who's responsible.) Whatever the group, as a practical matter one person will have to take charge of general planning and getting together whatever equipment and supplies are needed, simply to make sure nothing vital gets forgotten. That makes sense on the trip itself, too. Among the voyageurs, the leader of the party was

If you're traveling in a group (here, Brabant Lake, northern Saskatchewan), in calm weather on a big lake, leadership is less important than it will be when descending rapids, where it is sensible for the most experienced team to go through first, setting the course for the rest to follow. (Credit: Saskatchewan Department of Tourism.)

known as the *bourgeois* and had the authority of a ship's captain, not in the Captain Bligh sense but as a matter of respect and trust, based on experience and judgment. A modern canoe trip is likely to evolve its own bourgeois—someone with the sense to say no and make it stick when everyone else wants to run a dangerous rapids or ride out a sudden storm; who'll make sure the tent's pegged down tight, the food safe from animals, the fire really out before you leave. Indian tribes and bands seem usually to have developed a similar kind of leadership, reflecting not submission to power but a recognition of wisdom and responsibility. It's a working model for the kind of primitive society in miniature that a party of canoeists becomes for the days or weeks of its trip.

With several canoes in the party and marked differences in skill and experience, leadership needs to be more formal. In fast water, the most practiced twosome takes the lead and determines the course, which the others follow—*and no argument!* The number-two pair brings up the rear, assisting any weaker paddlers in between who have difficulty. Make the descent one at a time, with intervals of twenty or thirty feet, back-paddling while you wait for the one ahead to start on down. The same general rule applies in storms: the lead canoe sets the course, determines when and where to pull out, and the rest follow. Mutual adjustment is in order. The strongest paddlers should set a pace that's within reach of everyone, but the novices will probably have to push to keep up.

On the Move

If you have to travel any distance to get to the starting point of your trip, the chances are that you'll do so by car—either loaded with camping gear (if you're doing some or all of your own outfitting) or allowing time to pick up food and equipment from your outfitter if you've arranged things that way. In either case, *don't* try to start out by canoe late in the day, even if the vacation time you have is limited. You won't get very far with a late start, you're quite likely to wind up trying to make camp in the dark (tough on the best of dispositions), and being tired to begin with increases the risk of an accident that could ruin the trip. Instead, you and your car can probably pull into a camp ground in the area for the night. Or treat yourself to a hotel or motel and a good dinner in town. Whatever the formula, work it out so that you can start fresh, fairly early in the morning, with nothing else on your mind but the trip itself. (I try to reverse the procedure at the end of the trip: a motel with plenty of hot water for scrubbing and shaving, a change into going-home clothes, and a good dinner topped off by a night in a real bed—civilized touches that seem doubly luxurious after a stay in the wilds.)

Once you're under way, it's well to set a rough objective for each day's travel and then stick to it. It may be a lake where you've heard that this year's fishing is particularly good (there's always one) or an island in an otherwise populous river with an attractive and secluded camp site. A few canoers seem to like to paddle hard for thirty or forty minutes at a stretch and then break to lounge and smoke, like the voyageurs, while the canoe drifts. It's a matter of one's personal style, I guess. My own is to keep going fairly steadily and let the rest periods fall where they may. It may be no more than a cup of clear, cold water all around to sample the newest lake (hang a cup from a pack strap for the purpose so it will be handy without having to rummage through a pack).

As you travel, keep your eyes open for animal life in the water and along the shore: a beaver swimming a log back to his lodge; a bear or moose come down for a drink, as curious about you as you about him; a huge, ungainly-looking eagle's nest silhouetted against the sky at the tip top of a solitary tree. Those are moments for setting the paddles silently in the bottom of the canoe, for passing the field glasses around and digging out the camera for some pictures. In the North in spring and early summer you'll see, as well, a profusion of water-bird young—loons, several species of ducks and geese, gulls, perhaps, with luck, the great blue heron of the upper Midwest and southern Canada. If you sight a duck swimming erratically ahead of the canoe, it's probably a parent playing hurt to lead you elsewhere; look around for the string of ducklings hiding along the shore. Or perhaps even, if they're still very small, they may be concealed among the feathers on their mother's back. Gulls, which seem to like to nest on a rocky outcropping in the middle of a lake, will swoop at you with raucous cries if they have young to protect and you approach too close; since they nest in groups, you may find yourself with several white-feathered dive bombers darting and screeching around the canoe, not just a pair. They won't in fact strike if you paddle over to peer into the nest, but the mock assault is unnerving enough so that you may not want to find out.

It hardly needs repeating that in this season of cubs and calves, bears and moose should not be approached. Both will run from man in most circumstances, but with their young nearby they may be running *at you*. If you chance on either at uncomfortably close range, the old woodsmen's rule (which I've never had to test) is to stand still and talk soothingly until it decides to leave. Sudden movement on your part may be taken as a threat. (Some early explorers of North America tell tales of the stupidity and timidity of moose, but that's not how they look to me.)

Fishing doesn't combine very satisfactorily with traveling. With two paddlers and a passenger try-

A break from paddling: the end of a portage, where the next stage is loading up to cross a Quetico beaver pond. (Credit: JEM.)

Another kind of break: tying up at the riverbank for a chance to look around, stretch the legs— and study the map.

ing to troll, you'll be moving a little fast to catch anything. For casting, you need to drift along close to shore, taking several casts into each shallow little cove. Save the serious fishing for early morning and after dinner, the fishes' natural feeding times, with perhaps a few practice casts when you stop for lunch.

The passenger, if there is one, is the natural navigator and map reader; otherwise, the sternman had better keep the map handy in its case, perhaps tucked into the straps of a pack where he can glance at it from time to time without having it blow away. In lake travel, your primary concern is finding your way from one portage to the next, and if it's a good-sized lake, with deep bays and islands that may be hard to tell from mainland, that can be tricky. A compass, which I rarely use, is not much help; you can orient the map accurately enough by the sun. The key element is your own adjustment to the scale of the map so that you can relate its two dimensions to the physical features you actually see. That may take you a day or two, like arriving in Paris equipped with your college French courses, when everyone seems to talk too fast to follow. At first you'll do well to keep a close watch on the map, identifying each island and shoreline indentation as you pass so that you'll know constantly exactly where you are.

On a river, following the route is no problem, but the map helps you anticipate rapids, falls, and other hazards. Since a rapids or waterfall is made by a sharp drop in the river bed, you often can't see it from upriver, and if the wind's behind you, you may not hear it, either. Since the river will often be narrow as well as steep at a rapids, the current is generally slower along the banks, perhaps eddying back, stronger in the middle. If the rapids is short and easy enough so that you can see the whole length from the canoe, you may feel confident enough to run it without scouting from the shore. If not, look for a portage trail on either bank—signs of the wear of human feet; often an ax or paint blaze; perhaps, in a park, a sign of some kind. If there's a clearly defined portage, you'd better use it, but bear in mind that rapids feasible in spring high water may be too shallow for safety at other times, and one that looks easy enough at the start may be blocked by boulders or choked with deadwood farther down. If you have to cross the river to reach a convenient carrying place, work your way back well upstream along the bank, so you'll be able to stem the swift mid-river current without being pulled dangerously close to the fall. On a big river with a powerful mid-stream current above a drop of several feet, you may need half a mile or a mile of leeway for a safe crossing. *Don't take chances.* Even a comparatively gentle river will impose harsh penalties for carelessness or misjudgment.

At any portage, it's a sensible precaution for one canoeist to unload while the other holds the canoe steady in the water. If you're using a one-man carry for the canoe (see Chapter 3), you may want your partner to help you get it up or at least stand by just in case, then go ahead of you with a pack to scout the landing at the other end and help you get the canoe down and into the water. If you've chosen your packs with carrying in mind, you'll probably be able to make the portage in one go, particularly toward the end of the trip, as packs get lighter and it's easier for one person to carry two of them, one on top of the other (or canoe plus pack, the system most guides use).

On a long portage, you may need a rest part way, but try to do it without setting down the pack or canoe: it saves the energy required to get it up again. With a pack, look for a big rock or fallen tree where you can half sit while you take a breather. With the canoe, look for a natural canoe rest that will support the bow while you let the stern down to the ground—two trees growing close together in a V, a crotch or limb at the right height. When you're carrying the canoe, especially on a trail that's rocky or slippery with mud, don't hurry: take deliberate, wide-braced steps; if you come to a log across the trail that's too high to step across easily, let the canoe down on it, get across,

Above, picking up a loaded pack: take one shoulder strap near the top in both hands, then swing the pack up in a circular motion, sliding the strap along the arm and onto the shoulder; for short distances, the pack can be carried like this, on one shoulder.

Above right, fully loaded for a portage: pack, with tent (or another pack) balanced on top, tump strap over forehead to ease load on back.

Right, starting a portage: two people can carry all their gear in one trip if one can take two packs while the man with the canoe carries a light pack as well.

and then slide the canoe over along the gunwales until you can pick it up again. Unless there's something interesting to see at the beginning of the portage, I prefer to get the carrying over with and do my resting at the other end: travel is faster that way, with less waste time.

In lake country, the portages are generally clearly marked on the maps and at both ends of the trail, but matching those indicators with the physical geography isn't always so easy. The portages that exist today are mostly connecting links in voyageur and Indian trade and migration routes that have existed for centuries: near points between two lakes, rarely steep, often running beside a connecting stream—geological facts. Guided by the map, look for a low point in the horizon, a break in trees that indicates a stream, quite possibly with a portage trail beside it.

When you stop for lunch, all you should need to take out is the pack with your lunch foods in it— probably, as I suggested earlier, the cooking pack, since it's small and light and will have the stove in it, if you feel like a hot drink. Be sure to pull the canoe halfway up out of the water so it won't drift away—easy enough to do loaded by lifting one end and letting the other float while you draw it up. If it's windy, though, or waves are breaking hard against the shore, you'd better unload the canoe completely and carry it up above the water line: the chop might damage the bottom of the half-floating canoe even if it doesn't drift it away. With a soft bank and a calm day, you can use a painter line to moor the canoe, fully afloat, to the nearest tree, but make sure it's solid, not a half-rotten stump that may break or uproot if the wind comes up.

We've touched in earlier chapters on what to do if your canoe *does* get away from you or capsize. As with all such canoeing hazards, the best prevention is common-sense preparedness: practice canoe handling, with your partner, before the trip; keep within reach of the shore on big lakes so that you can get out quickly if a sudden squall blows up; avoid needless risks, such as rapids, unless you're certain your skill is sufficient. In the event you lose the canoe or an important part of your food and equipment, preparedness is, again, your best out. Be sure someone—outfitter, park ranger, friends, or family at home—knows your approximate route and schedule, and then stay put until you're missed and searched for. The emergency waterproof matches and sheet of plastic that I advise carrying

in your pockets will provide warmth and shelter in the meantime, perhaps assisted by a lean-to thatched with pine boughs to shed water. Berries and other wild plants you're sure of, such as flagroot and acorns (much boiled to leach out the bitter tannin), will provide food. Threads frayed from your clothes and braided give you a fishing line, with a safety pin for a hook; or with your belt knife whittle a hook, Indian-fashion, from a branching green twig. Porcupines and beaver— look for trees they've gnawed the bark from and follow their trails—are fairly easy to run down and not bad to eat. Keep calm, keep your spirits up, and you'll manage. But above all, with sensible preparation you won't get into such scrapes in the first place. I never have, and you needn't!

Making and Breaking Camp

Making camp at the end of the day really begins with getting a good start in the morning and then keeping moving without too many needless halts. In parks, camping may be limited to fixed sites, requiring a permit, so that you'll have no choice but to get to a particular place before stopping. Even in wild areas, though, it's well to have a general objective and arrange the day so you can reach it in time to make camp and eat with enough evening light left for after-dinner swimming, fishing, reading, or whatever. For myself, I start thinking about where to camp by mid-afternoon, and if an attractive site comes along, I'll take it—if possible, from the standpoint of enjoying the evening, no later than four or five o'clock.

As I've suggested earlier, a breezy, open point or island makes the best camp site, if you have a choice, because it will be relatively free of mosquitoes. For the same reason, I'd avoid a shady spot, thickly grown with trees or a beach backed by a fringe of trees with marshy ground beyond—it may be all right in bright sun but with the first twilight the insects will rise up in clouds and make you wish you were elsewhere.

In general, I prefer a compact site no bigger than strictly necessary for the size of the party. With water, fireplace, and tent site all close at hand and enough space to store the canoe for the night well above any storm-driven waves, you'll save steps and the scattering of food and equipment that may lead to loss. Although openness is preferable for the places where you'll be cooking

Above, a desirable camp site: a compact, open, wind-swept point on an island, free of mosquitoes and flies, moderately secure against bears, where after a long day's paddling even a rock makes a comfortable pillow while dinner cooks (here, a cobbled beach along the Mackenzie River, Northwest Territories).

Right, a final touch for the evening meal: a batch of dough goes into the frying pan over a beaver-wood fire that in minutes will bake it to a crusty slab of bannock. (Credit: Jim Mead.)

The start of a new day: a moment for paddling out into the misty stillness to try for a breakfast fish—or simply to enjoy the further solitude. (Credit: Grumman Boats.)

and eating, for the tent look for a flat area with a few trees around it—to rope the tent to, if need be, and provide shelter against strong winds; a space no bigger than ten feet square should be enough for any tent you're likely to use. Other things being equal, I try to face the tent east, for the unaccustomed pleasure of waking to early-morning sun.

Since making camp is work, so far as I'm concerned, I try to get through it as quickly as possible. Get the packs up where they're going to be used and then divide up the jobs. One person can probably put the tent up by himself, then unpack sleeping bags, pads or air mattresses, and so on, leaving everything that belongs there inside in case of rain (remember to leave the mosquito netting zipped when you're finished). Meanwhile, someone else can be gathering firewood (unless you're limited to a stove), getting the fire started, setting up the cooking gear, sorting out food for the evening meal. With these few tasks completed, you're ready for a swim, an exploratory walk, a little late-afternoon fishing (not, admittedly, the best time, but it's the one who keeps trying who gets the

fish), perhaps a cup of whatever's to your taste in canoer's grog.

No matter how meek the weather looks in the afternoon when you're setting up camp, make it a habit to pitch the tent as if you expected a storm: stake it tight all around, prop the poles with rocks, if need be, to get the tent walls and fly tight, and brace the poles with ropes at front and back. If the soil is no more than a thin, light loam with rock beneath so that stakes won't hold, brace them by one of the methods suggested in Chapter 5.

Also in Chapter 5, we touched on several other camp precautions, but reminders are in order. Use care in handling ax or saw and fire, keeping firewood dry. Small animals—squirrels, chipmunks, the wily raccoons—will attack and ruin any food they can smell if you forgetfully leave it unprotected, tearing holes in your packs in the process. Their likes include chocolate, bread, cheese, open cans of butter, anything in a soft container (including the supposedly airtight foil or plastic freeze-dried packages). At night, toss all such foods into a pack and take it into the tent, and you'll not be

Reinforcing the tent stakes: in the midst of a gale, the corner, side, and guy-line stakes of **this light nylon tent have all been weighted with driftwood logs laid across the stake loops.**

bothered; if you're away from camp for the day, you'll do well to use a length of that rope I advise carrying to string the pack over a tree branch well off the ground (or hang it from a tripod made of ten- or twelve-foot saplings tied together at the top). Bears seem to go quite nutty over food with a strong smell, such as bacon or butter, but I've never known them to show much interest in packaged stuff. In bear country, keep an eye out for fresh tracks or droppings suggesting that these excitable animals frequent your camp site. If they do, keep the food that tickles their palate *well away from the tent* and protect it by hanging it up out of reach. Except perhaps in Yellowstone, where they've been half tamed by foolish children and their parents, bears will stay well away from you unless lured by food tempting enough to overcome their natural fear.

The only other hazards you're likely to encounter are skunks and porcupines, and both, since they're well armed and fearless, are quite capable of wandering into camp for a tour of inspection. A porcupine is harmless unless you try to pick one up

in your arms (they *don't* "shoot" their quills); if one shows too much interest in your food, prod him gently with a pole and he'll waddle off again. Keep your distance from a skunk, stay in front of him, avoid sudden movements, and, again, he'll leave you alone when he's satisfied his curiosity. Dogs are notorious for attacking porcupines and skunks (and enraging bears)—with disagreeable consequences for all concerned—a good reason for letting your pet stay home.

And one last reminder: the canoe. While the light lasts, keep it handy to the water in case you want to paddle out in a hurry for something interesting—a big fish jumping, a gorgeous sunset to photograph. Before you retire for the night, however, remember to get the canoe well up above the water line in case big waves come up, and turn it over so that it won't be vulnerable to wind or full of water in the morning if it rains. I generally stow the paddles under the canoe, but if the bank's steep it's sensible to take them up to level ground and stand them against a tree (so that someone won't step on a blade and break it).

Getting started again in the morning is pretty much the reverse of the evening process. Again, it will go smoothly if you divide up the jobs: collecting additional wood; starting the fire; cooking breakfast (it helps if the cook happens to be an early riser); washing and drying pots, pans, and other cooking equipment. Meanwhile, open up the tent and let the bedding and nightwear air out, preferably hung over a line in the morning sun (your body, it is said, will exude at least a pint of moisture during the night, even if you don't feel sweaty). With breakfast finished, one person can repack the sleeping bags and clothes and take down the tent, while another deals with the cooking kit and food and sets aside something for lunch.

All this sounds simple enough on paper, but it can take up half the morning if you let it (pancakes, for instance, are a grateful part of the breakfast scene but slow work in a camp-sized frying pan, particularly when there are several mouths to feed). In a sense, that doesn't matter. Getting free of the time-bound schedules of modern urban life is one of the rewards of canoe travel. At the same time, however, whether the day is committed to moving on to the next destination or exploring, fishing, and loafing around camp, one wants not to spend too much of it sleeping the sun high into the sky, cooking, doing the camp-breaking chores.

Balance is the goal—between sun time and clock time. Whether or not you make the final break and leave your watch behind, you'll wake with the sun, sleep with the dark, eat (listening to what your body tells you) when you're hungry. Even if your natural cycle makes you a night person in the ordinary routine of life, you'll find yourself getting out of the tent while the others sleep and paddling into the misty half-light of a silent predawn, perhaps with the excuse of casting for an unwary breakfast fish—or simply to wait for the sunrise that, except on a canoe trip, you'll rarely see. And you rediscover out here that time is distance—the distance that takes you, paddle stroke by paddle stroke, from one end of a lake to the other, from portage to portage, from bend of river to rapids to evening camp site; and that the watch you may or may not be wearing on your wrist is not your master but a tool, measuring speed and distance as closely as need be, doubling in a pinch as a compass when set against the dawn or noonday sun. You are traveling free, and by a different and more fundamental time.

Chapter 7

VOICES OF EXPERIENCE

If you're thinking about going on your first canoe trip, you *can* do all the planning, make all the arrangements, on your own. The chief purpose of this book is to help you do just that. Nevertheless, you'll probably feel more comfortable if you supplement that help with specific information on the many kinds and levels of canoe travel that are possible in various parts of the United States and Canada. In addition, there's a good deal of in-person assistance to be had from national canoeing and wilderness associations and from local or regional canoeing and outing clubs, which offer everything from a chance to meet and talk with experienced canoeists who have "been there" to local canoeing maps and canoe-trail guides to training programs and organized canoe trips of anything from a weekend to a month or more. And, finally, at the entrance points to much of the best North American canoe country, there are outfitters who offer as much or as little as you want or need in the way of general planning and who, in most cases, can furnish most of the equipment you'll need, from a single rented sleeping bag to a complete outfit; and similarly with food and other supplies. Outfitting is a business, of course, but the canoe outfitters I've known are in it first of all because they love canoeing and the canoe country, and making sure you have a successful trip is their first concern. In this inflationary age, the costs of such services are still on the modest side for the value given.

Once the canoeist starts looking seriously for information and practical help, he discovers that the sources for both are so numerous as to be overwhelming. What we'll be doing here, then, is finding our way through this thicket, identifying some of the kinds of information and professional outfitting services that are available, with examples of what you can expect from each. From a canoeing standpoint, the most useful material about the canoe country is firsthand, local, and specific, meaning that much of it is available only in the areas concerned (or through the mail) or from a great variety of local, state, and provincial government agencies. Sources for the examples given in this chapter and for an abundance of similar material are given in the Appendixes, along with names and addresses of outfitters, in many parts of the continent, that I think you'll find reliable.

Where to Go

Deciding where to make what may be your first real canoe trip begins with shared experience. You get to talking to another canoer, he tells you about a trip of his own, last summer or years ago, and you think, why not there? Wanting to know more, you seek out the permanent record of many canoers' experience, in the form of books, pamphlets, canoe-trail guides, maps. Sooner or later, by that exploratory route, you will find your way in books and finally in fact to the Boundary Waters-Quetico canoe country of northern Minnesota and southern Ontario: the historic crossroads of Indian migration and trade, of voyageurs' fur-trade routes, of modern canoeing; the geographic and geological pivot point of lake and river routes that lead south and north, east and west, to the limits of the continent.

Probably no canoeing region in the world has been more fully written about than that border-lakes country, and among all the books it has inspired, none more beautifully evoke the land, its nature and history, and the essence of canoeing than those of Sigurd Olson, beginning with *The Singing Wilderness.* They're all worth reading, both for what they tell you about that part of the canoer's world and for the craft and wisdom of canoe travel that they communicate. Although the focus of these books is the Boundary Waters Canoe Area, what they tell is equally valid for the vast system of lakes and rivers that stretches north to the Arctic in the shape of an inverted triangle, its base a line running from Hudson Bay to the mouth of the Mackenzie River, its apex the Boundary Waters area.

This canoe country is essentially the area covered by the fur trade from its seventeenth-century beginnings until toward the end of the nineteenth century: an inexhaustible system of lakes and rivers between Hudson Bay and the Rocky Mountains, much of it Canadian but connected by history and geography via the St. Lawrence and the Great Lakes with New England and New York and the Mississippi and Missouri valleys. The literature describing every aspect of this huge area is correspondingly vast. One of the most useful books about it from the canoeing standpoint is Eric Morse's *Fur Trade Canoe Routes of Canada, Then and Now.* Using early records, Morse has reconstructed and mapped the routes themselves, but he has also traveled them by canoe. His book is both a history of North American canoe travel and a practical introduction to dozens of possible long-distance trips through country as unspoiled and remote as it was two centuries ago, when its only inhabitants were the voyageurs and the scattered bands of Indians with whom they traded.

For the first introduction to the wilderness canoe country of New York's Adirondacks and the lakes and rivers of northwest Maine, you can find no better guide than Thoreau. He was there first, more than a century ago, and mercifully, through the wisdom of two state governments, the country he described is still recognizable. The fruits of Thoreau's exploration of the Maine wilderness became *The Maine Woods,* published soon after his death. He did not live to write formally of the Adirondacks, but what he knew of that still-wild country is worth digging out of his journals for the summer of 1858, when he camped and paddled on Long Pond in company with Emerson and others hardly less eminent.

A modern sensibility, no less intent on wilderness waters, is to be found in Michael Jenkinson's re-

cent *Wild Rivers of North America.* The book describes in depth nine waterways as different from one another as the Suwannee (Georgia and Florida) and the Yukon: history and geography, what they're like now to travel by canoe. There are also brief introductions to more than a hundred wilderness water routes throughout the continent. Many of these are canoeable, though the author inclines toward those like the Colorado, which, for much of its length, is navigable only in oversize rubber rafts commercially operated; and warns of the strenuousness of the Boundary Waters area, which to me is as comfortable and familiar as my own living room. One man's meat, I guess.

Books like these, which you'll read primarily for general background on canoeing and the canoe country, simply whet the canoer's appetite for detailed guidance to specific rivers and lakes. Two canoeing guidebooks have the virtue of covering, in condensed fashion, canoeable rivers and some lake systems in every part of the United States and are therefore useful for getting your bearings. *Makens' Guide to U.S. Canoe Trails* summarizes something like eight hundred American rivers: location, access points, length of the canoeable sections, difficulty, special hazards, camping and fishing possibilities. Most are runs of a day or two, but some longer rivers are treated in sections (the Allagash in Maine, the Delaware River bordering New York, Pennsylvania, and New Jersey, the Rio Grande in the Southwest). The listings are not limited to remote or wilderness areas, but all are possible in an open canoe (as distinct from a kayak or rubber raft), though the range of difficulty is from beginner-easy to hazardously difficult.

Robert Colwell's *Introduction to Water Trails in America* provides a greater amount of information about a smaller number of canoe trails but, like *Makens' Guide,* systematically covers the country. He treats the big canoe routes (the Boundary Waters Canoe Area, for instance, or Missouri's Ozark National Scenic Riverways) only in general terms but provides mile-by-mile guidance, with sketch maps, for dozens of lesser streams. Most of these are short and easy (a day or two) but attractive: a sampler of the possibilities of canoeing within reach of the experienced beginner, but useful also for canoeists of any ability practicing up for an extended trip. Where *Makens' Guide* is a compilation, Colwell's accounts of the river runs he treats in detail seem to be based entirely on his own recent experience.

In *Canada Canoe Routes,* Nick Nickels has attempted for his country what Makens has accomplished south of the border: a condensed introduction, province by province, to the main possibilities for canoeing. Much of the material in this compilation is better set forth in Nickels's sources, free (or low-priced) pamphlets and maps available from the provincial governments. Where he reports from firsthand experience (his own or others'), however, he's useful, and there are bits of interesting canoeing lore scattered throughout.

Just where you do your canoeing, particularly if you're new to the sport, depends partly on where you live. The chances are, however, that with the help of the three comprehensive guides, you'll find attractive and varied waters within one or two hours' car-topping from your home. (Don't—to repeat—disregard a stream simply because you pass it every day going to and from work or whatever; it will probably look entirely different and a lot less tame from the seat of a canoe.) Nevertheless, for canoe routes that are comparatively long, demanding, or remote—or all three—you need more help than these introductory guidebooks attempt to provide. Large-scale, canoe-oriented maps will show rapids, falls, and portages, possibly camp sites as well in areas where they're limited by regulation or geography (on steep rivers, contours are a rough indicator of how fast a current to expect but not essential elsewhere). Verbal descriptions of the routes fill out the bare bones of two-dimensional line and color with details a map can't show—seasonal variations in water level, alternative portages, recommended courses for complex rapids or abrupt bends in fast-flowing streams. Finally, since the routes may vary from year to year, you'll have to supplement such published canoe guides with what you can learn face to face from local rangers, outfitters, or other canoeists.

For the canoe routes of the northeastern United States, nearly all you need in the way of detailed guidance is available in one compact, 600-page volume, *The A.M.C. New England Canoeing Guide,* published by The Appalachian Mountain Club. In an impersonal format similar to the A.M.C.'s trail guides for hikers (or the original Baedekers), the book includes a mile-by-mile account of just about every canoeable waterway in the region, with descriptions of access points, camp sites, seasonal variations, special hazards of all kinds, and a lively sense of the historic and geological actuality on which the canoe country rests.

Note, however, that the maps included primarily supplement the text (with ratings of all canoe routes for difficulty and attractiveness), do not show portages, and, at about eleven miles per inch, are a little small-scale for serious canoeing. For that, you'll need the large-scale maps of the U. S. Geological Survey, which are based on aerial photographs (see Chapter 8 for further discussion of maps and map sources).

If you're headed for Maine—and that, after all, is where American canoeing began as a sport rather than as a means of migration or commerce—Eben Thomas's guide to ten of the Maine rivers, *No Horns Blowing,* deserves to be consulted. It's less comprehensive and less thorough than *The A.M.C. New England Canoeing Guide.* Its advantage is that it was written by an individual rather than a committee—personal in tone, always in the context of the author's own canoeing with friends or a family that included young and growing children.

Outside New England, there's no one source you can turn to for the kind of inclusive coverage that *The A.M.C. Guide* offers for its six states. Every state government, however, produces at least one pamphlet on canoeing within its own jurisdiction, typically descriptive notes on the leading canoeable rivers and lake systems with sketch maps (free or at nominal cost—available materials, with addresses, are included in the Appendixes). While these materials vary greatly in quality, they'll usually tell you enough to get started with confidence, particularly if they're fleshed out with U. S. Geological Survey maps. There are also independently published guides to canoeing in Virginia, Wisconsin, California, Washington, and the Yellowstone River region, among others.

In addition to these state materials, where the canoe country falls within a national park, as in the Boundary Waters Canoe Area, you can get fine canoeing maps free, with advice on general preparation and route planning. Such maps and pamphlets are best obtained from the park headquarters (see Appendixes); the Park Service or Forest Service in Washington, whichever is in charge, doesn't always seem to know what's available out in the hinterlands. Unlike the river touring that's the norm elsewhere—conditions may vary from month to month, but the routes themselves, though often at the mercy of industry and competing forms of recreation, are fixed—the lake-and-river country stretching north from Michigan and Wisconsin through Minnesota to the farthest north will probably never be reduced to neatly schematized tours. The area is simply too big, the possibilities too various. The best approach to planning a trip is careful study of the available maps and general literature well in advance, refined by on-the-spot advice, before you set out, from local rangers and outfitters.

Finally, quite a number of local canoe clubs and miscellaneous outing clubs scattered around the country have produced useful materials of their own that are available to non-members at modest prices. For example, the Pittsburgh chapter of the American Youth Hostels publishes a guide to the wild rivers of western Pennsylvania and northern West Virginia, and they've also produced a durable and accurate canoeing map of the same region, with routes color-coded for level of difficulty (*you* fill in the colors according to mimeographed notes supplied with the map). Its counterpart in Minneapolis is similarly helpful for canoeing in that area.

In Canada, except for the tentative first step represented by the Nickels guide mentioned earlier, there's no one source you can turn to for at least a preliminary idea of where to find the best canoeing. (A few visionaries talk of feeding all known details of Canadian canoe routes into a computer for later retrieval on demand, but, thinking of the times computers have brought chaos into one's department-store statements, tax records, and magazine subscriptions, one hopes the machines will get a little smarter before that happens.) The provincial and territorial governments, on the other hand, do an outstanding job. A card to any one of them will be answered with an elaborate, free brochure describing the major canoe routes, with maps—supplemented, in many cases, by leaflets giving detailed routings for trips to match one's experience and available time. For Quebec, in addition, the French-speaking canoe association (the Fédération Québécoise de Canot-Kayak) has published a 300-page guidebook that manages to be both literate and highly informative, provided you read French; an English version is planned and should be available by the time you read this, though I haven't seen it.

In the United States, the areas of true wilderness suitable for canoeing are comparatively few and limited. They exist by virtue of careful management (sharply defined boundaries; regulations to exclude private development, roads, and sometimes aircraft, which can be just as threatening) and under fairly continuous pressure from lumber, mining, and power companies that would like to put them to other uses, and from speculators for whom "wilderness" means idle land ripe for development with lodges, hotels, or summer houses. Large parts of central and northern Canada, on the other hand, are still wilderness in the most literal sense, accessible only by small seaplane, on foot—or by canoe. Although the entire country has been surveyed from the air (the results are available to individuals), there are parts of the North for which these aerial photographs have not yet been converted into exact and detailed maps. Hence, for the venturesome and experienced canoer, Canada offers opportunities for traveling waters that are effectively uncharted, in the wake of the earliest explorers (if there were any). There are probably no canoeable Canadian lakes and rivers that have *never* been visited by white men, but there are many where the last outlander was a stray trapper, trader, missionary, or explorer whose scanty records have passed from public memory. For several years now, therefore, the Canadian federal government has encouraged proficient canoe parties to travel into these remote places and describe and sketch the routes—and for the serious canoeist the results of these expeditions are available in mimeographed form (details and addresses in the Appendixes). But because the canoe country is very nearly limitless, much remains that has not been touched even in that preliminary form. An exciting prospect!

Getting Organized

A liking for associations and interest groups is one of the traits that sets Americans apart from other nations. It's not surprising, therefore, that in the United States there are a great many national and local organizations concerned in one way or another with canoeing; the Canadians lag in this respect. Even if you're not by nature a joiner, there are practical reasons for hooking up with one of these groups. At the least, you'll be in touch with a clearing house for useful information about canoeing techniques, equipment, places. Several of these organizations sponsor group canoe trips during the summers in various parts of the country, an effective and not too expensive way for a beginner to learn the ropes under trustworthy leadership, the only drawback being that if the trip is oversuccessful and too big, the experience will be more like summer maneuvers at Fort Bragg than a vacation. In addition, some local groups organize training sessions in white-water technique, an indispensable safety factor for most river canoeing even if hell-for-leather rapids shooting doesn't happen to be your idea of fun. You can learn a good deal about such matters from books, but unless you can afford a smashed boat or two as part of the instruction fee, serious learning begins in the front end of a canoe with a master canoeist in the stern. Apart from these formal benefits, there's more than a little to be said for the chance to get together periodically and simply talk with others who share your interest in canoe and paddle.

Of the several national American organizations, the long-established American Canoe Association is the one most relevant to general or distance canoeing. As a member, in *Canoe,* the moderately interesting six-times-a-year magazine sponsored by the A.C.A., you have access to an up-to-date source of information on the multifarious state and local publications mentioned earlier, a fair number of A.C.A. pamphlets on techniques and canoe routes, and the large number of affiliated local clubs. A few of these local groups (notably the Minnesota Canoeing Association) are sufficiently strong and well organized to rival the national one in influence, activity, and general usefulness.

The American Whitewater Affiliation overlaps with the A.C.A. in interest (with an obvious difference in emphasis), and like it produces publications for its members. As the name implies, it's a federation of local clubs. Although kayaking (and rafting) have a larger place in Whitewater's sun than canoeing as such, what the various affiliates actually go in for depends on where they are; some are connected with the American Canoe Association as well as the American Whitewater Affiliation.

In Canada, the Canadian Canoeing Association is the organization corresponding to the A.C.A., but as in most other areas of Canadian life there are really two groups, one English-speaking (this one, based in Ontario), the other French, the Fédération Québécoise, mentioned a few pages back. Perhaps because the provincial governments do such a thorough job of providing information about canoeing, there is not, in Canada, the multiplicity of strong local canoe clubs to be found in the United States. Those that do exist are not forthcoming with help for inquiring strangers.

Although their primary concerns are elsewhere, two other organizations interest themselves in canoeing. Besides its *New England Canoeing Guide,* the venerable Appalachian Mountain Club publishes John Urban's *White Water Handbook,* a sensible, brief manual of the canoe and kayak techniques needed for getting through rapids. Headquartered in Boston, the A.M.C. has chapters throughout the East, several of which double as local canoe clubs. (Membership rather forbiddingly depends on coming up with a pair of sponsors, but you don't have to belong to avail yourself of the A.M.C.'s publications and other services.) The West Coast equivalent of the A.M.C. is the Sierra Club, based in San Francisco but with regional chapters that cover nearly all of North America. Although best known as a ferocious defender of what's left of the wilderness heritage (and a publisher of superb illustrated books dedicated to the same goal), the Sierra Club each year sponsors dozens of what it calls outings for its members: wilderness expeditions under experienced leadership at fairly modest rates that cover transportation and outfitting and leave the anxieties of group planning to someone else. Many of these are hiking or climbing trips (or depend on horse or burro power) and some are aimed at exotic portions of the globe, but several each year are family-oriented canoe trips down wild western rivers or through parts of the Canadian canoe country. For a novice canoer who wants the security of an organized group and informative leadership, the Sierra Club canoe trips are a good bet—and generally easier to find out about and join than the more casual group trips of the local canoe clubs and similar organizations.

Canoe travel forms an important part of the program of the Boy Scouts and the YMCA—provided you're young enough. Locally, both organizations sometimes provide instruction in canoeing technique (worth asking about). Don't, however, let yourself be talked into leading (or co-leading) a Scout or Y trip unless you're a proficient canoeist to begin with, already know the intended area, and possess a naturally winning way with kids in numbers. For those who are past the summer-camp stage of life, the American Youth Hostels are worth getting acquainted with. The hostels themselves are hard to find outside New England, but in cities as far west as St. Louis if an AYH branch is active at all there's a good chance that canoeing is one of the things it's involved in. In some places the AYH chapter is also *the* local canoe club.

Several organizations primarily concerned with conservation have, at least, interests in common with canoers and have played a part in the creation of the Boundary Waters Canoe Area and the national scenic waterways, for which we can all be grateful. Even if you're not a fanatical conservationist, you may well be led, through some aspect of canoeing—photography, the observation of and curiosity about plants and animals along the canoe-and-paddle routes, simple reverence for water and landscape—to the Wilderness Society, the National Audubon Society, or the Izaak Walton League. Depending on the terrain, strong local Audubon chapters will sometimes take to the water in pursuit of birds to watch—and do so by canoe.

Outfitter's Services

One index of the quality and popularity of a canoeing area is the number of outfitters it supports and the range of services they offer. By that standard, the Boundary Waters/Quetico region is preeminent, with dozens of long-established and reliable outfitters at the Minnesota entrance points to the south and in Ontario north of the Quetico Park. Other areas well provided with outfitting services are Maine, the Adirondack region of New York, Algonquin Park in southeastern Ontario, the Delaware River basin, and the Missouri Ozarks.

In general, in the eastern half of the continent, the minimum you can expect from a canoe outfitter is a canoe rental service, typically at a rate of around five dollars per day, with auxiliary equipment such as car-top carriers or trailers additional (in such crowded areas as eastern Pennsylvania, rates may be higher on weekends). Most canoe renters are dealers as well. Nearly all the outfitters listed in the Appendixes also provide food and—on a rental or sale basis—suitable packs and other equipment and maps for their areas. Particularly for the Boundary Waters/Quetico and Algonquin Park, *complete outfitting* is available, meaning that the outfitter supplies enough food for a trip of a specified length, with rental tents, sleeping bags, cooking equipment, and other basic equipment at a fixed rate per person per day. This is certainly the easiest and least expensive way to

handle your outfitting if you're making your first trip, and the costs are surprisingly modest, all considered: around fifteen dollars daily per person in the United States, closer to ten dollars in Canada. While some outfitters offer only complete outfitting, most also do *partial outfitting:* you can buy some or all your food from them and rent, at quite nominal charges, any equipment you don't happen to own. Even if you're well equipped for canoe camping and bring some of your food with you from home, you'll find it advantageous to do business with an outfitter simply for the sake of the contact. He can advise you on your intended route, current conditions, any special hazards, and it's well for someone to know where you're going and how long you plan to be out, in case you run into trouble, even in such areas as the Boundary Waters and the Maine wilderness, where registering with the local rangers is required. The outfitters' general advice and checklists of equipment and supplies help you make sure that you don't forget anything vital to the trip.

Most outfitters can also provide you with a *guide* if you want one, and, in a few places, that may be the only basis on which they'll work with you. Where it's available, you can expect to pay at least thirty dollars per day for guide service plus outfitting for the guide at the same rate you pay. In the major canoe areas, few people use guides any more—with systematic preparation and the help of a competent outfitter, you don't really need one—but in several respects it's an ideal way to make your first canoe trip. A good guide will know the route and the area as thoroughly as you know your own house, will do as much of the mere work as you'll let him, and will make certain you get to the spots where the fishing's best, if that's what you're after; even an experienced camper will probably learn a few things about canoeing, the canoe country, and the general lore of the woods. In the old days, the North Woods guides were generally full-time professionals, often Indian or part Indian—spiritually, direct descendants of the voyageurs and the original wilderness men. Today, they're more likely to be college students or young teachers, free for the summer; but the tradition continues.

In the American Southwest and the Canadian Northwest, "outfitting" has a meaning rather different from the one that applies to the east. In these areas, the big rivers—much of the Colorado, some of the steep tributaries of the Mackenzie—are *not* canoeable but can be run in big, inflatable rafts (heavily built wooden dories are also used on the Colorado). Outfitters in California, Nevada, and Edmonton, Alberta, organize such expeditions, trucking or flying their parties to the starting points, retrieving them, providing guides, camping gear, supplies—in effect, package tours through regions that by any other means would be absurdly dangerous or simply impossible but, in rafts or boats, with skilled leadership, are both safe and exciting; in the nature of things, the groups tend to be big—several ten-man rafts. The Edmonton outfitters will make similar arrangements for canoe travel on rivers where that's possible; otherwise, in the Northwest Territories, the canoer is pretty much on his own.

The prices for all-inclusive, organized river tours are not low. On the Colorado, for example, the rate for a recent five-day outing through the Grand Canyon by oar-powered raft was $275, including food and a professional guide but *not* camping equipment or transportation to the start or return. (The organization quoted in this example· is the American River Touring Association, a sort of club, which runs raft trips throughout the mountain states but also an occasional canoe trip on one of the easier rivers, useful for novices and less expensive; at least a dozen other commercial operators offer similar group tours, on the Colorado and elsewhere.) In the Canadian Northwest, typical costs run from a minimum of around five hundred dollars per person—all-inclusive, however—to two or three times that for a two-week trip, depending very much on the air distance from the base in Edmonton (the distances are great, air transport expensive, and most of the areas covered are still roadlss tundra, permanently frozen, just below the surface even in summer).

Somewhat closer to civilization, if your time is limited and your ambition is remote wilderness canoeing, flying in may be the solution. Canadian outfitters in the Quetico region, for example, can arrange to fly you to your starting point, fully equipped, in a light float plane and pick you up again at the end. Because these bush planes are small, the canoes are generally strapped on under the belly, across the pontoons, passengers and their equipment squeezed into the cabin; the ride, unless you're a born aerophobe, is no scarier than in any other light plane, and the seat-of-the-pants bush pilots who do the flying can be relied on to get you safely in and out of the lakes and rivers that make

a patchwork of the Canadian North. From, say, Atikokan, north of the Quetico in western Ontario, you can get to the headwaters of the Albany River, flowing northeast three hundred miles into James Bay, to the Hayes, Nelson, or Churchill river, each of which feeds Hudson Bay proper, or to literally hundreds of other famous and historic canoe routes than are still part of the canoer's heritage. Expect to pay a minimum of seventy cents per mile (for a small plane that will carry two people, their baggage and canoe), up to twice that for a bigger craft—an Otter, say. Bear in mind that air charter rates are always round-trip: a hundred air miles at seventy cents per mile will cost you $140—the distance to the drop-off point plus the return of the empty plane to its base.

On a smaller scale, similar fly-in arrangements are useful in the roadless canoe country of northwest Maine. You can, for instance, get to the headwaters of the St. John River by plane, and that's the way to do it if you want to take the river whole, from its source. The alternative is several days of arduous poling up shallow rivers that are on the wrong side of the watershed from which the St. John flows.

For the adventurous and experienced canoeist who has felt the call of the vast wilderness distances, there remains one further possibility: The Hudson's Bay Company's *U-Paddle service.* "The Bay" (as it likes to call itself) has dozens of posts dotted across the Canadian wilderness south, west, and north of Hudson Bay, nearly all of them on lakes and rivers that include the great canoe routes of the past and present. You can rent an aluminum canoe at most of these posts, paddle it downriver to the next outpost, leave it there, and return home (rental is about fifty dollars per week). The likely starting and stopping points are the mining and oil towns scattered across the North, bearing such romantic names as Yellowknife, Nelson House, Fort Chipewyan; many are accessible by the scheduled planes of Northward Airlines, Pacific Western, or Canadian Pacific (which can also arrange charters to points off their routes).

Obviously, any of these remote trips will take a lot of planning. For a start, The Bay has to know *in the fall* if you're going to want a canoe during the summer. The reason for this is that the canoes are hauled in by road, and many of the likely starting points can be reached only over frozen winter roads that vanish with the spring breakup around the middle of May. In addition, although many of the Hudson's Bay stores sell clothes and camping equipment (and a sufficient range of food to allow for resupplying along the route), they're *not* in the rental business; most of the camping equipment you need will have to fly in with you, and you'll have to make your own arrangements. And finally, the distances are considerable: any canoe trip you make will run to hundreds of miles and several weeks, and skill, experience, and long-term preparation will have to be in proportion. Cautions aside, though, as I study the maps, and the possibilities fill my imagination—my canoe parting those solitary waters, unlimited except by strength and ingenuity—I'm ready to start packing, and the only real question is *where*. You may feel that call yourself; when it comes, answer.

Chapter 8

ON YOUR OWN

You can usually find a canoe outfitter who, at a modest profit, will do your detailed trip planning for you. Even then, however, only you can decide where, when, and for how long—the decisions we've been concerned with in the preceding chapter. Moreover, because individuals vary, it's well to know what the outfitter had in mind when he rents you a sleeping bag or tent or sells you a carton of Bisquick. To my mind, though, the essential responsibility is bound up with the nature of canoeing itself. However much you borrow from others' experience, once you're under way, with food and equipment for a weekend or for several weeks fitted into your canoe, you're on your own, dependent on no one but yourself. That exhilarating self-reliance begins with the detailed planning, the checklists of food and equipment, that are the subject of this chapter. Doing your own planning and outfitting may save you a little money, but that's incidental. Even in tame country—but wilderness clings like an aura to a canoe traveling even the most civilized waters—a canoe trip needs a leader, one person, finally, who bears responsibility for what gets decided, what gets done: the *bourgeois*. We'll approach this final step in canoe-trip planning from that standpoint: what you, the leader, need to assemble, by whatever means, in order to ensure a successful trip, free of anxieties for yourself and others. For a start, it helps if you're a list maker.

Maps and Map Sources

Once you've decided in general where you're going for a canoe trip, your next step in planning is to get detailed and accurate maps. You'll study them in figuring out your route, matching distance and difficulties to available time, and you'll rely on them religiously for finding your way on the trip itself. Since the matter of what maps to get and where to find them is a little complicated, we've postponed specific discussion until now.

For the Boundary Waters Canoe Area, the map problem is easily solved. The B.W.C.A. was carved out of the Superior National Forest, and the Forest Service publishes an excellent free map that you can get by writing to the supervisor in Duluth (see Appendixes). The scale (1:250,000, or about four miles to the inch) is ideal for over-all planning and, although a little small, is adequate for use on the trip itself. The map shows portages and all geographic features with great exactness. In addition, commercial maps designed for canoeing are pub-

Planning a canoe trip: figuring the route, distance, and time, using a map measurer on a detailed, large-scale canoeing map, with a larger, planning map of the area underneath for reference.

lished in the area and cover both the B.W.C.A. and its sister Quetico region across the border—a total of about 14,500 square miles of canoe country in fifteen overlapping maps. These commercially produced maps are to a scale of a little over two miles to the inch, about right for canoe travel, are very accurate for portages and other features of the canoe routes, and are printed on a parchmentlike, waterproof paper for which you'll be intensely grateful the first time you have to consult one on a rainy day. The maps are available from the publisher or from outfitters in the area (under one dollar each—see Appendixes for addresses).

In a few other parts of the country there are Forest Service maps, comparable to the one for the B.W.C.A., for canoe routes that lie within national forests, but for most you'll have to start with maps produced by one or another state or local government agency (listed in the Appendixes along with Forest Service sources). These are good enough for planning, but for actual travel will generally have to be supplemented with topographical maps from the U. S. Geological Survey. Since thousands of these have been published in several different scales, figuring out which you need and actually getting them into your hands is rather a job in itself. The first step is to order the free index maps for the states you're interested in from the central map office in Arlington, Virginia, or Denver (see Appendixes).

From the index maps, you discover that the entire country is mapped to two different scales: 1:62,500, or about one mile to the inch (what the U. S. Geological Survey calls a 15-minute quadrangle); and 1:24,000, two thousand feet to the inch (7½-minute quadrangle). A few states, such as Pennsylvania, are also available in 1:250,000-series maps (four miles per inch). None of these scales is ideal for canoeing. The four-mile-per-inch series is on the small side: every inch represents an hour or more of paddling. The one-mile-per-inch maps typically show quadrangles about thirteen and a half miles square, with the consequence that you may need ten or fifteen maps to cover a trip of only a week or two, making a cumbersome bundle to carry and protect from weather. (One solution practiced by a number of serious hikers and canoers is to trim off the extraneous parts of the series of maps needed for a trip, then stick them together with rubber cement or transparent tape to show the intended route in a continuous strip that won't

be too bulky and can be folded, with care, to fit a map case.) The situation is further complicated by the fact that current U. S. Geological Survey policy is apparently to abandon the one-mile-per-inch series as the supply of each map is exhausted: eventually, there will be only the 1:250,000 series (still incomplete) and the 1:24,000 to choose from. Nevertheless, I'd recommend the 1:62,500 maps—while they last. The alternative is to use the 1:250,000 maps as your basic ones, where available, and supplement them (around rapids, for instance) with maps in one of the larger scales, but switching back and forth between two different map scales is something of a problem in itself.

Each state map index lists libraries and dealers that attempt to stock all the available maps for their region, and if you live near one of them you'll be able to examine or buy the maps you want in person. Or you can order the maps from one of the two map offices at the price most dealers charge, about one dollar per map. However you do it, don't order without first studying the appropriate index maps; it's a complicated matter.

From the canoeing standpoint, Canada is rather better off for maps than the United States. For the two major canoe areas in Ontario, the Quetico and Algonquin parks, excellent planning maps, showing portages, are available free from the park headquarters or from the Ontario tourist office in Toronto (see Appendixes for addresses). Both are to a scale of 1:250,000, which by now you know works out to about four miles to the inch—a little small-scale for actual travel but usable, once you adjust, since the maps are exceptionally accurate. There are similar maps for some other national and provincial parks that are good for canoeing, and, as we noted in the previous chapter, the provincial governments supply booklets describing other canoe routes, with route plans that will do for planning (free or at modest expense).

As in the United States, for a trip that's at all complicated, you'll probably want to supplement these planning maps with more detailed ones to a larger scale. The American set of two-mile-per-inch maps for the Boundary Waters Canoe Area also covers the Quetico, but elsewhere you'll need the maps published by the Canadian federal government in Ottawa (see Appendixes for address). There are two separate systems of interest to the canoer: one to a scale of 1:250,000, which covers most of the country, though not always with maps

Map case: homemade from two sheets of vinyl 12 × 13 inches, waterproof cloth tape and snaps.

in completely final form; and a large-scale system to a scale of 1:50,000 (one and a fourth inches to the mile), still only about half finished. The first step in ordering the 1:250,000 maps is to write for the index map (one covers the whole country); for the 1:50,000 series, you need to start with an *index of the index maps* (there are eighteen, not corresponding to provinces or territories), get the index map for the region you're interested in, and *then*

order specific maps. Current prices are one dollar per sheet for both map series. Generally speaking, since systematic mapping of Canada is a comparatively recent undertaking, the available maps are more up to date than their American counterparts.

One other Canadian map system will be ideal for canoeing, when completed: a 1:125,000 series, which (you guessed it!) works out to about two miles to the inch. So far, however, only a few maps are available in this scale, covering a large part of Ontario and scattered quadrangles elsewhere.

A clear-plastic map case is essential for protecting your maps in the course of a canoe trip. (Folding them to fit the case so that the route will be visible takes a certain amount of forethought.) Even in a case, however, maps printed on ordinary paper (all except the commercial maps for the Boundary Waters Canoe Area) will be subjected to moisture and dirt and will wear at the creases. You can prevent that by treating the maps, as some canoers do, with the kind of spray varnish you can get from art-supply stores or most hardware stores; put on several coats and let each dry thoroughly before spraying the next. Apart from making the maps last long enough to get through the trip or preserving them for the next time—considering the nuisance of getting them in the first place—I like to save my maps as a kind of visual summary of a trip I've enjoyed. Perhaps you will too.

There are a couple of map accessories that are moderately useful. A *map measurer* is an instrument with a revolving wheel geared to a gauge that converts map distances to inches, centimeters, miles, or kilometers, according to the scale of the map. They're handy in the planning stage, once you have your maps, particularly for a long trip, in which distance (and time) may be critical. They're available from downtown map stores and a few outfitters such as Eastern Mountain Sports, at prices ranging from about four to ten dollars (the less expensive versions are the better). A large-frame *magnifying glass* will also be handy at the planning stage, if you see through middle-aged eyes (as I do). Maps at a scale of four miles to the inch or more cram so much detail into a small space that I find them hard to follow without optical help.

I think of a *compass* as, first of all, an accessory to a good map. The best way to keep from getting lost on an unfamiliar lake is to follow the map closely all the way, identifying each point, island, and indent as it comes along. Even so, however, there will be times when it's difficult to relate what the map shows to the particular waterscape in front of you, and in such situations a compass can be decisive. If you're going to use a compass, I'd recommend one like the Silva Huntsman, which has a safety-pin arrangement for clipping onto your shirt so that it will never be buried in a pack if you happen to need it (about seven dollars).

Canoe Equipment

In chapters 2 and 4, we considered the various kinds of canoe equipment and the uses of each. The following list concerns items that are more or less essential. Check it in planning for any canoe trip, whether you're making all the arrangements yourself or leaving the details to an outfitter:

carrying yoke—positioned an inch or two ahead of the center thwart or mid-point of the canoe, so that it will balance with the bow up for visibility when carried.

spare paddle—same blade size as your regular paddles, tied in near the stern (for balance in portaging) with a hitch that can be released quickly, or with an elastic tie-down or a short webbing strap with buckle.

painter rings or loops—standard on most aluminum canoes but on others must be specified in ordering from the manufacturer; convenient for tying down the canoe on a car-top carrier and an important safety device in river canoeing involving extensive rapids.

bow and stern lines—twenty to twenty-five feet each of ¼-inch or ⅜-inch nylon rope securely tied to the painter rings and coiled so that it hangs inside the canoe (or use a heavy rubber band or short elastic tie-down); in rapids too shallow or treacherous to run fully loaded, the long lines can be used from the bank to let the canoe down or tow it up or to rescue the canoe if wedged against rocks by a strong current; *not essential* for flat-water lake canoeing.

repair tape—1½-inch waterproof cloth adhesive tape (or furnace tape, wider), for quick repair of canoes of all kinds or for mending rips in any fabric; so that it will always be there if you need it, put it in a small plastic bag and tie it into the canoe. *Epoxy*, perhaps a sheet of heavy vinyl, can be used for more serious canoe repairs.

life preserver—one for everyone in the canoe, to satisfy the law; you'll want the compact, expensive types only if you're canoeing the kind of wild river in which it's prudent to wear one most of the time—or if you don't swim.

Clothing

The only special purchases more or less necessary for canoeing are adequate boots and rain gear.

A fully equipped canoe: painter loops with painters at bow and stern, long decks (or white-water end caps), carrying yoke, paddles, with a spare paddle lashed in under the stern seat.

Everything else can be improvised from old clothes or work clothes you probably already have. The quantities suggested in the following checklist are for a two-week trip:

hat with brim—water-resistant cotton is better than wool or felt.

wool shirt with button pockets—with a change; or flannelette or a wool-cotton blend if you really can't stand the feel of wool, but neither is as functional; or if the weather's likely to mix hot with chilly (cold nights and some cool days, probable in northern climates), take one warm shirt and one of heavy cotton twill (any work-shirt type).

trousers—with a change; a tough cotton twill, cut roomy, is fine for most canoeing, with extra layers for cold weather (see below); fitted cuffs are a protection against bugs.

belt or suspenders.

socks—wool or a wool-synthetic blend; four pairs.

boots—preferably all leather and nine to ten inches high, with a tongue sewed right up to the top on both sides (a low-cut tongue lets the water in); since you'll be stepping in and out of water, not standing in it, really waterproof boots are not strictly necessary (expensive), but the boots should be treated before the trip with a *waterproofing cream* or *liquid,* and a supply of the latter is worth carrying on a long trip.

sheath knife—4–5-inch blade, so useful that I always have one on my belt when camping and regard it as an article of clothing; or a folding pocket knife with a blade of comparable size.

rain shirt or parka—by whatever name, an over-the-head kind reaching at least to the knees; don't waste your money on a poncho.

sweater.

windproof jacket—not essential if you want to travel light.

underwear—four changes, more if you're fastidious (easy to wash out, though, to keep bulk down).

Dressed for canoeing: hat with brim, bandanna neckerchief, wool shirt, tightly woven trousers (water-repellent and insect-proof), waterproof boots (the author and his eldest son at a lunch stop on a rocky beach of the Great Slave Lake in the Northwest Territories).

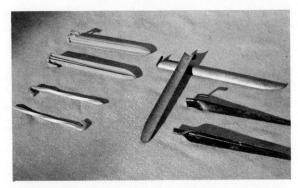

Some types of tent stakes: Cycolac plastic, I-beam design, as strong as steel (upper left); aluminum alloy, twisted for strength (lower left); galvanized steel (upper right); steel, painted, with hooks (lower right).

handkerchiefs—four.

bandanna—useful in addition to ordinary handkerchiefs.

head net (or hat with attached net)—a nuisance but advisable off the water in the Far North or the coastal Southeast, where insects may be a serious menace in midsummer.

for cold weather—add to the list a second sweater, long underwear with a change, warm waterproof gloves, and suppress your objection to wool for shirts; you might also want to substitute whipcord trousers (a tough wool twill) for the cotton suggested above—or another wool of comparable warmth and durability.

Sleeping Gear

I've included here several items that don't strictly have to do with sleeping arrangements, on the theory that they're most conveniently packed with the tent or sleeping bags:

tent—with poles and stakes (supplied with most current designs); if light wire tent pegs are standard with your tent, substitute heavier stakes of metal or plastic, at least at the corners—the light pegs are easy to put in but pull out if the ground's soft or the weather windy.

nylon rope—twenty to thirty feet or the equivalent in elastic shock cords, for anchoring the tent to a tree in a storm—particularly if yours is the kind of high-profile tent recommended in Chapter 5.

sleeping bag—the kind known in the trade as a "three-season bag"; rated for +10° or +20°; with waterproof stuff sack.

air mattress and/or *foam sleeping pad*—depending somewhat on the temperature and your notions of comfort.

pajamas—even if you're not normally a pajama person they help keep your sleeping bag clean and dry with less nuisance than a sleeping-bag liner; can be rolled up with the sleeping bag for packing.

candle lantern—saves the flashlight for emergencies and lights the tent adequately until everyone's in bed or on those late nights when you have to cook or wash dishes after dark; can be packed with the tent or a sleeping bag so that it ends up in the right place when needed.

six candles—a 6-inch candle with a diameter of three-fourths inch or less is about right; those sold in most supermarkets tend to droop in warm weather; some outfitters offer a more resistant kind.

flashlight—again, conveniently packed with the tent or sleeping bags which will protect it.

spare batteries and bulb—for a long trip; but start out with fresh ones.

aerosol insecticide—for use in the tent, after the mosquito netting's zipped up for the night.

books, playing cards—here again, my theory of keeping together things that are likely to be used together, though you may have your own set of packing associations.

Personal Accessories; Repairs and Emergencies

I've grouped together here quite a few miscellaneous items, mostly because they're small and are best kept together in bags to avoid loss or damage in a pack. The few that you'll need only in the event of such an ultimate emergency as losing the canoe and much of your camping equipment—flexible saw, waterproof match case, plastic sheet—belong in your pockets:

ditty bag—cloth or leather bag with drawstring top, for carrying toiletries and other small items.

personal-care supplies—toothbrush and toothpaste; comb and brush; razor (if you want to bother) with steel shaving mirror; nail clippers and fingernail brush; wash cloth; soap (or equivalent) in plastic or aluminum soap dish with cover; liquid soap (a tube can be carried in a shirt pocket); two bath towels; prescription medicines if any.

first-aid kit—in tight-fitting rigid case: iodine or equivalent, aspirin, laxative, adhesive bandages, gauze pads and bandages, adhesive tape, elastic bandage, a burn remedy such as Unguentine.

needle and thread—with a few *safety pins* and spare *buttons* which, being small, can be squeezed into the first-aid kit; extra *shoe laces*.

snake-bite kit.

Halazone—or an equivalent water-purifying chemical.

sun-tan lotion—or a sun-shield cream if you burn easily.

insect repellent—but in most areas and most seasons a well-chosen camp site, the smoke from the camp fire, and care in keeping the tent's mosquito netting closed will be your major defenses.

plastic rescue blanket—a survival item; on a long trip, you might do well to tuck a large sheet of heavy-gauge plastic into a pack as insurance against serious damage to the tent (and on wet days in camp it can double as a tarp; four plastic Versa-Ties at the corners will serve as instant grommets for roping the plastic to the nearest trees).

Versa-Tie, used to convert a sheet of plastic to a tarpaulin: a disk goes inside the plastic sheet and a ring snaps around it to form a grommet through which a rope can be tied.

waterproof match case—another survival item (include the striking surface if you use wooden safety matches), which might be backed up with a disposable *butane lighter*.

flexible steel survival saw.

sunglasses.

binoculars.

wallet, with money.

camera, with film—keep it simple.

small notebook with ballpoint pen—useful for making notes on places, route, or pictures, or for leaving messages.

fishing rods and tackle—again, avoid non-essentials to keep the tackle box light and compact; a rigid, tubular *rod case* is essential; include alligator-jaw *pliers,* with wire cutter, in the tackle box, with *reel oil* and an extra-sharp *knife,* in a case, reserved for cleaning fish (or keep the knife with tableware).

rope—fifty feet, say, for miscellaneous camp uses, in addition to what's with the tent or on the canoe.

twine, heavy rubber bands—for resealing plastic bags, odd jobs in camp; with, perhaps, a handful of *nails* (but *don't* drive them into live trees).

watch—unless you're determined to cut free of anything but sun and moon time.

whistle—well, *I've* never used one, but some experienced canoers wouldn't venture into the wilderness without one, for general signaling or emergencies, particularly if there are youngsters in the party who may wander off by themselves, exploring.

cigarettes, cigars, pipe tobacco—if you're a smoker, you'll know how much tobacco you need; for a pipe, don't forget your *pouch, pipe cleaners,* a metal *pipe tool,* and possibly a *windproof cover.*

Food

Making out a food list is a bit forbidding, simply because the range of choice is so considerable and one wants as varied a diet as possible. Quantities, too, are difficult to estimate. Individual appetites differ greatly to begin with, and someone doing sedentary work most of the year may double his intake under the stimulus of a strenuous canoe trip. It helps to break the meals down into types—so many breakfasts, lunches, and dinners for each person in the party—multiplied by the number of days in the trip; and that's what we'll be doing here. I won't attempt to prescribe quantities for each type of food, but I will list the number of servings you can expect from various standard packages—and leave it to you to decide the proportions according to your particular tastes. On a trip on which you plan to do some fishing (and catch some fish!), take enough food for the full number of days planned for the trip: the fish will then give you leeway for emergencies or a feast on the last night out. If you don't fish or don't expect the fishing to be good, allow enough food for an extra day or two, in case the trip for any reason runs longer than you plan.

In general, I prefer a heavy breakfast when I'm canoeing (fuel for the day's travel), a light, uncooked lunch (so as not to waste the best part of the day for travel), and a moderate dinner. I try to keep all the cooking as simple and non-time-consuming as possible; from the standpoint of preparation and clean-up afterward, I prefer a one-pan stew to any dinner that takes three or four pans and proportionately more time and attention. Although I enjoy elaborate cooking at home, on a camping trip I carry a minimum of condiments and seasonings—a matter of taste, but I view the extra jars and bottles as that many more breakables that have to be packed, protected, and carried. And, as a final prejudice, I don't like dried or canned soups of any kind—not enough nourishment for the price, weight, and bulk.

So much for personal tastes. In the following lists, I've mixed canned or bottled foods with plastic- or foil-wrapped freeze-dried foods, with the aim of balancing the lightness and comparatively high cost of the latter against the weight, low prices, and (usually) quick preparation of the former. In the Boundary Waters Canoe Area, however, cans are forbidden—and anywhere, courtesy and common sense should dictate that you carry out all containers that can't be burned, including foil wrappers, which are no more disposable than tin cans. From the standpoint of total weight, the mix of canned and dried foods should be feasible for a two-week trip, but for a longer one you'd want a smaller proportion of heavy cans; and vice versa. Quantities, where given, reflect not a scientific count of calories but my seat-of-the-pants experience of what's satisfactory for a person of average size and appetite. Big people or heavy eaters should adjust accordingly.

General

sugar—white sugar comes out to four teaspoons per ounce. If you use it in coffee or tea, cereal, and lunch-time lemonade, you'll need about one pound per person per week, about one third more if you prefer brown sugar (less refined, heavier, less concentrated).

dried milk—bulky but worth carrying, particularly if there are children in the party; you'll use it on cereal, in cocoa and other hot drinks; most convenient for mixing in boxes of foil-wrapped one-quart portions (and drink up what's left over at breakfast).

coffee—making it strong, I get about fourteen cups per ounce of freeze-dried coffee, so if you drink it at breakfast and dinner you'll need one ounce per person per week; tea seems to be favored among canoers, but I'll leave it to you to figure the quantity (less than coffee).

cocoa—an extra unless you or your children drink it in preference to coffee or tea; allow about one half ounce (two and one half teaspoons) per cup, and make it with milk.

Bisquick—an old-time mix that saves carrying flour and baking powder separately, good for making morning pancakes or evening biscuits (such as pan-baked bannock) even if you don't carry an oven; or for breading fish; the recipes on the carton recommend mixing with milk and a fresh egg but plain water will do.

butter or margarine—canned if available and permitted (or liquid margarine in a plastic jug); a welcome topping to biscuits or pancakes and luxurious for all frying, saving the need for a separate shortening; if you use it in that generous fashion, allow up to one pound per person per week.

jam or jelly—the sweetness seems awfully good on dinner bread of any kind and can substitute for syrup on pancakes if you run out; one of the Gerry squeeze-tubes (available from many camping outfitters) holds about two thirds of a pound, enough for two weeks for anyone but a jelly freak.

bread—ordinary store bread is a pleasant addition to the dinner menu for the first few days of a trip (or as an alternative to crackers for luncheon sandwiches, or as french toast for breakfast), but it's bulky, soon gets moldy (rye or whole wheat lasts a little better than white), and is likely to get crushed in a pack unless you carry it in a rigid aluminum provision box; there are a few canned breads (9-ounce size, from Stow-A-Way Sports Industries), but I've never, myself, been enough of a bread eater to bother.

salt—a waterproof shaker-container, if you can find one, holds about two ounces, enough for two people on a two-week trip, and is preferable to a one-pound carton or individual picnic-size shakers, both of which spill and soak up moisture; I don't usually bother with pepper or other seasonings.

tartar sauce—the one condiment that, being a fisherman, I don't like to be without; fresh lemons, which keep well, are useful for the same reason.

liquor—a bottle of whatever you like will last two people a couple of weeks if used sparingly.

Breakfast

powdered orange drink—Tang or equivalent; an easy way to start the day with a few vitamins; the current biggest size (twenty-seven ounces net) makes six quarts, which is enough generous 1-cup servings to last two people just about two weeks if they drink it every morning.

dried fruits—prunes or whatever else is available in the stores at the moment (apricots, apples, pears); an alternative to the orange drink for breakfast (a possible dessert, too, but better soaked overnight), or can be eaten as is as a lunch-time sweet; one pound per person should provide a modest serving each day for a two-week trip, but you probably won't want them that often.

oatmeal—a light, filling breakfast second course, fairly quick to prepare, more nutritive for the price and weight than even the best of the "concentrated" cold cereals; or another hot cereal you happen to like; figure about one ounce of oatmeal (dry weight) per person, and multiply by the number of people and the days of the trip if you have it every day.

bacon—unsliced bacon, if possible with rind attached (also called "slab bacon" or "a side of bacon"), keeps better and is infinitely less messy in a pack than the presliced variety, either plastic-wrapped or in a can; slicing it thin and neat with a knife takes a little patience in the morning; save the fat from cooking for frying pancakes or eggs. Note that in warm weather a little mold may form on the outside of a side of bacon, but it's harmless and doesn't seem to affect taste; scrape it off with your knife before slicing.

eggs—even in summer, you needn't feel anxious about their keeping up to a week if you carry them in a plastic egg container to prevent breakage; useful in camp cookery and a welcome break by themselves from pancakes; packaged *freeze-dried eggs,* though less tasty and more expensive, will fill out the second week of the trip. If you're planning for several people for a couple of weeks, buy the freeze-dried eggs in bulk, in a No. 10 can (the equivalent of at least forty eggs, as nearly as I can figure); much less expensive that way but also for some reason better tasting than the smaller packages; transfer the contents of the can, once opened, to a watertight plastic bag.

pancakes—use a mix or good old Bisquick (see above); a break from a breakfast of eggs and/or bacon and oatmeal; a cup of Bisquick, weighing six ounces, makes enough pancakes for a moderate two-man breakfast (ten pancakes), so two people would consume a 60-ounce carton per week if they had pancakes every morning.

syrup—for pancakes, in an unbreakable plastic jug; or a drop or two of Mapleine, a synthetic maple extract, added to one cup of sugar and ½ cup of boiling water makes enough syrup for breakfast for two to four people (a 2-ounce jar of extract will last through any trip with plenty left over).

Lunch

When I'm traveling, the only lunch-time cooking I normally do is a little hot water on a small stove for a cheering cup of coffee, tea, or cocoa, if the weather's cold or rainy. If I happen to catch a fish about lunch time, however, I either throw it back or, if there's time, cook it immediately—it will never taste better than when freshly caught; carrying it all afternoon is awkward (you *could*, of course, put it in a spare plastic bag in a pack, but it would be stiff by evening) and could be an irresistible temptation to any feisty bears within smelling distance. For a day in camp, I'd still eat the same sort of lunch (rather than dip into the foods reserved for dinner) but would hope to have some fish instead.

In my view, *none* of the packaged trail lunches or snacks put out by the producers of freeze-dried food can compare, in nutritive content or cost, with the following traditional items which you can buy in most supermarkets:

lemonade (or *orange drink*)—I use Realemon or an equivalent reconstituted liquid in preference to the powdered kind (tastes better and costs a lot less); allowing two teaspoons of lemon juice per cup of lemonade (with two teaspoons of sugar), a pint of Realemon will last two people through a two-week trip (if the possibility of breaking the glass bottle in a pack makes you nervous, transfer the contents to a plastic jar).

summer sausage—a hard sausage in a tough casing that keeps well even in warm weather (the herbs and spices that help preserve it also make it tasty); supplemented by cheese, one half to one pound per week should be enough for one person. (Since the sizes and shapes of sausages of this general type vary quite a bit, go by weight.)

cheese—American processed cheese is bland but nourishing, and it keeps well; use it as an alternative or supplement to sausage, in about the same quantities.

Ry-Krisp—or equivalent; not very nourishing but tastes pretty good and travels better than fresh bread, which you might use instead for the first few days of the trip; one standard box per person per week should be more than enough; if you run out or want a change, make a slab of bannock in the morning after breakfast, let it cool and dry, and carry it with you for lunch. In some places, you can get what the British call pilot biscuits—thick crackers about four and a half inches in diameter, each equivalent to a slice of bread.

chocolate—a small chocolate bar per person makes a good lunch dessert (the 1-ounce size, packed twenty-four per carton); Hershey makes an inexpensive, melt-resistant tropical chocolate bar that you can get from some outfitters, but you needn't bother except in the hottest weather.

raisins—a small handful (don't overdo it) will do instead of a chocolate bar (I like them in the morning oatmeal, too); one half pound per person per week should be plenty if used as a supplement.

Dinner

Not all the freeze-dried-food packagers are prepared to discuss the calorie values of their products, but from experience I think the portions are skimpy for most people and I also have doubts about their nutritional value for long-term use: a one-pot dinner rated for four persons (the usual packaging) is about right for three, and two could finish it without feeling gluttonous. Plan your quantities accordingly; that's one reason I prefer to split the dinner ration, where that's permissible, between freeze-dried foods and the heavier cans, which are generally more filling and cost less (another reason is that the canned foods are ready to eat when heated or in a pinch can be eaten cold,

where the feeze-dried kind take about half an hour of *slow* cooking and soaking). On the whole, the simplest thing is to stick with packaged foods, whether canned or freeze-dried. A pair of canoers traveling alone should try to finish each canned product in one meal: open foods are messy to carry, an invitation to animal invaders, and, in hot weather, possibly hazardous. Excess freeze-dried food can be saved, uncooked, in screw-top plastic jars.

For dinner main courses, I lazily incline toward dishes that are more or less complete in one pot—stew, hash, mixes of macaroni, noodles, rice, or beans, with meat or cheese—supplemented by canned or freeze-dried vegetables or potatoes. All these, admittedly, can be cooked from scratch from standard ingredients that keep well, but that means extra preparation time, on top of the cooking, which I prefer to keep for other uses. The freeze-dried main courses and vegetables in the following list are available in some form from most producers, generally taste good, and—most important—are higher in calories than other possibilities:

freeze-dried main courses—beef hash, beef Stroganoff with noodles, macaroni with ham and cheese; vegetables needed for balance.

freeze-dried vegetables—peas (hard to tell from fresh), green beans (for good flavor, must be cooked over low heat, hot coals rather than leaping flames).

Camp chores: a small boy entrusted with the responsibility of drying the after-dinner wash-up. (Credit: JEM.)

canned main courses—stew (separate vegetables not needed), hash, pressed ham (such as Spam), pork and beans, spaghetti, ravioli; corned beef or chipped beef, which with a canned soup for gravy, onions for flavor, and a canned or freeze-dried vegetable makes a filling one-pot meal.

canned vegetables—peas and green beans are reliable, but the variety of canned goods is greater than in the freeze-dried form, allowing more room for personal taste.

instant mashed potatoes—useful filler with any of the above and, mixed thick, can be fried as potato cakes to make an easy main course; one half pound makes twelve servings of mashed potatoes, about enough for one person for two weeks if you serve them nearly every night.

bread or *bannock*—with butter and jam or jelly, fills a need for something sweet.

desserts—instant pudding (the no-cooking supermarket variety); canned fruit; dried fruit, stewed, unless you're reserving it for breakfast; freeze-dried instant applesauce or pudding (both particularly good and high in calories).

hot drinks—coffee, tea, or cocoa, the latter if you have trouble adjusting your sleeping habits to the early hours of camp life.

Cooking and Related Equipment

The rationale for this list was discussed in Chapter 5. I've included a few things not directly connected with cooking, either by association or because they can conveniently be packed with the cooking kit.

frying pan—with folding handle.

pots—bucket type, with attached handles, tight lids, in aluminum or stainless steel; 8–10-quart, 6- or 4-quart, and 2-quart sizes are convenient, with a small coffee pot (useful for all hot drinks); pots and frying pan should nest and fit into a drawstring bag; cut grocery bags to cover each pot for protection against soot.

work gloves—cotton or leather, for handling hot or sooty pots; pack them in the cooking kit.

plates—aluminum, steel, or plastic, nesting; enough to go around, with one or two spares.

cups—nesting, to match other utensils.

bowls—for juice, cereal, desserts, with a couple of extras for mixing things in; or take a duplicate set of cups if you can't find bowls.

spatula.

long-handled fork.

can opener, bottle opener.

knife—extra-sharp, for cleaning fish, cutting meat; you can use the one on your belt, but if you reserve one specially for these jobs it will keep its edge better.

Carborundum or *steel*—for sharpening knives; but check the edges before the trip and they should last.

paring knife—if you carry fresh potatoes and fruits.

tableware—knives, forks, teaspoons, cereal spoons (also useful for cooking and serving), enough to go around with one or two extras each.

camping caddy—a roll-up, fitted bag to hold all tableware.

grill—preferably with folding legs.

stove—a small hikers' size as an auxiliary or a big one with two or three burners, depending on whether or not you're traveling country in which open-fire cooking will be the norm.

fuel container—for white gasoline or other liquid fuels, if your stove is that type; heavy-duty aluminum or plastic with a really tight top; don't waste your money on a cheap fuel can, almost certainly leaky and dangerous.

small funnel—for filling stove fuel tank.

fire lighters—and a little dry newspaper in a plastic bag, if all else fails.

matches—one box per day of wooden safety matches (or equivalent) for a party of three or four.

plastic jars or *bottles*—with airtight screw tops, wide mouths (*if* you can find them—inexplicably scarce); you can use several big ones (one quart or 1,000 cc. or larger)—for mixing dried milk, juice, lemonade, puddings, pancake batter, scrambled eggs, or for saving leftovers or storing the sugar supply (better than a bag); small ones are good for salt, emergency matches.

food boxes—rigid aluminum, various sizes; an optional extra but useful for protecting such crushables as bread, small items that are likely to get lost in a big pack and need protection against spillage or damp—salt, pepper, other condiments, Mapleine, and so on.

Some watertight plastic containers, all with screw tops: (clockwise from lower left) half-liter and liter, 1½-quart and pint, quart calibrated in ounces, 1½-quart with wide mouth—all useful for mixing dried foods or for storing and carrying dry foods (such as sugar, flour, cereals) or liquids.

two wash rags or small sponges—for washing dishes.

two dish towels—for a party of three or four on a two-week trip.

soap—in a rigid soap dish; one bar per week is adequate for a party of three or four.

scouring pad.

small scrubbing brush—optional but useful for cleaning the oatmeal pot.

scouring powder—Bon Ami in cake form (carry in a soap dish) is ideal, because it doesn't spill, but it is another scarce item.

liquid detergent—an extra, since you have to carry soap for your own use anyway.

ax—24–28-inch handle, full head, with leather case; may not in fact fit in cooking pack, but that's where it belongs.

small file—for sharpening ax; but sharpen it well before you leave for the trip.

folding saw—an optional alternative to an ax, in my view; in addition to the recommended emergency saw, which should be in your pocket.

canteen—only if the water's so dubious that you have to carry it from one safe supply to the next, in which case you may want a big *folding jug* or *bucket* as well (choice of 2½- or 5-gallon size).

vaccuum bottle—a luxury, but it allows you to carry the breakfast coffee hot for lunch without having

to make more; if you use one, get the unbreakable kind with a steel liner.

cutting board—a convenience for cutting meat or cleaning a fish (flat surfaces are scarce around camp), though all these jobs can be done on a paddle blade.

paper towels—a few, folded flat, will save the dish towels when drying dirty cooking pots (a last-resort toilet paper, too).

toilet paper—one full roll should be enough for three or four people on a two-week trip; squeeze it flat to save space and carry it in a plastic bag.

Packs

If you use Duluth packs or the Canadian equivalent, as I recommend, you needn't waste time trying to decide among the multitudes of less suitable packs, mostly designed for hiking. Instead, you can devote your ingenuity to packing *inside* these cavernous canoe packs (beginning with a supply of plastic bags, the first item on the following list), which should provide generous carrying capacity for two people for two weeks and be adequate, with a little restraint, for four on a trip of the same length:

plastic bags—get at least two sets of the three sizes made by Gerry (or something equally tough, if you can find it), and take any extras with you on the trip; although waterproof canvas sheds rain well when new, anything that *must* be kept dry should be in a plastic bag for protection against the day the pack has to stand for hours in a puddle in the bottom of the canoe: extra clothes, dry food of all kinds in cartons (or empty the contents into a bag, saving the directions), dry drink mixes that come in bottles (in case of breakage), bacon, with an inner wrap of waxed butchers' paper. The plastic or foil packages of freeze-dried food are fairly tough, but if you're carrying a lot it's convenient to sort the different kinds into separate bags; ditto such small oddments as sun-tan lotion, so they'll be easier to find again. Plastic-coated twist-ties are best for closing the bags, but take some spares: kids (mine, anyway) have a talent for taking them off and throwing them away; rubber bands or twine will do if you run out of ties.

two Duluth packs—full size, twenty-four inches wide by twenty-eight inches high; with tump straps, though two people on a short trip won't carry enough weight to need the latter.

cooking pack—a small Duluth pack or a European Alpine-style pack; be sure to check the dimensions of your cooking kit before buying the pack.

waterproof stuff sacks—supplied with most sleeping bags and tents, but if not, or if they're lost or damaged, replace them; you can use the same thing for other items that have to be kept dry, but they're expensive, and a good plastic bag does just about as well.

camera pack—keep the outfit simple (saving weight and bulk) and camera and film will be safe in a plastic bag, in the top of a pack where you can get at it (include one or two small bags of *silica gel* to soak up incidental humidity); most gadget bags I've seen are fine for padding camera and lenses, but I wouldn't trust them out in the rain. With a rubberized, waterproof *Flote-Bag* you can have the camera out in the canoe with no fear of its getting wet or being lost if it falls overboard (a good container for other indispensables, such as your wallet and money).

Rec-Pac—an extra (described in Chapter 5); watertight and proof against most animals (except, probably, bears), hence a safe place for photographic equipment and supplies; money; perhaps, to fill it up, a reserve stock of any foods you think might be fragile, such as the freeze-dried packages; in the unlikely event you capsize the canoe, losing everything else, this pack should float, stay dry, and ensure both your survival and your comfort, if you've selected the contents with an emergency in mind (and with your camera, you could always record the adventure in pictures!).

The several lists in this chapter are, I realize, lengthy—rather like the bewildering list of personal possessions that results when you inventory the contents of your house on moving day. As you review these lists and check them off in planning your own canoe trips, you might therefore reflect for a moment on just how many civilized products it takes to sustain life on your own, in the comparative isolation of a canoe trip, and make it moderately comfortable. All the things suggested derive from the lists I've put together over the years for my own canoe trips; I've winnowed out, by trial and error, the non-essentials, and very few of the items mentioned in this chapter are really optional. The outfit that results is simple; compact; quick and easy to portage, pack, and repack—on the Spartan side, if you like. Some outfitters, other canoers, you yourself in time will probably have other ideas at some points—things you'll leave out, others you'll add. And that's fine too. Start from a base of experience and common sense and the rest follows. It's what makes us individuals.

Chapter 9

CANOE COUNTRY

Canoeable waters are, quite literally, everywhere. There is not a major city on the continent more than a day's travel from attractive, often challenging, lakes and rivers; and in most cases the distance is even less. These are the waters the canoeist can turn to for a day or weekend of relief from the pressures and anxieties of a densely urban life, for the fresh and refreshing perspective that is one of the rewards of slipping from behind the steering wheel of a car and gripping one's means of propulsion, a paddle, in one's two hands. Yet the canoe country we've been heading for all through this book is something more, grander, bigger, generally more remote. That is the landscape we'll be exploring in the present chapter.

The major canoe areas are as various as the North American continent itself, but in a canoeing context they have several things in common. For one, all are big enough for extended canoe trips, from at least a week to a succession of weeks or even months—the kind of long-distance canoeing that was once as normal and indispensable a means of travel in much of the central and northern United States and Canada (and still is in the Canadian Far North) as horseback riding on the plains of Texas. In addition, the great canoe country is also in some sense wilderness country, which is to say that it's comparatively remote from the most tightly packed urban corridors; unless you're exceptionally lucky in where you happen to live and work, you'll probably not be able to set your canoe on one of the major water systems for a casual weekend: you'll undertake such a trip only with the thorough advance planning that, in effect, we've been doing in this book. Conversely, the canoeing regions I've picked *deserve* that kind of preparation: all, in their different ways, are worth

crossing a continent to experience, even if the chance comes only once in a lifetime.

Finally, all the canoeing waters discussed are within the capacity of canoeists of moderate ability and experience, properly equipped. And all are reasonably accessible: you won't have to mortgage your back teeth to get there, and, in most cases, you'll be able to count on local outfitters for some or all of your equipment and supplies, and for seasoned advice and other services.

These common characteristics of the canoe country—my standards, if you like, for selecting the areas described—require some comment.

Most of the values we connect with wilderness are positive: land where plant and animal life, earth, water, air, light exist in something like a natural balance; where men intervene on comparatively even terms, with a minimum of those material props that most of us twentieth-century humans unconsciously depend on. Ironically, in most of the United States, wilderness in that positive sense is an artificial and quite sophisticated arrangement, expressed in state and national parks, the newer wilderness areas, with their sharply defined boundaries and multiple exclusions—of lumbering, mining, hydroelectric dams, homesteading, private property of all kinds, whether for summer cottages or for vacation lodges and hunting and fishing camps. In the little more than a century since Yellowstone, the first of the national parks, was created, we have learned that any area penetrated by railroads, highways, airplanes ceases to be wilderness; where difficult access and physical remoteness are not enough to preserve the fragile natural balance, limits on human numbers and increasingly complex rules for their behavior, with the means of enforcement, do the job.

All this is at odds with the strictly human value of wilderness: the freedom to go where one will, unimpeded by outside regulations and the pressures of human society, with no limits but one's own strength, skill, endurance. Yet the canoe traveler can hardly complain. You cannot canoe a river that has been blocked by log booms or turned into a series of lakes by dams. You cannot pitch your tent on the lawn of someone's summer cottage or on land that has been stripped bare by logging or turned into a slag heap by strip mining.

Wilderness in the original sense—wild land still virtually unpeopled, unregulated—has not disappeared from our continent. Across its northern third sprawls a nearly limitless land, where hunting and fishing remain the serious means of livelihood they have been since the earliest men wandered the earth, and on the vast lakes and endless rivers, the canoe is still the natural mode of travel that it was when the Indians taught the first European explorers the use of paddles: the northland frontiers of the Canadian provinces, the Alaskan interior, above all the Northwest Territories, where scarcely forty thousand Indians, Eskimos, and whites cluster in settlements scattered across almost a million and a half square miles, and population densities are reckoned not, as elsewhere, by the square mile but in hundreds of square miles.

Sooner or later, if you come to care deeply about canoeing, you will want to paddle your vessel into those northern waters. The rewards are commensurate with the actual remoteness, the personal challenge: not least, the possibility of living in something like a balance with the natural world, not set apart from it by all our civilized dependencies. There is no real alternative if you are to travel that land even for a few weeks of the northern summer. Living *with* that world—not against it and the unrestrained forces that play across it unpredictably, not with the preposterous notion that you will somehow conquer it—is simply a matter of survival, natural in the fullest sense. In the process, you may learn also a few other fundamentals the northland's peoples have not yet forgotten. It is a great teacher, that land; demanding but just.

The canoe country of the Far North is not necessarily in itself more difficult or demanding than some you can find nearer to home. Within easy reach of most American and Canadian cities, you can, if that's your taste, paddle rivers (or big lakes and tidal bays) that reach or exceed what the white-water people call "the limits of navigability"—what's humanly possible in an open canoe propelled by paddles. In the northern wilderness, remoteness, the huge scale of the landscape and the waters that fill it, and the scarcity of people are simply an extension of the conditions you face wherever you set your canoe, answering to the same skills. The moment of bravado or misjudgment that wrecks your canoe or sinks food, clothing, or tent in heavy rapids may, in the Far North, leave you weeks away from help rather than days or hours, but the difference is not fundamental.

Nevertheless, as I said at the outset, all the canoe country I'll describe in this chapter is within the ability of experienced canoeists of moderate ability, properly equipped. You needn't be an Olympic slalom medalist or a flat-water racing champion to make any of these possible canoe trips successfully and pleasurably. You *do* need to have mastered the basic paddling skills outlined in earlier chapters, practicing them in varied and increasingly demanding conditions, where possible under the eye of more experienced friends or in company with a local canoeing or outing club. Strengthening your canoeing muscles and learning to use them effectively are only part of the preparation for a canoe trip. Experience is also a state of mind, a level of judgment: knowing what you and your canoe are capable of and recognizing the limits when you reach them; knowing, for instance, when to portage around a rapids instead of attempting to run it, when to head for the lake shore before those scattered whitecaps build up to ocean-size surf that can swamp you.

To be properly equipped for a canoe trip means that your canoe and paddles will be adequate for the waters they'll have to negotiate, the loads they'll carry; that clothing, food, tent and sleeping bags, cooking equipment, first-aid supplies will suit the geography, climate, and probable weather. Some of these items are basic, the same wherever you travel. Others depend largely on the particular locale of the trip; to reduce them to checklists like those in Chapter 8, you'll need to inform yourself as fully as possible about where you're going. The notes that follow are a first step. They should be fleshed out with books about the region, preferably with the focus on canoeing; with descriptions of the canoe routes, whether in guidebooks or the many pamphlets on canoeing available from state, provincial, or national government agencies; with the firsthand reports of other canoeists who have been there and of local canoeing outfitters; and with large-scale, detailed maps such as those described in Chapter 8, which you'll study with care.

With the analytical precision that their language seems to encourage, the French-speaking canoeists of Quebec speak of the preparations for a canoe trip as "moral, physical, and material" and attach greatest importance to the first. By that they mean not only that you'll inform yourself about where you're going, what to expect; you'll travel with confidence in your own strength and skill balanced by caution in the face of the unknown, the unpredictable, that is likely whenever we venture away from the familiar routine of daily life. It's a good point. The right equipment for the particular canoe trip is important, of course, but what counts, finally, is your own state of mind, both in your preparations and on the trip itself. Wherever you travel, under whatever physical conditions, every canoe trip is first of all an interior journey. Its most important events take place in your mind.

In what follows, I'll indicate in general what's available for the main canoe routes in each region in the way of background information, guidebooks, maps, and outfitters. Sources for all such material and the addresses of selected suppliers and outfitters are given in the Appendixes.

Mid-Continent

Through the heart of north-central North America stretches a vast region of connected lakes and rivers, flowing generally north to Hudson Bay and the Arctic Ocean: the finest, most varied, most extensive canoe country on earth. Bear with the superlatives. It was here, as a child, that I got my first exposure to canoeing and canoe travel, here that I return, in imagination, as to a touchstone for the thousands of miles of canoeing I've done since then.

The pre-eminence of this central canoe country of the continent is programmed into its geology. Across it, like a great bowl curving gently upward around the rim, lies the Canadian Shield, the most ancient exposed rock on earth, its surface glacier-scoured into gentle mountain shapes and etched with the wild rivers and tranquil lakes left behind by the retreating ice sheet. The Shield covers much of Quebec, Ontario, and the Northwest Territories, holding Hudson Bay in its immense embrace and

extending below the Canadian border into northern Minnesota, Wisconsin, Michigan and, in New York, the Adirondack Mountains. Along the southern edge of this region, extending west from Lake Superior for two hundred miles on both sides of the Minnesota-Ontario border, something over two million acres have been set aside primarily for canoeing: the Boundary Waters Canoe Area in Minnesota and, adjacent to it in Ontario, Quetico Provincial Park.

Boundary Waters-Quetico. The border-lakes country has formed a natural highway probably for as long as it has held human inhabitants—which is to say since roughly nine thousand years ago, when the first people to leave a trace, ancestors of the later Indian tribes, arrived, at the end of the last ice age. Montreal-based fur traders, in the eighteenth and nineteenth centuries, using big freight canoes, followed these immemorial waterways to reach the great lakes and rivers of the Northwest, crossing the mountains to the Pacific and the Alaskan interior, descending the Mackenzie River to the Arctic Ocean—distances, paddled for the sake of beaver pelts, that make most modern canoe trips seem tame by comparison. Their long-established trade routes eventually determined the international boundary in the border-lakes country, leaving the main route open to traders of both nations.

For the French-speaking voyageurs, who manned the trade canoes, the border-lakes country was *le beau pays*—beautiful country, certainly, but also gentle country, soft country, easy in its currents and portages, rich in food of all kinds free for the taking; a description one appreciates fully only after traveling, as they did, the harsher country stretching to the north and west. For the modern canoeist, part of the attraction of the Boundary Waters-Quetico area is the knowledge that the routes he paddles, the portages he makes, the camp sites where he pitches his tent have been imprinted on this land by thousands of years of Indian and voyageur history.

For those who care about canoeing or about wilderness and its preservation, the more recent history of the border-lakes country is equally instructive. For a century on both sides of the border, it has been subjected to various forms of exploitation—for iron ore and other minerals, lumber, water power, marginal homesteads, vacation homes, and fishing camps. Repeatedly, it seemed that the border lakes were destined for irrevocable

The Boundary Waters-Quetico: looking up the Agnes River from a portage at the north end of **Agnes Lake, in the heart of this canoe country. (Credit: JEM.)**

change—to be logged over, mined out, built up. That did not happen. That it did not has been due largely to the perceptions of a few men who over the past fifty years succeeded in communicating their ideas to the two national governments: the perception simply, that whatever value wilderness may have lies not in what it may produce but in its very existence.

The practical expression of that idea—the preservation of the border-lakes country—has been a series of compromises. In 1909, Superior National Forest was set aside in the northeast corner of Minnesota and in the same year Quetico Provincial Park was created. On both sides of the border, logging, mining, and existing private property were to be regulated but not abolished. In the mid-twenties, the nucleus of the Boundary Waters Canoe Area was outlined within the national forest as a roadless area, though logging roads continued to be cut, away from the lake shores. It was not until thirty years later that the Boundary Waters Canoe

Area took its present form, confirmed by the Wilderness Act in 1964, for which it had been the working model: a million acres set aside for canoeing, from which not only roads but airplanes have been excluded (earlier, fly-in fishing parties had begun to exhaust the more remote lakes—canoe travelers can keep no more fish than they actually eat). In the years since, the encroaching summer cabins and fishing camps have been bought up, dismantled, and removed, and their traces have disappeared under the renewed growth of black and red pine and birch. Consciously and deliberately, the land was returned to something like its original state.

Today, the two parks together embrace what is estimated as twenty-five hundred miles of canoe routes, though, since all the waters are connected, the possibilities are really beyond numbering. The lakes are comfortably scaled to the size of a canoe and its human occupants: a big lake, such as Saganaga, Basswood, Crooked, or Lac La Croix, which formed the voyageurs' main line along the border, may be as much as three or four miles across at its widest point, twenty or so miles long (with the wind blowing and the waves rolling, that can, of course, seem an ocean from the seat of a canoe); most are considerably smaller. The Laurentian Divide crosses the Boundary Waters Canoe Area about thirty-five miles west of Lake Superior. East of that point, the waters flow into the Great Lakes, to the St. Lawrence, and ultimately to the Atlantic; west of there, the flow is west and north through Lake of the Woods and Lake Winnipeg to Hudson Bay.

The connecting streams are generally narrow, shallow, and rocky, expanding here and there into short stretches of river broken by small rapids and, along the border, by spectacular waterfalls—Basswood, Curtain, Rebecca. Canoeing these waters rarely involves as much as a full day of solid paddling. The natural rhythm of border-lakes canoeing alternates an hour or two of paddling with, typically, a quarter-mile portage along a well-worn woodland trail beside one of the connecting streams or around a waterfall. As a boy, I thought of the portages as something of an ordeal, toiling under a heavy pack in the sharp clarity of the mid-summer northern sun, but now I welcome them. Just as the paddling begins to seem tedious, you reach the next portage and a chance to stretch the legs, pause by a waterfall to take some pictures, perhaps gather blueberries or the tiny, sweet wild strawberries. Since the portages do come up several times in the course of a day, you'll plan your gear accordingly, to fit into as few packs as possible, with no loose odds and ends to dangle from hands and catch on shrubs and tree branches along the trail (see Chapter 5). Two people on a two-week trip should be able to fit *everything* they need into a pair of medium-sized packs, plus a smaller cooking kit—meaning not more than two portages per person on any trail, and if you're feeling strong you'll double up the packs and make the portage in one go.

From the American side, the town of Ely is the most central to the Boundary Water Canoe Area and is also within a day's paddle of the Canadian border and the Quetico (most Americans spend at least part of their trip in Canada). Other possibilities are Crane Lake to the west and, to the east, Grand Marais on Lake Superior, at one end of the Dawson Trail, a road that leads north through Superior National Forest almost to the border,

with entrance points to the B.W.C.A. on either side and to the Quetico at the terminus. From the north, Atikokan on the edge of the Quetico is the usual Canadian base town, within easy reach of entrance points on Nym or French Lake. Ely and Atikokan can be reached by plane, train, or road (Ely is about half a day's drive north of Duluth). All four towns are generously served by outfitters, Ely particularly so (see Appendixes for a selected list); most will provide either complete or partial outfitting (see Chapter 7) and can also arrange for a guide, a service that makes an easy initiation for the inexperienced but is far from necessary. Both the U.S. and the Canadian park authorities or any of the outfitters will supply, free for the asking, planning maps for their respective areas; for the trip itself, you'll want the more detailed commercial maps.

The canoeing season in the border-lakes country extends from about mid-May to mid-October. If it's solitude you crave, you'll go early or late, when it's quite possible to make the entire trip without seeing another canoeist. The spring fishing is likely to be particularly good, with cold-loving lake trout up on the surface, which by midsummer will have retreated to the depths; a light frost will often have put an end to the mosquitoes by late August or early September, and a little later you can expect, as a bonus, a display of autumn colors hardly less gaudy than in New England. (In the summer months, the mosquitoes live up to their northland reputation, but if you're suitably prepared—with an insectproof tent, the sort of clothes recommended in Chapter 5, insect spray, mosquito repellent—and choose your camp sites judiciously, they'll not trouble you.) Through most of the season, you can expect warm and sunny, not hot, days, interspersed with rain in a three- or four-day cycle; cool nights may make you put on a sweater or warm jacket in the evenings and get the breakfast fire going in a hurry in the morning, but will rarely go below the capacity of a medium-weight sleeping bag (such as I suggested in Chapter 5).

On our family canoe trips in the thirties, it was unusual to meet more than one or two other parties in the two or three weeks we were out on the lakes. A year ago, traveling the same routes with two of my sons, I saw dozens. The country did not *feel* crowded: the blue-gray smoke from another campfire at the opposite end of a lake is not a crowd. Nevertheless, the change is an index of the area's growing popularity and of a new hazard, still potential, for country that has survived so many others: overuse. The Canadians and Americans have treated it in accordance with their rather different national styles.

The 150,000 or more canoeists who enter the Boundary Water Canoe Area every year must have permits issued either by their outfitters or by the Forest Service. (In Ely the handsome Voyageurs' Center has a fine exhibit of the area's natural history, worth perusing when you get your permit.) There's no charge. It's simply a means of keeping track of numbers—and of making sure each party has a responsible leader and is not overlarge (ten, currently, is the maximum)—but the same system could also be used to ration use of the area if that ever becomes necessary. In the B.W.C.A. now one is required to camp at one of hundreds of official camp sites, each equipped with a permanent grill for wood-fire cooking and, usually, a rustic toilet at a short distance—a way, apparently, of concentrating the leavings in a comparatively few places and making them easy to clean up. For the same reason, canned and bottled foods are illegal, a rule enforced with fines (freeze-dried foods in their foil or plastic packages have become the norm), and other cans (aerosol insect sprays, for instance) must be carried out. Resident hydrologists, assisted by computers, monitor the water quality as one means of determining if any of the lakes are becoming saturated with people; so far, the water seems to be as good as ever and purer, probably, than any you drink at home. At the start of each portage trail, an unobtrusive sign, identifying the portage and giving the distance, has replaced the older ax blazes; rangers walk the trails periodically, clearing fallen wood, filling in the wet spots. Although on paper the system sounds overregulated, in practice it's tactful and doesn't seem restrictive; given the alternatives, one accepts it.

Across the border in the Quetico, the Canadian system is a little more easygoing than the American "management" approach, relying on fees to keep the numbers of users within bearable limits. There's a modest charge for the permit to bring a canoe in and another for camping: for Canadians, one dollar for entrance and one dollar per canoe per day for camping. The charges for foreigners—Americans—are higher: two dollars per day for the canoe plus the irritating Canadian duty on food brought in from the United States, currently interpreted as a flat forty cents per person per day.

There are no official camp sites in the park; terrain, personal preference, and a camping history going back to Indian days determine where you'll set your tent. Portages are marked by blazes, as they've always been, not by signs. Visitors are encouraged to carry out any non-burnable refuse, but there's no law compelling them to do so.

The border-lakes country has been much written about, and several of the books it has inspired are listed in the Appendixes. Among them, there is no better introduction to the region (or to the pleasures of wilderness canoeing generally) than those of Sigurd Olson, beginning with *The Singing Wilderness,* whose devotion to the canoe country and whose lifetime of persuasive eloquence, more than any other, have been responsible for the creation and preservation of the Boundary Waters Canoe Area.

Elsewhere in Ontario. Although the Boundary Waters-Quetico area comes close to being the ideal canoe country, Ontario—with what are said to be 250,000 lakes and twenty thousand miles of rivers within her borders—offers limitless alternatives. The best of these for family canoeing is Algonquin Provincial Park in the southeast corner of the province, midway between Ottawa and Georgian Bay. Older as a park and bigger (2,910 square miles), Algonquin, like the Quetico, is a region of connecting lakes and rivers sculptured by the last ice age in the southern rim of the Canadian Shield. The water routes are more loosely formed in Algonquin, however: portages of a mile or two, almost unheard-of in the Quetico, are commonplace. Nor does the canoe reign supreme: there are summer camps and lodges; two highways and a railroad cross the park, though not near the main canoe routes. Being close to several of the biggest Canadian and American cities means that the park is heavily used but is also an advantage: if you live in the northeastern United States or Canada's populous southern tier, you're no more than a long day's drive, at most, from this very attractive canoe country, a welcome time-saver for anyone limited to a two-week vacation. The usual entrance points are by way of Whitney, Ontario, and the park's East Gate, near the midpoint of the southern boundary, or via Dwight, Ontario, and the West Gate, in the southwestern corner. There are semiofficial outfitters inside the park just past both these entrance points and a few others in the adjacent towns. Those who want to get a little farther away can go in by way of South River, Ontario, near the park's northwestern corner, and here again outfitting services are available. All the outfitters provide both complete and partial outfitting; Northern Wilderness Outfitters also offers organized trips for the young and inexperienced, with the aim of developing canoeing skills.

A descriptive planning map (scale: three miles to the inch) is available free from any outfitter or from Ontario's Department of Lands and Forests. Detailed travel maps in the several Canadian topographic series can be ordered from the national Map Distribution Office in Ottawa (see Appendixes).

Ontario's Ministry of Natural Resources publishes booklets detailing dozens of the province's other canoe routes. Most of these are in southern Ontario, easy to get to, comparatively short, and not too demanding. Of particular interest are the several in the North Georgian Bay Recreational Reserve, which includes a number of provincial parks and the historic French River, a link in the voyageurs' water connections with the West and still beautiful and comparatively unspoiled.

In a quite different category are the river systems of northern Ontario that flow northeast into Hudson Bay or James Bay (the narrowing southern extension of the former): the Missinaibi, Albany, Attawapiskat, and Winisk. Each is several hundred miles long and requires from two to four weeks, depending on your starting point. All, too, are big, fast, and thickly sown with rapids, particularly in the upper stretches. I consider them within the ability of medium-level canoeists who are properly cautious (you'll inspect the rapids, and portage or line any you're not dead sure of), but they require thorough preparation and, for safety, are best attempted with parties of two or three canoes. The logistic problems are considerable. There are few sources for supplies or emergency help along the way; except for the Missinaibi (which ends at Moosonee, with scheduled air service and a branch rail line), you'll need chartered bush planes to get in and get out again. The Hudson's Bay Company's one-way U-Paddle canoe rental service (about fifty-dollars per week—see Chapter 7 and Appendixes) simplifies the problem somewhat, and The Bay's stores at the put-in points can sell you some staple foods, though not much in the way of camping equipment (bring it!). The local Bay manager can also put you in touch with competent guides (worth considering).

For the Missinaibi, the natural place to start is Mattice, which is on the Trans-Canada Highway and the Canadian National Rail Way as well as the river, about two hundred miles from James Bay. The Albany, which has its source in Lake St. Joseph, about 250 miles north of Thunder Bay on Lake Superior, was one of the lesser fur-trade routes linking Hudson Bay with the Far West and North. Although you can, therefore, canoe there from several places farther west, the most promising jumping-off place is the village of Osnaburgh House, near the end of a gravel road running north from the Trans-Canada Highway and just east of Lake St. Joseph, roughly five hundred miles from James Bay. The best way out from Fort Albany, at the mouth of the river, is a charter flight to Moosonee to the southeast, thence by train or scheduled plane. Paralleling the Albany to the north is the Attawapiskat. Lansdowne House, on Attawapiskat Lake, is something like three hundred miles from the river's mouth and as yet beyond the reach of any road; you'll need a chartered bush plane to get there and another to return at the end of the trip (or else arrange to fly to Moosonee and proceed from there).

Finally, for the Winisk River, the put-in point is the village of Webequie on Winisk Lake, about 250 miles from the river mouth at Winisk on Hudson Bay. To fly to Webequie, the nearest charter point is at Nakina about 250 miles to the south or at the slightly larger town of Geraldton 40 miles farther down (both can be reached by road, train, or plane).

Upper Midwest. Wisconsin, Michigan, and central Minnesota all have extensive lake and river systems which historically were significant canoe routes and still have their attractions. Nearly all, however, are so thick with summer cottages and motorboats, so broken up by dams, that they can't be seriously compared with the great wilderness canoeing to be had in the nearby Boundary Waters Canoe Area. Nevertheless, all three states offer a good many short, challenging stretches of whitewater river which make effective training grounds for the wild rivers of the Far North. There are also a number of longer rivers flowing through rural or semiwilderness country, affording a week or more of fairly easy canoeing for experienced beginners and their families—preparation for more demanding canoe trails elsewhere. All three states publish useful free guides to their best-known canoeing rivers, and descriptive leaflets for several individual rivers are available locally; in addition, for Wisconsin there are three comprehensive regional guidebooks, detailed and professionally produced (see Appendixes for sources). The Minneapolis-based Minnesota Canoe Club is the strongest such group in the country, a good source for firsthand information and organized instruction at all levels; Minneapolis itself is especially well provided with canoe-oriented outfitters (branches of EMS and Eddie Bauer, among others).

In our grandparents' time, the exact Minnesota source of the Mississsippi River was a matter of considerable controversy, and it was leaders of the first generation of American sport canoeing who finally solved the problem. Modern canoeists can retrace their explorations. The attractive headwaters—meandering northeast before the river swells and swings southward—are narrow, shallow, and swampy, flowing through quite wild country and crossing several good-sized lakes. The distance for this section, from Lake Itasca to Ballclub Lake, is about a hundred miles, but the whole upper portion of the river as far as Anoka just north of Minneapolis (a total distance of 370 miles) is frequently canoed.

In Wisconsin, probably the best river for extended canoe travel is the Wisconsin itself, which rises in Lac Vieux Desert on the border of Michigan's Upper Peninsula and flows generally southwest about five hundred miles until it empties into the Mississippi. Camp sites, mostly in state parks, occur at regular intervals. All considered, the most interesting, least spoiled sections are above the town of Merrill. The river as a whole is generally easy, interspersed with dams (mainly in the central portions), reservoirs, and fair-sized lakes, some fast water, big riffles, and a few rapids that prudent canoers will prefer to portage. The Wisconsin Dells, where the river flows deep and swift through a series of canyonlike channels, are of great inherent beauty much vulgarized by tourism (the backwash from the motorboats speeding sightseers through the Dells is the most serious hazard the canoer will face on the Wisconsin).

The Wisconsin River connects with a number of worthwhile shorter canoe routes. The Kickapoo (yes, there really was an Indian tribe by that name), a tributary, joins the Wisconsin not far from the Mississippi—125 miles of easy canoeing through hilly country that can be stretched to a week's trip; a canoe-rental agency at La Farge will

shuttle you to the starting point and pick you up at the end. The Fox River, flowing northeast from the town of Portage, has the interest of being a connecting link in the voyageurs' route that led from Sault Ste. Marie south through Lake Michigan, Green Bay, and Lake Winnebago to the Wisconsin River, the Mississippi, and points south (there was a long and arduous carry at Portage—as the name suggests). Near Lake Winnebago, the Fox joins the Wolf River, which in the sixty-five miles below Post Lake offers several days of semi-wilderness canoeing spiced with frequent rapids and falls.

Although Michigan is sprinkled with French and Indian place names that recall the voyageurs (from Detroit to Sault Ste. Marie), the state has no long canoeing rivers comparable to the Wisconsin. Several rivers in the northern part of the state are, however, good for pleasant trips of up to two weeks, covering one or two hundred miles. The Menominee, which forms the boundary between Wisconsin and the Upper Peninsula before emptying into Green Bay, has the recommendation of avoiding the few towns in the sparsely inhabited region east of the Iron Mountain ski resort—from a canoe, it *seems* wilderness. To the east, on the Lower Peninsula, the gentle Au Sable, flowing into Lake Huron, is much traveled by canoers. The Big Manistee and Muskegon both wander more than two hundred miles through attractive country east of Lake Michigan before falling into the lake.

Northeastern United States

Geography did not endow the American Northeast with the limitless waterways that made the canoe the Pegasus of the Indians and voyageurs in the center of the continent and in the Canadian North. It is perhaps that smaller scale, however, that has made the region synonymous with canoeing as a sport since its inception little more than a century ago. Quite apart from their intrinsic attractions, the modern paddler will be drawn to the lakes and rivers of western Maine and New York's Adirondacks by the knowledge that he is following in the paddle strokes of Thoreau, the painter William Remington, and other canoeists hardly less noble. Although of more regional interest, the big rivers of New England and the Middle Atlantic states provide varied and often challenging waters for distance canoeing in the backyard of several of the biggest American cities. It is no coincidence that two of the leading American canoe builders, Old Town in Maine and Grumman in New York, are long established in this section of the canoe country.

The canoeist headed for the waters of the Northeast has no excuse for venturing unprepared. In its sober detail and comprehensiveness, the *New England Canoeing Guide,* published by The Appalachian Mountain Club, is a model of what such a book should be. There are also useful free canoeing guides for Maine, Vermont, New York, and Pennsylvania published by the states (see Appendixes). The Maine wilderness, the Adirondacks, and the Delaware Valley are served by knowledgeable canoe outfitters (names and addresses in Appendixes).

Dozens of Maine rivers offer a day or two of paddling ranging in difficulty from easy to barely canoeable. Among them, the Allagash Wilderness Waterway, with its lovely Indian name and its Thoreau associations, is unique in providing distance canoeing of considerable variety for the experienced canoeist of moderate ability. A narrow band of much-regulated wilderness that the state in 1966 carved from the surrounding millions of lumber and pulpwood acres, the waterway begins west of Mount Katahdin, northern terminus of The Appalachian Trail, in a series of lakes feeding the north-flowing Allagash. Telos Lake, the official starting point, is accessible from Greenville, Millinocket, or Patten by way of private paper-company roads (advance permission required). The Waterway ends ninety-two water miles north, just below the forty-foot Allagash Falls, but in practice, having portaged the falls, one continues the few miles farther downstream to the village of Allagash and the juncture with the parallel St. John River, making a trip of a week or a leisurely two; several alternative approaches to the system's headwaters may be used to extend the trip, but they're hard work (upstream stretches, long portages).

Since high spring water following the mid-May breakup and low water in late summer are both inimical to enjoyable canoeing, the best season for the Allagash is from about June 15 to early August (also the peak period for mosquitoes and black flies). Camping along the route is at official camp sites only (grills, toilets), which may be crowded. State-licensed guides are encouraged but not required and are unnecessary for first-timers who've prepared for the trip with reasonable thoroughness.

No other New England river matches the Allagash's combination of distance canoeing with country that approximates wilderness. The Connecticut River, however, has several characteristics that recommend it to the average canoer. Its four-hundred-odd miles are canoeable from near the river's source on the New Hampshire-Quebec border to the mouth at Old Saybrook, Connecticut, on Long Island Sound—a three- or four-week trip, if that's your pleasure, that breaks readily into shorter segments. The country along much of the route, while not wilderness, has the scenic attraction of New England's half-mountainous hills alternating with lovingly tended farmland, and even in populous areas the river can seem quite secluded; many of the riverside villages possess great charm and are worth visiting. Finally, unlike other New England rivers, the Connecticut has a long season: for most of its length, it carries enough water for good canoeing through late summer and into the fall.

The upper half of the Connecticut, forming the Vermont-New Hampshire border, is best, varying fast water and easy rapids with longer sections of gentle current and lake-like reservoirs (the Hartland Rapids six miles below White River Junction are serious, though, and must be portaged). The most practical starting point for paddling this section in its entirety is on the Vermont side just below the village of Canaan, and the water levels should be satisfactory from late May or early June onward, after the spring runoff (earlier, high water may be troublesome). Apart from the one big rapids, the main hazards are dams and their attendant portages; most of the latter are short and pleasant enough, but at Bellows Falls, two hundred miles downriver, the portage is a long one down a village street, and you may want to arrange there for someone to truck you over it, or end the trip at that point.

In Massachusetts, the Connecticut River has good possibilities for carefully selected day trips but cannot be recommended as a whole (the human, industrial, and agricultural effluvia, which make the water unsafe to drink farther north—like virtually every other New England stream—here become noxious to eye and nose as well as intestines). From Windsor Locks in Connecticut to Long Island Sound, the river is broadly meandering, moderately attractive, and mercifully unbroken by dams. For the river's whole length, state and private camp sites occur just about frequently

The Allagash Wilderness Waterway, Maine: a party of youngsters push their loaded canoes up Allagash Stream, one of several approaches to the headwaters of the Allagash River. (Credit: Maine Department of Conservation, George Tooze.)

enough to be practicable. In addition to the detailed description of the Connecticut in *The AMC New England Canoeing Guide,* there is a separate, moderate-priced *Connecticut River Guide* and a free booklet about the northern section, *Canoeing on the Connecticut River,* published by the state of Vermont (see Appendixes).

In northern New York, the large area of wilderness enclosed by Adirondack Park is recurringly threatened with final disappearance by road building, summer homes, large-scale real estate development, the several famous and long-established resort hotels that rim its lakes—yet it survives. The canoe routes at the heart of this region form a kind of Quetico in miniature sculptured in a final outcrop of the Canadian Shield: a system of scenic, stream-connected lakes winding among mountains that rise to three or four thousand feet. The main route between the towns of Old Forge and Saranac Lake is good for five or six easy days by canoe and can be stretched with a number of variants or side trips; the developed camp sites along the way are numerous and attractive. If your imagination is excited by a sense of the past, you feel the presence not only of Thoreau and Remington but of the early canoeing writer George Washington Sears ("Old Nessmuk") and J. Henry Rushton, one of the first canoe builders of the modern sporting era, whose designs are still unsurpassed. The foot trails that in places link the waterways are known as *carries,* not portages, the traditional American term still used in parts of Maine as well.

The Hudson River has its source as a narrow, east-flowing stream in mountains a few miles south of Long Lake, the main axis of the Adirondack canoe country. The upper river is a revelation if you know only the grandiose, much-polluted sections near New York City—swift and wild in the seventy-five or so miles above Glens Falls, demanding spring water conditions and skilled canoemanship, then widening out but still attractive as it turns south toward Troy, another thirty-five miles.

New York and Pennsylvania share two important distance-canoeing rivers, quite different in character in the two states: the Delaware and the Susquehanna. The Delaware's East and West branches rise near each other in the Catskill highlands and come together at Hancock, New York, to form the New York-Pennsylvania line. The river is canoeable from Hales Eddy a few miles up the West Branch from Hancock, pleasant and surprisingly unspoiled as far as Trenton, New Jersey, a distance of 210 miles that makes a good and quite varied ten- or twelve-day trip. Throughout the route, easy stretches alternate with fast water and riffles and occasional serious rapids that, in the upper section, should be portaged by those who haven't had a lot of practice in white water (below Port Jervis, New York, the river is wide enough to offer routes around most of the hazardous rapids); between Hales Eddy and Port Jervis, the river is best reserved for the high-water conditions of May and early June. The scenery along the route is generally attractive as far as Trenton, spectacular in the Delaware Water Gap around East Stroudsburg, Pennsylvania, where the river slices through the Appalachians. Considering how much of the river's banks is privately owned, the camping possibilities are pretty good (on the Pennsylvania side between Easton and Point Pleasant, there's a state park formed around a sixty-mile stretch of the old Delaware Canal paralleling the river—a pleasant bit of safe water, incidentally, in which to introduce young children to the art of canoeing).

Canoe-oriented maps of the Delaware are published by the Delaware River Authority (two dollars per set—see Appendixes). There are several places to rent canoes within reach of Philadelphia on both sides of the river (seven to eight dollars per day, generally less by the week or for groups). One, at Point Pleasant in Bucks County, Pennsylvania, has the distinction of being a comprehensive canoe outfitter comparable to those that serve the Quetico-Boundary Waters area, Algonquin, and the Allagash: complete or partial outfitting with food and camping equipment in addition to canoes, plus trip-planning advice and delivery or pickup service at the start and/or finish of your trip (see Appendixes).

Winding more than four hundred miles in a nearly endless series of loops, the Susquehanna can be rewarding for the canoeist who can manage his logistics without the kind of outfitting help available on much of the Delaware. The river is generally swift and shallow, with few natural obstructions. Although the dark valleys and rugged mountains along its course have been battered since the eighteenth century by coal mining and various other industries, the country, like an aging *grande dame,* retains much of its inherent beauty. It is really two widely separated rivers. The North Branch of the Susquehanna has its source in Lake Otsego at Cooperstown, New York, not far from the headwaters of the Delaware; three hundred miles downstream, at Shamokin Dam, Pennsylvania, it is joined by the West Branch to form the broad waterway that empties into Chesapeake Bay 125 miles farther down. At fairly regular intervals throughout its known history, the cramped tributaries of this system have combined in devastating floods, most recently in 1972.

The narrow upper section of the Susquehanna's North Branch is best run in the high water of spring: after June 1, the flow is likely to be inadequate, the going tough on your canoe. Below Binghamton, New York, the river widens to make a pleasant week's trip to the coal town of Wilkes-Barre 135 miles distant, or on to Shamokin Dam sixty miles further. The West Branch flows through similar country no less attractive, with mountains of considerable grandeur, the towns fewer and smaller (here, too, coal mining has left its marks). The more interesting section is the 115 miles between Clearfield and Lock Haven; allow about four days, about the same for the shorter distance and slower current between Lock Haven and Shamokin Dam. Below the confluence of the two branches, there are half a dozen power dams to portage around, and the broad, slow-moving river hardly repays the week's paddling to the Chesapeake; on the other hand, if you do continue as far as the bay, the shores opposite the river mouth—with several marshy streams flowing in, and abundance of waterfowl, fairly good fishing, and pleasant camping in a Maryland state park at Elk Neck—are worth exploring.

Southeastern United States

The Indians around Chesapeake Bay and in the subtropical swamps farther south built intriguing dugout canoes in a variety of forms burned and chipped from single logs or from several joined together. So did the white trappers and fishermen who succeeded them. The Southeast as a whole, however, was never the natural canoe country that produced the sophisticated bark-covered canoes developed in the northeastern quarter of the country and in most parts of Canada. Here and there, particularly in the mountains of Virginia, West Virginia, and Tennessee, white-water enthusiasts have searched out sections of wild rivers that are good for strenuous trips of a day or two. The hair-raising rapids of the upper Potomac, for instance, are not much more than an hour's drive

from downtown Washington, and the country around Harpers Ferry is as splendid to look at as when the young Jefferson first saw and described it, but the river itself and its banks have suffered shamefully from every form of pollution.

The scattered stretches of white water are not the whole story of canoeing in the Southeast, but everywhere in the Appalachian states dam building and pollution, particularly from mining, have taken their toll of the longer rivers, and those that remain are threatened by overuse. Virginia and Tennessee have both taken steps to establish scenic river systems, sections of several rivers that have some chance of being preserved for canoeing and fishing and are of at least local interest. In Virginia, the South Fork of the Shenandoah—winding northeast through a lovely valley between the Blue Ridge Mountains and the lesser Massanuttens to the west—is a possible five- or six-day trip throughout the year: close to a hundred miles between Port Republic and Front Royal, with some fast water but generally easy (midway, near Luray, there's an all-around canoe outfitter offering everything from partial outfitting at reasonable rates to guided tours for beginners—see Appendixes); below the meeting of the two forks at Front Royal, parts of the broad expanse of the Shenandoah proper are also worth trying as far as Harpers Ferry, where the river joins the Potomac. The historic James River, rising in the mountains south of the Shenandoah, is potentially important for distance canoeing, but its future depends on legislative wisdom to preserve and restore it.

In western Tennessee, the Buffalo River is comparable to the Shenandoah: 110 miles between Henryville and its confluence with the Duck River near the Tennessee, year-round canoeing of modest difficulty, comparatively clean water flowing through pretty country. (The Duck River, about the same canoeable length, also has some attractive sections interrupted by serious pollution but is reportedly scheduled to disappear behind two projected dams.) Both the Buffalo and the Duck are described and mapped in leaflets available from the state's Game and Fish Commission (see Appendixes).

Kentucky's rivers have suffered like those of Virginia and Tennessee, and so far less has been done about them. The Green River, flowing 370 miles through the middle of the state between McKinney and the village of Basket on the Ohio River, offers several possibilities for easy trips, notably in the protected sections in and near Mammoth Cave National Park. There are canoe renters in the area.

Nevertheless, the rivers mentioned are exceptions. There simply aren't many canoeable rivers in the Southeast long enough for real canoe travel and sufficiently unspoiled to repay the effort. The best possibilities are far south, in Georgia and in Florida. Here the venturesome canoer will discover a world of water and exotic plant and animal life unlike any other where he is likely to dip his paddle.

Most of Georgia's Okefenokee Swamp lies within the three hundred thousand acres of a national wildlife refuge. It is not the stagnant waste that its name implies: the waters *flow;* the swamp is the focus of several important canoeing rivers that can carry the traveler east to the Atlantic or southwest through Florida's panhandle to the Gulf of Mexico. The swamp itself is set aside for canoeing in an experiment in controlled and limited use that may well be the future of American wilderness waterways, if they are to survive. Parties of not more than ten canoes make advance reservations; the park authorities assign dates that will ensure their having their chosen route to themselves (see Appendixes for address). The half dozen water trails are clearly signposted, a feature you'll be grateful for in this featureless wilderness of narrow channels winding among cypress trees and islands of clustered vegetation that may float away with the current, but detailed maps and some skill with a compass are also necessary. Most camping will be on wooden platforms built for the purpose, and a suitable frame tent should be chosen with that in mind: there is not much solid ground in this country, whose Indian name means "trembling earth." Possible trips through the interior of the swamp range from two to six days, the latter a fifty-mile circuit; the constricted channels, often shallow and thickly laced with roots, make for slow going.

The Okefenokee is canoeable throughout the year. From about October through April, you can expect pleasantly cool weather, occasionally chilly, not much rain, a scarcity of mosquitoes, and an immensely varied cast of aquatic birds—the majestic sandhill cranes, for instance, which have their summer nesting grounds north of the Arctic Circle, spend the winter here. Alligators, on the other hand, sluggish and somnolent when it's cool, are more likely to be seen during the summer months. With luck, you may see other animals with fear-some reputations—black bears, several species of poisonous snakes, possibly even scarce panthers, wildcats, or wild hogs—but they're not likely to threaten you: like other wild creatures, they'll recognize you as the ultimate predator and treat you accordingly.

The Okefenokee forms the headwaters of both the Suwannee (the "Swanee" of Stephen Foster's song) and the St. Mary's rivers, which flow in opposite directions through Georgia and Florida. A short portage in the southwestern corner of the wildlife refuge links one of the swamp canoe routes with the Suwannee for a 250-mile float to its mouth on the Gulf, a leisurely two- or three-week extension of the Okefenokee trip, if you have the time; the upper 106 miles, designated by the two states as an official canoe route and ending at Suwannee River State Park, is generally wild, undisturbed by motorboats, with numerous camp sites—but the whole river is attractive. Two tributaries permit longer variants on the Suwannee trip, and both are official canoe routes: the Withlacoochee for the fifty-six miles from just east of Valdosta, Georgia, to the Suwannee, at Suwannee River State Park; and the Alapaha, running eighty-three miles from Willacoochee, Georgia, to Statenville near the Florida line, thence another twenty-five miles to the Suwannee. Both offer good camping and are punctuated by minor rapids that may be difficult in the high water of late spring.

From its source in the Okefenokee Swamp to its mouth in the Atlantic, the St. Mary's River forms part of the boundary between Georgia and Florida, a distance of about a hundred miles. The upper sixty-odd miles is another jointly designated canoe trail, but you can, if you like, continue through the tidal lower portion to the ocean. Nearly every bend in the river encloses a bar of pure-white sand that offers good swimming and makes a pleasant natural camp site.

Swinging in a great arc north and east of the Okefenokee Swamp, the Saltilla River is among the loveliest rivers in the area for canoeing. The best section is the 149 miles between Waycross and Woodbine, Georgia, designated by the state as a canoe trail, with abundant camp sites similar to those on the St. Mary's. The river is canoeable for nearly a hundred miles above Waycross, but the season must be chosen with care: in summer and fall, low water makes the river a tedious succession of snags to avoid or pull over, while in the spring it may become a raging torrent. In its final miles

Saltilla River, Georgia: slow and meandering through wild country east of the Okefenokee to the Atlantic—but more energetic farther up.

(Credit: Tourist Division, Georgia Department of Industry and Trade.)

below Woodbine, the river swells into St. Andrew's Sound, where it empties into the sea, broad and tidal, with swampy shores, and the canoer faces increasing competition from motorboats.

Except for the upper Saltilla, the advice about the canoeing seasons given for the Okefenokee applies equally to the surrounding rivers, and in the unobtrusive silence of your canoe you have a good chance of encountering a comparable range and variety of wildlife. There are several places in the area where you can rent canoes, but there are no general outfitters. The Okefenokee and the Georgia rivers are described in leaflets, with maps, that are useful for trip planning, available from the regional Slash Pine Area Planning and Development Commission. Florida, which prides itself on its sailing and motorboating waters, has also in-

terested itself in canoeing, and the result is a system of canoe trails, mostly in the northern half of the state, that currently includes twenty-two rivers; all are described and mapped in the *Florida Canoe Trail Guide,* a free booklet available from the state's Department of Natural Resources. (See Appendixes for the Georgia and Florida addresses.) You'll find both agencies helpful in planning a specific trip. Check particularly on the current state of the water: the waterways are generally in good shape, but you may have to purify what you drink or cook with or else provide yourself with containers to carry what you'll need for the duration of the trip. Okefenokee water, for instance, looks and tastes odd (dark brown, infused with tannin) but is said to be harmless.

Florida holds one other intriguing prospect for

the canoer. If you've seen the Everglades only from the causeway west of Miami or the front seat of an airboat (that particular noisemaker is banned within the boundaries of Everglades National Park), consider the advantages of traveling *through* this tropical wilderness of mangrove swamp by canoe. You'll come across patches of wild sugarcane and banana trees among the mangroves, cypresses, and sawgrass; wading the shallows you'll see egrets, storks, spoonbills, possibly flamingos, several species of heron, and other remarkable shore birds you're not likely to encounter anywhere else. A well-marked hundred-mile inland waterway leads through a series of sheltered bays, river mouths, and narrow channels from Everglades City at the north end of the park to Flamingo on the south coast. (Motorboats are also allowed, but the nature of the route restricts their size and speed, so they're not likely to be a nuisance.) You can make the trip in a week from either end (current is not a factor); or add a couple of days for side trips. Cleared camp sites on solid ground occur frequently enough for leisurely travel, though most are off the main route. As in the Okefenokee Swamp, the channel markers are helpful in finding one's way, but you should carry a compass, the detailed navigational charts produced by the U. S. Coast and Geodetic Survey, and the careful description of the route by the park naturalist William G. Truesdell, *A Guide to the Wilderness Waterway of the Everglades National Park* (order from the Everglades Natural History Association or the University of Miami Press—see Appendixes).

Before we leave the Southeast: In case you read James Dickey's novel *Deliverance* (or saw the movie) and wondered what river he had in mind, it's the Chattooga. It rises on the slopes of 4,900-foot Whiteside Mountain just over the North Carolina line from Georgia, then furnishes about thirty miles of the boundary between Georgia and South Carolina before vanishing into a series of reservoirs. Although short, it's wild white water nearly all the way, with several rapids that are extremely dangerous. What remains of the Chattooga is among the candidates for inclusion in the National Wild Rivers System.

The Central Midwest

Illinois, Indiana, Iowa, and Ohio have all made official efforts to encourage canoeing, and all four states publish pamphlets on their canoeable rivers. A private organization in Ohio called Ohio Canoe Adventures has done a similar job (and is also a source for an immense body of material on canoeing elsewhere—see Appendixes). Nevertheless, the pickings are slim. Too many of the rivers that in their natural state would make for interesting canoe trips have been turned into sewers or garbage dumps or have simply been swamped by urban growth. Of those that survive, the Fox and Spoon rivers in Illinois (the latter the inspiration for Edgar Lee Masters) offer easy, short trips in rural surroundings. Indiana's Sugar Creek is ninety miles of fairly fast water; the Wabash, whose 450 miles form much of the border with Illinois, has quite a number of possibilities for trips you needn't feel nervous about making with small children or the family dog.

It's only as you travel south and west of these much-developed states that you reach canoe country bearing serious comparison with, say, Algonquin or the Allagash: the Ozarks. The region's borders are elastic, but within it are the southern third of Missouri, below the Osage River, and the northern quarter of Arkansas. This is highland country with mountains rising to two or three thousand feet, deeply slashed by rivers that all, sooner or later, find their way into the Mississippi.

Some of the best of these have been dammed into great rambling sources for power or drinking water such as Lake of the Ozarks, formed from the Osage, but strong canoeing and conservation organizations in the two states have managed to preserve dozens of others. The area's history since World War I has been one of small farmers driven from their land by poverty, of the gradual return of something like wilderness. One regrets these human losses, but for canoeists the unpeopling of the Ozarks is mostly gain.

The centerpiece of Ozark canoeing is the Ozark National Scenic Riverways in southeast Missouri, the first (1966) area to gain such protection under a complex program that can only rejoice canoeists and wilderness lovers everywhere. The riverways, administered by the National Park Service, embrace more than a hundred miles of the Current River, close to fifty of its tributary the Jacks Fork River. Much of the Current River route lies in the shadow of high limestone bluffs, thickly grown with hardwoods, with many big cold-water springs along the banks, some waterfalls, and water-hollowed caves to explore; riverside camp sites are frequent. The fishing is pretty good; among the wildlife are many varieties of water fowl, beavers returning to the area after long absence, and at least a few wild turkeys. While the water in the springs and in the river itself is generally clean, there are enough exceptions so that precautions are advisable.

The Current is an all-year river, though the winter weather can be quite chilly and in mid-summer the park gets crowded. The Jacks Fork may be too shallow in summer to be practicable. The 105 miles of the Current within the park, between Montauk Springs and the Hawes camp-ground, make a pleasant five- or six-day trip, enlivened by some fast water and riffles but with no sections that require highly developed white-water skills. You can continue the voyage on down into Arkansas (thirty-four miles to the state line), but below the park the motorboat traffic becomes increasingly heavy.

Two other Ozark rivers offer relaxed semiwilderness canoe travel comparable to the Current: the Gasconade, a tributary of the Missouri (250 miles) and the Meramec, which flows into the Mississippi (193 miles). These and other Missouri canoe routes are all covered in *Missouri Ozark Waterways,* a very competent guidebook by Oz Hawksley, published by the Missouri Conservation Commission (well-drawn two-color maps for all the rivers, too). A map-brochure for the Current and Jacks Fork rivers is available from the park headquarters in Van Buren. At Akers Ferry, a few miles below the nothern entrance to the park, there is a competent canoe-rental agency that will provide a shuttle service to any put-in or take-out point along the Current.

Southwest of the Current in Arkansas is another fine canoeing river on a somewhat grander scale—higher bluffs, bigger bankside caves, a generally faster, more strenuous current that on occasion can rise to dangerous flood, wilder, less traveled, less peopled: the Buffalo. For a decade now the river has been the scene of a tug of war between the Army Corps of Engineers, which proposes to improve it with dams into something on the order of Lake of the Ozarks, and the Ozark Society, which likes it just the way it is. Along the way, the National Park Service put forward a plan to make the Buffalo a national river, like the Current, but that, so far, has not happened either. Canoeists within reach of the river will do well to enjoy it while they can: it's worth it.

With the right water conditions, the Buffalo can be canoed between the villages of Boxley and Buffalo City, where it meets the White River—a distance of about 150 miles for which you'll want to allow a couple of weeks (why hurry?). Low water, beginning in early June and getting worse as the summer progresses, may make it necessary to start farther down. Provided there's enough water to float a canoe in the first place, the upper section between Boxley and Pruitt (about thirty miles) has several shallow rapids that require a fair degree of skill; look them over before you attempt them and line or portage if in doubt. As in the Missouri part of the Ozarks, there are informative publications concerned with the Buffalo, a good index of the esteem in which the river and its countryside are held: *Buffalo National River,* a pamphlet describing the Park Service plan; *Buffalo River Canoe Guide,* a booklet; and *The Buffalo River Country,* a comprehensive guidebook. All can be ordered from the Ozark Society in Fayetteville (see Appendixes). The state's Fish and Game Commission puts out a map of the river, but for actual travel I'd get the appropriate U. S. Geological Survey maps as well.

Western United States

When you turn your mind to water sport in the great West, quite possibly the first image to form is of the Colorado River in its plunge through Grand Canyon: clumps of elephantine inflatable rubber rafts lashed together, steered through cascading falls by powerful outboards or professional oarsmen while the paying customers cling to the grab loops. Personally, I'd as soon take a two-week tour through Disneyland in a wheelchair, but each to his pleasure.

There are some grand and awesome rivers in the mountain states and along the West Coast, but too many of them are like that stretch of the Colorado: splendid to look at, photograph, explore on horseback or possibly on foot, but navigable (unless the likelihood of getting your irreplaceable body smashed is your idea of fun) only with the kind of elaborate mechanical assistance that has turned climbing in the Himalayas into a branch of industrial technology. Or else the big western rivers have been swallowed by the gargantuan reservoirs that supply water and power to places like Los Angeles, Denver, and Phoenix; or their banks have been sprinkled with towns and industry; or, since many of the rivers have their sources in high mountains and drain country that was either half desert to start with or has been made so by over-grazing and modern strip mining, they offer few months in the year when they're not either in mur-derous spate or too nearly dry to paddle. Never-theless, when all these subtractions have been made, there remain a number of important west-ern rivers that, seen through canoer's eyes, are both wild and beautiful, exciting but not suicidal.

Near the top of any western canoer's list is that part of the Rio Grande that forms the border be-tween Texas and Mexico. Texas paddlers, an in-trepid and well-organized bunch (and a generous source of current information on their river—see Appendixes) speak of the Rio Grande with the same kind of reverence and affection that Down-easters use for the Allagash, and with reason. The river is unlike any other that can be traveled for extended distances by canoe: coursing deep can-yons that very nearly rival those on the Colorado, through arid, mountainous country that feels as remote from homely human activity as it is in fact; a land rich with history, from Indian cliff dwellers to Cortez and his dogged search for the fabulous cities of gold, from the first great herds of long-horns to the badmen from both sides of the river for whom the river was more gateway than barrier.

The canoeing from Presidio to the archetypal Texas frontier town of Langtry is good all the way, a distance of about 250 miles; the best of it, wildest, most isolated, is the ninety-mile section near the middle, within the boundaries of Great Bend National Park, the only segment that can easily be taken separately from the whole in this almost roadless country. You'll need at least two weeks for the run from Presidio to Langtry, twice that if you take time to explore the many inter-esting side canyons that slash the river's rocky banks. The current is generally swift, interspersed with fairly difficult rapids; get local advice and equip yourself with detailed U. S. Geological Sur-vey maps so you know where the tough ones are, then be sure to go ashore and inspect them, lining or portaging when in doubt; this is harsh country, and misjudgments won't get off lightly. The camp-ing along the river is good; purify the water and plan to carry big jugs that you can fill from the oc-casional reliable spring. The best season extends from fall through about the end of February; the flood levels of spring can be dangerous, and in the summer, low water and excessive heat make the going tough.

The Rio Grande is as big as its name, and there are other wild and remote sections farther up-stream, in particular the 150 miles or so north of Santa Fe, New Mexico, now part of the National Wild Rivers System. Only short and carefully selected segments of the upper Rio Grande are within the capacity of canoe and paddle, and the approaches involve steep trails descending banks several hundred feet high. In between these ca-noeable sections are fearsome rapids that can be outright killers, beyond the reach even of the gas-bags that ply the Grand Canyon.

Farther north, in Montana, two other major rivers deserve the attention of the canoe traveler: the Missouri and the Yellowstone. The Missouri has the dual distinction of being the longest Ameri-can river—and also, for much of its length, the most despoiled by damming and a great variety of pollution. Its upper reaches, however, cutting deep canyons through the living rock, are still wild and remote and can be enjoyed by canoemen of quite modest experience. As preparation for canoeing the upper Missouri, there's no better first step than a reading of the journals of Lewis and Clark describing their expedition up the river to the Pacific coast: it is so little changed since that time. (A modern guide to the river is available from Montana's Fish and Game Department, which also publishes a booklet on other canoeable rivers in the state—see Appendixes.) The section between Fort Benton, Montana, and Robinson Bridge is about 160 miles long and good for a trip of a week to ten days.

Within the park to which it gave its name, the Yellowstone is hazardous, but its course from the Montana line to its confluence with the Missouri has several possibilities for pleasant, fairly easy trips. Probably the best is that between Livingston and Billings, again a week or so (160 miles). There is a useful guidebook for the whole river, privately published (see Appendixes).

In this same general area, Wyoming's Green and North Platte rivers, flowing in opposite directions, on either side of the Continental Divide, provide a few days' paddling each. The Green rises in a series of small lakes south of Yellowstone Park—a transplanted fragment of the border-lakes country, complete with portages—and can be followed for about a hundred miles south, when it disappears into the Fontanelle Reservoir; or cross the reser-

The Rio Grande, Texas: Mariscal Canyon in Big Bend National Park, where two skilled canoers successfully negotiate The Slot. (Credit: Will Thompson.)

voir, with its motorboats, and continue the 150 miles to Dinosaur National Monument in northeastern Colorado. West of Laramie, you can put in three or four days on the North Platte, paddling north from the Wyoming-Colorado border, before the way is blocked by a series of dams and reservoirs at Fort Steele, a distance of sixty-seven miles.

The three coastal states all have short stretches of daredevil white water but few attractions for the purposeful distance canoer who doesn't happen to live in the neighborhood. Oregon, solicitous of every aspect of its environment, is in the process of creating a scenic rivers system. Among those included are the Rogue in the southwestern part of the state (difficult and treacherous for open canoes); the Deschutes, a tributary of the Columbia (attractive and not unduly demanding in the hundred miles north of Bend); the John Day, flowing north to the Columbia through the arid moonscape west of the Cascade Mountains (about 150 miles below the village of Service Creek, easy but restricted by water level to late fall and early spring). Paralleling the coast, the Willamette (natives accent the second syllable) is longer and easier than any of these but is punctuated by a series of good-sized towns and shadowed by a heavily traveled interstate expressway before it empties into the Columbia amid the southward-thrusting urbanization of Portland.

Wild Waters of the Far North

Canada is the natural homeland of the canoe. Before the first Europeans sailed up the St. Lawrence, her immense system of rivers and lakes served the thinly scattered Indian and Eskimo population as routes for fishing and hunting, migration, warfare, and, in some cases, trade over considerable distances. With few exceptions, the earliest explorers followed these routes, borrowing the Indians' skills. The canoe-borne fur trade spawned by the pathfinders, in time settling the country and shaping it into a nation, is an inland epic to rival the transocean voyages of the Vikings and the Polynesians. In parts of the Canadian Far North, the canoe of necessity holds its own against other forms of transportation, though it's more likely to be driven by a multihorsepower "kicker" than by a set of paddles. The modern canoer can discover these historic routes for himself, sometimes in a quite literal sense.

In traveling this north country, you'll use essentially the same canoeing and camping skills that serve you in other parts of the continent. The routes described—a few selected from the nearly infinite number of possibilities—are ones that I consider within the ability of canoers of moderate skill and experience: enough experience, to repeat, to recognize the rough waters that may be dangerous *for you*, enough skill to act on that judgment. There is, however, a very real difference in scale. Even such rivers as the Mackenzie and the Yukon, which are generally easy canoeing, require an extra dimension of those who would travel them: their sheer size demands endurance; the few settlements occur at intervals of one or two hundred miles, and since they're the natural starting and stopping points, any canoe trip on them will be a three- or four-week expedition rather than the week or two that would be sufficient elsewhere. This is not the circumscribed and protected wilderness that canoeists experience in southern Canada and most parts of the United States. The northland is wild because people and their means of livelihood, their industries, have still hardly penetrated; or where they have come, they have not stayed. Preparations for such a trip must be made accordingly, starting months in advance.

To begin with, there's the canoe itself. Starting points for many great northern canoe trips can be reached by a road such as the Alcan or Mackenzie highway, so that it's feasible to car-top your own canoe there and use it on the trip (the road, gravel-graded, is likely to be an adventure in itself). The canoe should be chosen for toughness and carrying capacity: you'll be heavily loaded on a long trip, and an extra margin of freeboard will help keep you dry and safe when the water's rough. If the route includes rapids and/or much portaging, a 17- or 18-foot canoe with a hull designed for maneuverability is probably as big as you'll want; if long stretches of straight paddling are going to predominate, think seriously about a 20-foot canoe, though you may have less use for it later unless you return to the North (see Chapter 2). Where flying in or flying out is necessary, however, using your own canoe will be a big expense and a substantial nuisance. In that case, your best bet will be a one-way rental from the Hudson's Bay Company's U-Paddle service. The Bay has stores or trading posts throughout the Canadian North, and you can arrange to pick up one of their canoes (generally a 17-foot standard-weight Grumman) at just about any starting point you settle on. Remember, though, that since the canoe may have to be tractored in over a winter road that ceases to exist when the spring thaw comes, early planning is essential: make your reservation in early fall for a trip the following summer.

The chances are that on any route you pick you'll never be more than a week or two from a Hudson's Bay post where you can replenish your food. You needn't, in other words, carry all you'll need for the trip. You can count on standard canned goods (including canned butter, bacon, and those great canned Canadian jams that inexplicably are unobtainable in the United States), such staples as flour, sugar, and coffee, sometimes fresh or frozen meats, vegetables, and bread. On the other hand, to save weight and bulk, you'll probably want to take a fair amount of freeze-dried food and supplement that with systematic fishing (but see comments in Chapter 8): The Bay does *not* stock freeze-dried foods. In addition, as a cushion against accident or delays caused by bad weather, you should keep your basic food supply about a week ahead of actual need; for example, if you figure a week's travel between supply points, carry enough food for two weeks.

The northern summer weather is not as cold as you might think. Even within the Arctic Circle there will be bright, warm days in July and early August when the temperature is in the eighties. There will also, of course, be days (and nights!) in the thirties. Clothes and sleeping gear should match this considerable range: the sort of three-season clothes and down bags I've recommended for less northerly climates (Chapter 5), supplemented by long underwear, a jacket that's both warm and windproof, and heavy pajamas. Warm, waterproof gloves provide insurance against wet days when the temperature hovers in the mid-thirties and you make the uncomfortable discovery that the hands are the most vulnerable parts of a canoer's anatomy.

The size of your party may be an important consideration. The easier trips through the North are practical for two people reasonably experienced in canoeing and camping. For mutual safety in emergencies, the more difficult routes are best attempted by parties of two or three canoes with an agreed-on leader, even though the larger party complicates planning and logistics and limits camp sites to those with room for two or three tents.

Sources of information for the regions described below are listed in the Appendixes. The provincial governments of British Columbia, Alberta, Saskatchewan, and Manitoba all publish materials on their canoe routes: guidebooks in the case of Alberta and British Columbia (currently two and two and a half dollars respectively); separate booklets, including maps, on twenty-seven Saskatchewan routes; detailed canoeing maps for Manitoba. For Quebec, the same job is admirably done by the *Guide des rivières du Québec,* compiled by the province's canoeing association and published commercially by Éditions du Jour in Montreal. There is not as yet anything comparable for the Northwest Territories, but there are several accounts of canoeing there (including my own *Ultimate North*) and of travel generally. Finally, for the past several years the Canadian Department of Indian Affairs has been sending out teams of canoeists to survey some of the best of the wild rivers in various parts of the country, and their reports are available in mimeographed form.

Quebec. In canoeing, as in most other things, *la belle province* goes her own way. This is an effect partly of geography, partly of history. The European fur trade, with bases in Montreal and the city of Quebec, had exhausted the easily accessible sources by the end of the seventeenth century. This was the practical motive that pushed the traders west, but Montreal, with its ocean-going link to Europe, remained the eastern terminus of those immense waterways, and French-Canadian voyageurs supplied the strength and skills that drove the canoes along the trade routes—in the process, scattering French place names across what was to be the northern United States and all of Canada, west to the Pacific, north to the Arctic Ocean. But where the western waterways were connecting veins and arteries in the growth of the future provinces of Ontario, Manitoba, Saskatchewan, Alberta, British Columbia, in Quebec they were barriers, not highways. Except for the Ottawa River—the boundary between Quebec and Ontario and the first link in the chain of trade and communication laid through the Great Lakes and the Quetico region to the farthest west and north— Quebec's major rivers flow north into the James and Hudson bays and never had the importance of the rivers farther west; or they drain into the eastern St. Lawrence and lead, if anywhere, to Europe; or north to the ice-bound Hudson Strait and Ungava Bay at the mouth of Hudson Bay. Yet the characteristics that made Quebec's big rivers unrewarding for the early explorers and traders are precisely the ones that make them attractive to modern canoeists: their size, extent, direction, and remoteness.

To the outlander acquainted only with Montreal or Quebec, the sheer size of the province is difficult to take in: more than twelve hundred miles from south to north, nearly a thousand east to west; from the small farmers along the St. Lawrence, living in conscious continuity with *paysans* ancestors in central France, to the Indians and Eskimos of the sub-Arctic tundra, whose second language is not English but French. In this huge area, innumerable wild rivers invite the canoeist, but there are serious qualifications. Some of the biggest long-distance rivers are so thick with murderous rapids and high waterfalls—the Rupert, which leads to James Bay, or the Kaniapiskau, emptying into Ungava Bay in the Far North—as to be impractical for all but the most skilled, daring, and persistent canoemen. Or they suffer from mammoth hydroelectric and logging operations, such as those spreading across the eastern shore of James Bay. In addition, the provincial government so far seems more attuned to the interests of hunters than canoeists, though the young canoe-kayak association attempts to fill that gap (besides the general guidebook mentioned earlier, it can provide descriptive notes and maps for quite a number of routes, exactly the kind of firsthand information a canoer likes to hear). The three routes I've chosen to describe are *comparatively* accessible and (for well-prepared moderate canoers like me) feasible. They'll also give you an idea of the possibilities in three distinct regions of Canada's biggest province.

Easiest to get to is the upper section of the Rivière des Outaouais (the Ottawa, to English speakers) about 150 miles due north of Ottawa. The river's source is the Lac des Outaouais east of La Vérendrye Provincial Park, which you can reach by rough logging roads that lead northeast from near the park entrance. (La Vérendrye, with Laurentides Provincial Park farther east, is one of the areas where canoeing is officially encouraged by the provincial government.) The river flows generally west through La Vérendrye, linking a series of big lakes, to Lake Timiskaming on the Ontario border, a distance of 330 miles. Except for the first forty miles, where there are some fairly difficult rapids (they can be portaged), it's easy and varied travel through nearly uninhabited wilderness, with good camping and potable water. What more can a canoeist ask? From Lake Timiskaming, you can, if you like, continue to Ottawa or the St. Lawrence, but this long stretch of voyageur water is urban and uninviting. (For crossing La Vérendrye or canoeing within it, get a permit at the park headquarters, Le Domaine, a few road miles beyond the turnoff to Lac des Outaouais.)

A number of important south-flowing rivers drain the North Shore of the St. Lawrence. Among them, the Moisie is particularly intriguing and not too tough. Not the least of its interest is the means of getting to it. You can drive along the North Shore to Sept Îles or the village of Moisie (at present, the end of the road) near the mouth of the Moisie, or, if you have plenty of time, you can take the weekly ship from Rimouski, at the base of the Gaspé Peninsula, across the St. Lawrence from Sept Îles. (Rimouski is accessible by road or rail.) Either way, you then avail yourself of the Quebec, North Shore and Labrador Rail Way, which runs north from Sept Îles, to reach your starting point, mile 19 on the branch line to the towns of Wabush and Labrador City (be very clear about your destination when you buy your ticket). That particular point is within easy reach of the Moisie River, which runs 265 miles from its source nearby to the St. Lawrence, an attractive three-week trip. Since the mouth of the river is swampy, arrange in advance to be picked up by truck at the bridge that crosses the river between Sept Îles and Moisie. Except in the river's upper reaches, where there is a lengthy series of moderate rapids, the trip is demanding but feasible, the country wild and virtually uninhabited. For a longer and more strenuous trip, you can continue on the branch rail line to Wabush, thence through a series of lakes to the Rivière aux Pékans and down it to the Moisie.

Schefferville, the northern terminus of the Quebec, North Shore and Labrador (an 11-hour trip) gives access to several north-flowing wild rivers in the Ungava Bay basin—the Swampy Bay River, for instance—but they're generally too hazardous to be attempted by any but the hardiest canoers unless provided with local guides.

In the great drainage basin of James Bay, there's one river the Quebec canoe association, little given to superlatives, describes as "a paradise of canoe camping": the Mégiscane. It's also relatively easy to get to. You can drive as far as Senneterre, about thirty-five miles north of La Vérendrye Provincial Park, use train from there seventy miles east to

The Ottawa River, Quebec: the start of a difficult portage on the upper river, in La Vérendrye   **Provincial Park. (Credit: Gouvernement du Québec, Direction Générale du Tourisme.)**

Monet near the source of the Mégiscane (or take the train all the way from Montreal or Quebec). The Mégiscane flows north and west about two hundred miles through a series of lakes, emptying into Lac Parent at a point only a few miles from Senneterre. It's a small, energetic river with frequent rapids (about half will have to be lined or portaged) but no falls. It also provides access to several much longer routes. From Lac Parent, for example, you can travel north down the Bell River to the Nottaway (difficult and hazardous, with several big falls), then to James Bay. Or from near Monet you can cross over into a different watershed, traverse the big Gouin Reservoir, and from there paddle down the St. Maurice River 235 miles to Trois Rivières on the St. Lawrence, midway between Montreal and Quebec. (The best section is the 135 miles above La Tuque, wild, much used by canoeists, and not difficult except for portages

around five big rapids; farther down, the river is quite industrial and may at times be blocked by dangerous log booms.) For the energetic canoer, there are several other good possibilities using the Mégiscane as a starting point.

Across the Prairie Provinces. Like a great hand spilling toward Hudson Bay, the Canadian Shield supports half a dozen mighty river systems that flow generally east and north: the Albany (mentioned earlier in this chapter); the Assiniboine and Red, feeding the south end of Lake Winnipeg, linked by that big and always treacherous lake with the Hayes and Nelson rivers; the Saskatchewan, with its two large branches rising in the Rockies; above all, the Churchill. These rivers, with their immense drainage basin, formed the main highway that led from Montreal west and north by way of the Great Lakes and the border-lakes region; or from the Hudson's Bay Company outposts on Hudson Bay. They connected, in turn, across two divides, with the headwaters of the Columbia River and the fearsome Fraser, falling into the Pacific; and with the Fond du Lac, Athabasca, and Peace rivers, draining through a series of huge lakes into the Mackenzie River and, ultimately, the Arctic Ocean.

All these lakes and rivers are set in remote and generally wild country that has changed remarkably little since they first floated the big birch-bark canoes of the voyageurs. Although they differ greatly in character and difficulty, collectively they're a Promised Land for modern canoemen. Given the unique conjunction of history and geography, the best introduction to this vast region is Eric W. Morse's *Fur Trade Canoe Routes of Canada, Then and Now* (see Appendixes). Morse has traced the routes through the accounts of the early explorers and the records of the fur traders (often the same people). More importantly, he has paddled many of the routes for himself and set down what he observed with exactly the concrete attention to rapids, currents, and portages that his fellow canoers will appreciate when they set out to follow.

The Saskatchewan River proper is formed by the meeting of two large branches in central Saskatchewan. The upper part of the South Saskatchewan, from its beginning near Grassy Lake, Alberta, to a big reservoir just over the Saskatchewan border (Lake Diefenbaker), makes a fairly easy trip that you can take in a leisurely ten days. The river course stays away from the few towns in the area, but there are enough access points along the way so that you can break the trip or get additional supplies if you need them. By starting at Fort McLeod, Alberta, on the Oldman River, a tributary, you can lengthen this trip by 160 miles (above Fort McLeod, the Oldman is canoeable but difficult, with rapids rated from moderate to impossible). The South Saskatchewan is worth picking up again outside the city of Saskatoon, Saskatchewan, for another easy two hundred miles as far as Nipawin; or, if you're ambitious and have plenty of time, you can continue to Cumberland House, a voyageurs' crossroads for several historic routes to Hudson Bay (see below). The North Saskatchewan, which flows through Edmonton, Alberta's capital, and joins the South Saskatchewan east of Saskatoon, is more populous, less interesting.

Till near the end of the eighteenth century, while the French traders from Montreal and their Scottish and English rivals and successors pushed into the Canadian interior to procure the furs at their ever-receding source, the Hudson's Bay Company stayed put, operating from one or another base at the mouth of one of the rivers emptying into Hudson Bay: Fort Churchill, Fort Nelson, York Factory (on the Hayes River), Fort Albany. From as far west as Lake Athabasca and the modern site of Edmonton, the Indians brought their furs to these points to exchange for guns, powder, shot, cloth, metal tools, the rum or brandy and the glass beads that were staples of European trade everywhere in North America. The Indian canoe routes led east down the Saskatchewan River to Cumberland Lake, then northeast to the Grass River and a meeting with the Nelson halfway down to Hudson Bay; or through Moose Lake, avoiding treacherous Lake Winnipeg, to the Carrot River or the Bigstone and Fox rivers, both connecting with the lower Hayes. Later, with inland outposts at Norway House northeast of Lake Winnipeg and Cumberland House on Cumberland Lake, the Hudson's Bay traders made the Hayes their main route, partly solving the problem of crossing Lake Winnipeg by using heavily built boats with sails, manned by rugged boatmen from the North of Scotland.

None of these routes was entirely satisfactory. The Nelson is a big, rocky river with a torrential flow of water for canoes and small boats to negotiate, rapids and falls (and, today, dams on the lower river). The Moose Lake connection with the lower Hayes involved a long and difficult portage across a height of land. The Hayes, tedious and mud-banked in its lower section, is broken by fifty miles of rapids halfway up, and the crossing of Lake Winnipeg that it leads to, with its threat of fierce and sudden storms, is hazardous for canoes and boats no matter how big or stoutly built. Yet for the modern 'canoer these routes retain the attraction of their history, and parts of them, accessible by road or rail, make good, extended trips that are not excessively difficult. Long since abandoned and now established as a national historic site, York Factory, with its links to the seventeenth century, serves as a magnet at the end, pulling the adventurous canoer into the past.

One interesting trip along a part of the historic route can be made starting from Cumberland House, today at a road end, from there northeast through Namew Lake and the Goose River to Grass River and its confluence with the Nelson at Split Lake about 325 miles downstream. Hudson's Bay stores at both ends make possible one-way canoe rental. From Split Lake you can fly out or connect with the Churchill branch of the Canadian National Rail Way. A variant on the same route, about seventy-five miles shorter, starts from Cranberry Portage, which you can also reach by road. Another possibility is to fly in to Norway House northeast of Lake Winnipeg (scheduled service). From there you can follow the traditional main track to York Factory down part of the Nelson, the Echimamish, and the Hayes rivers as far as Oxford Lake, returning from there by plane and avoiding the toilsome lower section of the Hayes; or continue on to York Factory, again about 325 miles. (To get back, you can fly the whole way by prearranged charter, or only as far as Gillam, a station on the Churchill rail line where there's also a Hudson's Bay post.) An alternative near the start would be to follow the Nelson to Cross Lake, thence to Oxford Lake via the Carrot River or else through Utik Lake to the Bigstone and Fox rivers, joining the Hayes about ninety miles above York Factory and bypassing the long stretch of rapids on the Hayes.

Cumberland Lake was a junction not only for the Hudson's Bay traders but for the Montrealers headed up Lake Winnipeg for the Saskatchewan River and the west—or for the arduous connection with the Churchill by way of Amisk Lake and the Sturgeon Weir River. Traveling up the Churchill to its source, the intrepid voyageurs crossed the northern divide (over the twelve-mile Methye Portage, one of the longest and steepest on the entire route) into waters that carried them ultimately to the Arctic and across the mountains to the Pacific coast and into Alaska at a time when it was still a little-explored extension of Russian Siberia. The Churchill remains, as it was when the voyageurs paddled it, one of the grandest watercourses on the continent, a thousand-mile succession of large and beautiful wilderness lakes periodically narrowing to wide, fast river thick with rapids.

For canoers who feel the pull of the Churchill—and the more you know of it, the more you will be drawn—Sigurd Olson has captured its history and present state in *The Lonely Land,* which is, among other things, an account of his own trip down the river. It is not an expedition for the inexperienced or the imprudent. Between Churchill

Lake and the river's mouth at Fort Churchill on Hudson Bay there are well over a hundred major rapids, some of them miles long, the exact number depending on water conditions in any given year and month; fewer than half can be run by even the most expert canoeists. But there are portages around most of these danger spots, kept up by the Indian hunters and fishermen who are still the river's chief inhabitants. With careful preparation, good maps and due caution along the way, the Churchill offers experienced canoeists possibilities for several exciting trips of from two to six weeks.

Two hundred miles north of Saskatoon, Saskatchewan, the headwaters of the Churchill at Buffalo Narrows on Lake Churchill can be reached over a long stretch of northland gravel road. From there it's about three hundred miles and at least twenty rapids that will have to be portaged—three weeks—to the village of Missinipe on Otter Lake, the next access point by road, on the north edge of Lac La Ronge Provincial Park. (Or you can cut fifty miles from the start of the route by putting in at Île-à-La Crosse on the lake of the same name.) You can start (or continue) from Missinipe or, a little farther east, from Pelican Narrows, another road end, connected with the Churchill by the historic and fairly easy Frog Portage (or paddle to the same point from Cumberland House, though the rapids in the connecting Sturgeon Weir River are difficult and tiring). From Missinipe it's still more than six hundred miles to Fort Churchill, but it's possible to fly out halfway along (or resupply) at South Indian Lake; from Fort Churchill, one gets back to civilization by scheduled plane or by the train, which has its terminus there. Since there are Hudson's Bay posts at all of these access and exit points, their rented canoes are advisable, particularly on the lower half of the river (they're also the *only* places on the river where you can count on buying food, a further reason for careful planning).

For less experienced canoers or those who are short of time, the Saskatchewan Department of Natural Resources has worked out a number of shorter and easier routes, with some circuits, centering on Lac La Ronge, all designed to give the modern voyageur, for a week or two, an authentic taste of the mighty Churchill. The routes are described in individual booklets and 'shown on the province's laudable canoeing maps (see Appendixes).

If, like the voyageurs, you were to paddle *up* the

The Churchill River: Nistowiak Falls in north-central Saskatchewan, one of the many hazards to be admired and portaged on this grand but strenuous river. (Credit: Saskatchewan Department of Tourism.)

Churchill to its source instead of down and carry canoe and packs across the back-breaking Methye Portage to the Clearwater River, you would enter an entirely new system of waterways, draining north and west two thousand miles to the Arctic Ocean: the vast Mackenzie River system, second only to the Mississippi-Missouri in North America. The *if* in that sentence is, admittedly, a big one for most of us. Yet the route is followed, the portage made, since there is in fact no other way of getting to the Clearwater. And it is appropriate that so radical a change in geography, with all it implies of history and human culture, should be marked by the harsh climb up and over the Methye Portage.

From the portage, the Clearwater flows about eighty-five miles west to Fort McMurray through a beautiful narrow valley. Apart from its remoteness and physical attractiveness, the river has the interest of having served as a funnel through which passed nearly all the early explorers of the far Northwest—a kind of pantheon of North American canoeing. There are some bad rapids in the upper half of the Clearwater but the portages around them are fairly clear, well documented. Access is by gravel road to La Loche on the lake of that name (Hudson's Bay store) eight easy water miles from the start of the portage.

Before we turn to the Northwest, two big southern tributaries of the Mackenzie are worth noting: the Athabasca and the Peace. Historically, their importance was that several heroic expeditions traveled up them to their sources in the Rockies, thence over high passes and down the western slopes to the Pacific. The modern voyageur will reverse the procedure.

From high mountains near Jasper, the Athabasca offers about 650 miles (three or four weeks) of isolated semiwilderness canoeing as far as Fort McMurray, Alberta—modern towns where the few roads cross (access points for shorter trips), not many other evidences of a human presence. The current is fairly strong most of the way, with dangerous rapids near Fort McMurray, the present end of the road north from Edmonton, at the confluence with the Clearwater. Beyond Fort McMurray there are no hazards, and the Athabasca, once a highway for barge traffic to Lake Athabasca and Fort Chipewyan two hundred miles north (there being no road) is now virtually deserted.

The Peace River, rising north of the Athabasca, is comparable in size, character, and difficulty. For a not too difficult two- or three-week trip, you

could pick it up at the town of Peace River at the start of the Mackenzie Highway, or farther north at Fort Vermilion. From where the river empties into the Slave River, you're half a day's paddle from Fort Chipewyan (fly out), a couple of days south of Fort Smith (scheduled plane service or road north to Great Slave Lake and a connection with the Mackenzie Highway for a return to the starting point).

The Far Northwest

The Mackenzie River is the great axis of the Northwest. Around it, like spokes on a wheel, its tributaries offer limitless possibilities for long-distance canoeing at every level of skill and experience.

The Mackenzie itself is easy canoeing, assisted by a fairly strong current that periodically boils up into a big riffles or short rapids. Given its size (a couple of miles across in places), its hazards are more likely to come in the form of storms driven by the prevailing north wind, which will tie the canoer down for a day in an average summer week. The half dozen settlements occur at intervals of a hundred miles or so. Apart from them and an occasional distant barge or team of prospectors, you'll see no people. In a shrinking world, it is a last frontier, and that is one of its attractions; another is the chance to share, if only in a limited way, with much support from the civilization to the south, in the life of the Indians and Eskimos for whom the river, with its trapping, hunting, and fishing, is still the natural means of existence. Since World War II, the frontier in the form of the Mackenzie Highway, gravel-graded and arduous but passable in all seasons, has pushed north to Fort Providence at the beginning of the Mackenzie, now another 160 miles downriver to Fort Simpson. In time it will extend the whole length of the river, to its Arctic delta. The transformation will be slow, but the river and its people are worth seeing before it comes.

The river distance from Fort Providence to Inuvik in the delta is close to 950 miles. With cooperative weather, you can paddle it in three or four weeks—or take twice the time, if you can, and explore the settlements, the attractive side rivers along the way. A good shorter trip would be from Fort Simpson (so far, the end of the road) to Fort Norman (fly out), about three hundred miles, with

The Mackenzie River, Northwest Territories: breakfast on a cold morning near the Arctic Circle, the Camsell Range cloud-hidden to the south.

Camsell River, Northwest Territories: rapids on Marian Lake, near the start of the river-and-lake system connecting two giant lakes of the Far North, Great Slave and Great Bear. (Credit: Information Canada Photothèque, Paul Baich.)

Yukon River, Yukon Territory and Alaska: near Lake Laberge, one of the sources of this big river, north of the Yukon capital of Whitehorse.

(Credit: Government of the Yukon Territory, Tourism and Information Branch.)

rugged northern mountains on both sides of the river. Or start from Fort Good Hope near the Arctic Circle (regular but infrequent plane service) and travel down to Aklavik or Inuvik (on opposite sides of the delta). From either of these half-Eskimo towns, you can continue another hundred miles to the edge of the Arctic Ocean itself. Getting back is not easy, but when you've gotten that far the pull of the icebound sea is irresistible.

Fort Simpson, with the beginning of a canoe-oriented outfitting service, is a base from which to explore the steep mountain rivers to the west, particularly the South Nahanni, enclosed by the recently created Nahanni National Park. You can charter a float plane to a point above the Virginia Falls (316 feet high). The two-week trip down the South Nahanni to the Liard River and Fort Simpson is difficult and fraught with rapids and portages (not least the one around Virginia Falls) but grand. Bighorn sheep are among the rare animals you may see en route.

A comparable but less demanding circuit can be made starting from Fort Norman farther down the Mackenzie, at the mouth of the Great Bear River. A local Indian outfitter can arrange to fly you, with a canoe and supplies, to one of the lakes east of the river (spectacular fishing). From there, you can paddle through lakes and rivers to the swift Great Bear and down it to the starting point.

An intriguing but more difficult trip is the 250 miles of wilderness water between Great Slave and Great Bear lakes: the Camsell River. Like the Churchill River, the Camsell is a sequence of lakes connected by rivers that have their due share of rapids. The start is the Indian village of Rae near the head of the North Arm of Great Slave Lake, on the road to Yellowknife, the gold-boom town that is now the capital of the Northwest Territories. The Camsell empties into Conjuror Bay on Great Bear Lake. From there, unless you've arranged to be met by a chartered plane from Yellowknife, it's necessary to paddle sixty miles northeast to Port Radium, where you can return to Yellowknife by a scheduled flight. With unlimited time, you can, as an alternative, reach the starting point from Fort Resolution on the south side of Great Slave Lake, going around the lake's superb rocky east end; or return from Conjuror Bay by heading west on Great Bear Lake to Fort Franklin or down the Great Bear River to Fort Norman. Both lakes are, however, big, slow, and tedious for canoers, and even close to the shore they can be dangerous in the periodic storms that blow down from the Arctic.

One other canoe route in this·far-northwestern corner of the continent is worth thinking about: the Yukon. Like the Mackenzie, it's big, remote, easy, and wild for much of its length, with settlements just frequent enough to remind even the confirmed misanthrope of the necessity of human society. Again like the Mackenzie, it's been dyed by many layers of history and only since World War II has it begun to be probed by highways of a sort. Indeed, rumors that the Yukon existed across the mountains were the motive that led to the discovery of the Mackenzie toward the end of the eighteenth century. The long-sought Northwest Passage became a reality when traders some years later struggled up tributaries of the Mackenzie to mountain passes, from there to the Yukon River and the Pacific by way of the Pelly River nearly six hundred miles up the Liard from Fort Simpson, or the Porcupine, north of the Arctic Circle. In the 1890s, gold added its glamour to these man-killing backdoor routes to Alaska—as it still does.

The 435-mile section of the upper Yukon between Whitehorse and Dawson, in the Yukon Territory, is a popular two-week canoe trip, with gold-built ghost towns to explore along the way as well as the live frontier towns at either end. Whitehorse and Dawson are both easy to get to or from by plane or by loops of the Alaska Highway. Another three hundred miles carries you to Circle, Alaska, the last point on the river that's accessible by road. The Bering Sea and the end of the river are still close to nine hundred miles for those with the time and the inner stamina. Getting back is the difficulty, but there, too, modern canoemen have dipped their paddles. It can be done.

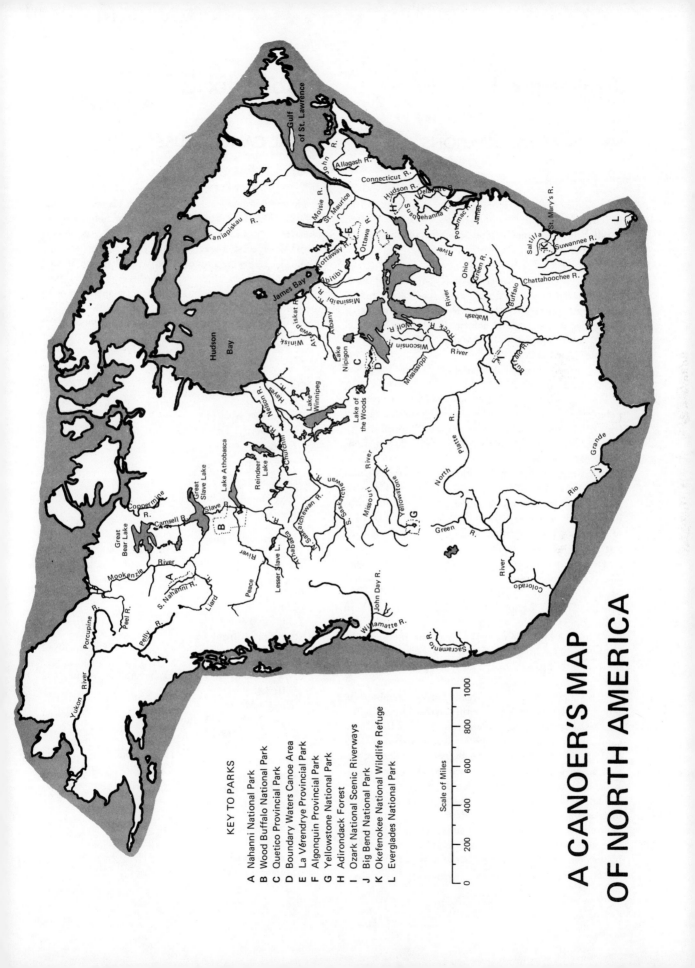

A CANOER'S MAP
OF NORTH AMERICA

KEY TO PARKS

A Nahanni National Park
B Wood Buffalo National Park
C Quetico Provincial Park
D Boundary Waters Canoe Area
E La Vérendrye Provincial Park
F Algonquin Provincial Park
G Yellowstone National Park
H Adirondack Forest
I Ozark National Scenic Riverways
J Big Bend National Park
K Okefenokee National Wildlife Refuge
L Everglades National Park

Scale of Miles

0   200   400   600   800   1000

Appendix 1

NATIONAL ASSOCIATIONS

In addition to the four canoeing associations, I've included four environmental groups whose goals often parallel those of canoeists and which occasionally sponsor related activities.

American Canoe Association. $6.00 per year for adult voting members plus $1.00 initiation fee: *Canoe* magazine (semimonthly); books and leaflets about canoeing and canoe routes, general information, access to local clubs; races and regattas. *Address:* 4260 East Evans Avenue, Denver, Colo. 80222.

American Whitewater Affiliation, P. O. Box 1584, San Bruno, Calif. 94066.

The Canadian Canoe Association. $5.00 per year; no publications, but a source of general information and has on file reports on specific canoe routes, furnished to members on request. *Address:* 805 Valetta Street, London N6H 2Z2 Ont.

Fédération Québécoise de Canot-Kayak, Inc. Primarily a federation of local clubs (in effect, Canada's French-speaking canoe association), but individuals can join for $25 per year: *Guide des Rivières du Québec* (Éditions du Jour, Montréal); materials on specific canoe routes, available to members on request; maintains a non-profit workshop aimed at improving canoe design and construction. *Address:* 881 Boulevard de Maisonneuve Est, Montréal 132, Que.

Izaak Walton League of America, 13711 Parkland Drive, Rockville, Md. 20853.

National Audubon Society. $15 per year, family membership: *Audubon* (semimonthly), workshops through local clubs. *Address:* 950 Third Avenue, New York, N.Y. 10022.

Sierra Club. $22.50 per year, family membership, plus $5.00 admission fee: monthly magazine and bulletin, discounts on publications (guides to hiking and camping as well as the superb illustrated books), organized wilderness trips, some by canoe; collective action on environmental issues. *Address:* P. O. Box 7959, Rincon Annex, San Francisco, Calif. 94120.

The Wilderness Society. $7.50 per year, regular membership: *The Living Wilderness* (quarterly), organized wilderness trips that include canoeing, information and action on conservation matters with the emphasis on legislative issues. *Address:* 729 Fifteenth Street, N.W., Washington D.C. 20005.

Appendix 2

LOCAL CANOE CLUBS

There are a few local canoe clubs in Canada, but the only one I've found at all responsive or helpful to an outsider (for whatever that may be worth) is: North West Voyageurs, 10922 88th Avenue, Edmonton 61, Alta. The following groups, then, are all in the United States and all are affiliated with the American Canoe Association, though several also have connections with the American Whitewater Affiliation or with other national organizations concerned with the outdoors.

California
  Cakara
  E. R. Leach
  675 Overhill Drive
  Redding 96001

  Feather River Kayak Club
  Mike Schneller
  1773 Broadway St.
  Marysville 95901

  Haystackers Whitewater Canoe Club
  Tom Johnson
  P. O. Box 675
  Kernville 93238

  Marin Canoe Club
  Gordon Young
  744 Penny Royal Lane
  San Rafael 94903

  Powell Boating Club—University of California, Berkeley
  Charles Martin
  5499 Claremont Avenue
  Oakland 94618

  Sierra Club—Loma Prieta Paddlers
  Ron Williams
  85 Blake Avenue
  Santa Clara 95051

  Sierra Club Yokut R. T. S.
  Sam Gardall
  914 Standord Ave.
  Modesto 95350

Southern California Canoe Association
Ron Cuervorst
3966 South Menlo Avenue
Los Angeles 90037

Valley Canoe Club
Bob Blackstone
10363 Calvin Avenue
Los Angeles 90025

YMCA Whitewater Club
Gary Gray
640 North Center Street
Stockton 95202

Colorado

Colorado Whitewater Association
Mike O'Brien
2007 Mariposa
Boulder 80302

Fib Ark Boat Races, Inc.
Phill Noll
P. O. Box 762
Salida 81201

Connecticut

Amston Lake Canoe Club
Robert G. Dickinson
Deepwood Drive
Amston 06231

Columbia Canoe Club
Mrs. Pat Murphy
Lake Road
Columbia 06237

Waterford Canoe Club
Ralph Clark
Box 111
Waterford 06385

Delaware

Wilmington Trail Club
George M. LeClercq
324 Spalding Road
Wilmington 19803

District of Columbia

Canoe Cruisers Association
E. Dennis Conroy
6400 MacArthur Boulevard
Washington 20016

Potomac Boat Club
Jerry Welbourn
3530 Water Street, N.W.
Washington 20007

Washington Canoe Club
Jack Brosius
3700 K Street, N.W.
Washington 20007

Florida

Everglades Canoe Club
Charles Graves
239 NE 20th Street
Delray Beach 33440

Florida Sport Paddling Club
Phil A. Rhodes
133 Hickory Lane
Seffner 33584

Seminole Canoe & Yacht Club
Noble Enge
5653 Windermere Drive
Jacksonville 32211

Georgia

Explorer Post 49
Doug Woodward
1506 Brawley Circle
Atlanta 30313

Georgia Canoeing Association
Margaret Tucker
2816 De Foors Ferry Road
Atlanta 30318

Hawaii

Hawaii Kayak Club
Virginia Moore
1560 Murphy Street
Honolulu 96819

International Hawaiian Canoe Association
A. E. Minvielle
1638A Kona
Honolulu 96814

Idaho

Idaho Alpine Club
Dean Hagmann
1953 Melobu
Idaho Falls 83401

Sawtooth Wildwater Club
Roger Hazelwood
1255 Elm Street
Mountain Home 83647

Illinois

American Indian Center Canoe Club
Roger D. Harper
1630 North Wilson Avenue
Chicago 60640

Belleville Whitewater Club
Linda Seaman
3 Oakwood
Belleville 62223

Chicago Whitewater Association
Bruce Weber
5652 South California Avenue
Chicago 60629

Illinois Paddling Council
Lynn Snarr
2316 Prospect Avenue
Wanston 60201

Lincoln Park Boat Club
Frank Dallos
2236 North Burling Street
Chicago 60614

Prairie Club Canoeists
Ray Lessner
17 West 373 Belden
Addison 60101

Prairie State Canoeists
Louis Boehm
6320 North Hermitage Avenue
Chicago 60626

University of Chicago Whitewater Club
Bruce Campbell
933 East 56th Street
Chicago 60637

Indiana

Connersville Canoe Club
Arlington M. Hudson
R. R. 3
Connersville 47331

Elkhart YMCA Canoe Club
James Trader
229 West Franklin Street
Elkhart 46514

Hoosier Canoe Club
Dave Ellis
5641 North Delaware
Indianapolis 46220

Kekionga Voyageurs
George A. Parker
1407 Kensington Boulevard
Fort Wayne 46805

St. Joe Valley Canoe & Kayak Club
Leroy Rohrer
229 West Franklin
Elkhart 46514

Kansas

Johnson County Canoe Club
George Weiter
7832 Rosewood Lane
Prairie Village 66208

Kentucky

Viking Canoe Club
Joseph Venhoff
3108 Rockaway Drive
Louisville 40216

Maine

Penobscot Paddle & Chowder Association
William F. Stearns
Box 121
Stillwater 04489

Maryland

Baltimore Kayak Club
Al Karasa
7118 McLean Boulevard
Baltimore 01234

Monocacy Canoe Club
Lawrence Swann
Route 1
Walkersville 21793

Massachusetts

A. M. C. Berkshire
Forrest House
33 Knollwood Drive
East Longmeadow 01028

Cochituate Canoe Club
Guy Newhall
99 Dudley Road
Cochituate 01760

Foxboro Canoe Club
Paul Neely
32 Taunton Street
Bellingham 02019

Lake Chaogg Canoe Club
William R. Graham
P. O. Box 512
Webster 01570

Waupanoag Paddlers
Ray Paulson
345 Forest Street
Pembrook 02359

Westfield River Whitewater Canoe Club
Merritt Andrews
90 West Silver Street
Westfield 01085

Michigan

Kalamazoo Downstreamers
James Tottle
6820 Evergreen
Kalamazoo 49002

Lower Michigan Paddling Council
Edward Woods
8266 Patton
Detroit 48228

Michigan Canoe Race Association
Al Robinson
4735 Hillcrest
Trenton 48183

Michigan Trailfinders Club
David Groenleer
2680 Rockhill, N.E.
Grand Rapids 49505

Niles Kayak Club
Mrs. William Smoke
Route 1, Box 83
Buchanan 49107

Minnesota

Minnesota Canoe Association, Inc.
Box 14177
Union Station
Minneapolis 55414

Missouri

AYH—Ozark Area
P. O. Box 13099
St. Louis 63119

Central Missouri State College Outing Club
Dr. Oz Hawksley
Department of Biology
Warrensburg 64093

Meramec River Canoe Club
Al Beletz
3636 Oxford Boulevard
Maplewood 63143

Ozark Wilderness Waterways Club
Box 8165
Kansas City 64112

Nebraska

Fort Kearney Canoeists
Ward Schrack
2623 Avenue D
Kearney 68847

Nevada

Basic High School Canoe Club
John Shannon
751 Palo Verde Drive
Henderson 89015

New Hampshire

Androscoggin Canoe & Kayak Club
John Wilson
Lancaster 03584

Ledyard Canoe Club of Dartmouth
Fritz Meyer
Robinson Hall
Hanover 03755

Mad Pemi Canoe Club
Dennis F. Keating
93 Realty
Campton 03223

New Jersey

Knickerbocker Canoe Club
Joe Corbiscello
6115 Washington Street
West New York 07093

Mohawk Canoe Club
Charles Schrey
11 Thomas Street
High Bridge 08829

Murray Hill Canoe Club
W. J. Schreibeis
Bell Telephone Labs
Murray Hill 07974

Neversink Canoe Sailing Society
William Reed
Oak Tree Lane
Rumson 07760

Red Dragon Canoe Club
221 Edgewater Avenue
Edgewater Park 08010

New Mexico

Albuquerque Whitewater Club
Glenn Fowler
804 Warm Sands Drive, S.E.
Albuquerque 87112

New York

Adirondack Mountain Club
Arthur L. Wickborn
Hamburg Savings Bank
315 Wyckoff Avenue
Brooklyn 11227

Adirondack Mountain Club
Doug Smith
769 John Glenn Road
Webster 14580

AYH—New York
Jim Naven
6 Cardinal Court
West Nyack 10994

A. M. C.—New York
Canoe Commission
John Neirs
Midland So. Box 1956
Syosset 11791

Inwood Canoe Club
Stephen Kelly
509 West 212th Street
New York 10034

Ka Na Wa Ke Canoe Club
Harold J. Gray
26 Pickwick Road
Dewitt (Syracuse) 13214

KCC—Cooperstown
Agnes Jones
Riverbrink
Cooperstown 13326

KCC—New York
Ed Alexander
6 Winslow Avenue
East Brunswick 08816

New York-New Jersey River Conference Canoe &
    Kayak Council
William Weiler
564 River Road
Chatham, N.J. 07928

Niagara Gorge Kayak Club
Michael J. McGee
147 Lancaster Avenue
Buffalo 14322

Sebago Canoe Club
Alfred E. Musial
9622 Avenue M
Brooklyn 11236

Sierra Club—Canoe Commission
Don Scott
875 West 181st Street
New York 10033

Tasca
P. O. Box 41
Oakland Gardens 11364

Wanda Canoe Club
Larry Guyre
315 Cross Street
Fort Lee, N.J. 07024

Wellsville Downriver Paddlers
Leroy Dodson
Proctor Road
Wellsville 14895

Yonkers Canoe Club
Joe Beczak
360 Edwards Place
Yonkers 10701

North Carolina

Carolina Canoe Club
Bob Moyer
121 Turner Street
Elkin 20621

Ohio

AYH—Columbus
Charles H. Pace
565 Old Farm Road
Columbus 43213

CMAC Kayak & Canoe Club
Dr. Paul J. Szliagyi
35124 Euclid Avenue
Willoughby 44094

Dayton Canoe Club
R. C. Deppner
1020 Riverside Drive
Dayton 45405

Keelhaulers Canoe Club
John A. Kobak
1649 Allen Drive
Westlake 44145

Madhatters Canoe Club
Christ Wolk
2647 Norway
Perry 44081

Warner & Swasey Canoe Club
Wayne McRobie
406 Mill Avenue, S.W.
New Philadelphia 44663

Oklahoma

O K Canoers
B. L. Smith
3112 Chaucer Drive
Village 73120

Tulsa Canoe & Camping Club
Jean Estep
5810 East 30th Place
Tulsa 74114

Oregon

Mary Kayak Club
Rob Blickensdorfer
3312 Elmwood Drive, N.W.
Cornwallis 97330

Oregon Kayak & Canoe Club
Lloyd Likens
2955 N.E. 49
Portland 97213

Pennsylvania

Allegheny Canoe Club
Walter J. Pilewski
362½ Circle Street
Franklin 16323

A. M. C. Delaware Valley
Donald M. Demarest
306 Crestview Circle
Media 19063

AYH—Delaware Valley
Fred Rosen
4714 York Road
Philadelphia 19141

AYH—Pittsburgh
George Robertson
6300 Fifth Avenue
Pittsburgh 15232

Benscreek Canoe Club
Roger Hager
R. D. 5, Box 256
Johnstown 15905

Bucknell Outing Club
Ray Charles
Box C-1610
Bucknell University
Lewisburg 17837

Buck Ridge Ski Club
William Wright
1728 Earlington Road
Havertown 19083

Delaware Canoe Club
William Woodring
14 South 14th Street
Easton 18042

Endless Mountain Voyageurs
Louis Hopt
285 Shorthill Road
Clarks Green 18411

Explorer Post 65
N. Hosking
22 Catalpa Place
Pittsburgh 15228

Fox Chapel Canoe Club
Bill Henderson
610 Squaw Run Road
Pittsburgh 15238

Indiana University Outing Club
David Cox
Department of Chemistry
Indiana 15701

Kishacoquillas Canoe & Rafting Club
c/o Wilderness Voyageurs
P. O. Box 97
Ohiopyle 15470

Mohawk Canoe Club
Charles Lopinto
6 Canary Road
Levittown 19057

North Hills YMCA Whitewater Club
Tim Hawthorn
1130 Sandlewood Lane
Pittsburgh 15237

Oil Creek Valley Canoe Club
Ray Gerard
214 North First Street
Titusville 16354

Paoli Troop I, BSA
Douglas Hoffman
432 Strafford Avenue
Wayne 19087

Penn Hills Whitewater Canoe Club
James Catello
Penn Hills Senior High School
12200 Garland Drive
Pittsburgh 15235

Penn State Outing Club
John Sweet
118 South Buckhout Street
University Park 16801

Philadelphia Canoe Club
Dr. Paul Liebman
4900 Ridge Avenue
Philadelphia 19128

Post 42, BSA
James Oro
Route 2
Palmerton 19053

Scudder Falls Wildwater Club
Dave Benham
795 River Road
Yardley 19067

Shenango Valley Canoe Club
E. K. Holloway
863 Bechtal Avenue
Sharon 16146

Sylvan Canoe Club
Don Hoecker
132 Arch Street
Verona 15147

Wildwater Boating Club
Robert Martin
Lock Box 179
Bellefonte 16823

Williamsport YMCA Canoe Club
John L. Houser
343 West 4th Street
Williamsport 17701

South Carolina

Sierra Club—Canoe Section
Gordon E. Howard
P. O. Box 463
Clemson 29631

Tennessee

Bluff City Canoe Club
Lawrence Migliora
P. O. Box 4523
Memphis 38104

Carbide Canoe Club
Herbert Pomerance
104 Ulena Lane
Oak Ridge 37830

East Tennessee Whitewater Club
Reid K. Gryder
P. O. Box 3074
Oak Ridge 37830

Tennessee Scenic Riders Association
Dr. William McLean
P. O. Box 3104
Nashville 37219

Tennessee Valley Canoe Club
James C. Mahaney
Box 11125
Chattanooga 37401

University of Tennessee Hiking & Canoe Club
William R. Krueger
Route 6
Concord 37730

Texas

Heart of Texas Canoe Club
Bob Burleson
Box 844
Temple 76501

Houston Canoe Club
Harold W. Walls
3116 Broadway
Houston 77017

Utah

Wasatch Mountain Club
J. Calvin Giddings
904 Military Drive
Salt Lake City 84108

Virginia

Appalachian Transit Authority
G. Hechtman
11453 Washington Plaza, W.
Reston 22070

Blue Ridge Voyageurs
Ralph Smith
8119 Hillcrest Drive
Manassas 22110

Coastal Canoeists
R. L. Sterling
309 Mimosa Drive
Newport News 23606

Washington

Cascave Canoe Club
Ray Parker
2333 Harris Avenue
Richland 99352

Paddle Trails Canoe Club
Ev Woodard
Box 86
Ashford 98304

Seattle Canoe Club
Ted Houk
6019 51, N.E.
Seattle 98115

Spokane Canoe Club
Norm Krebbs
N 10804 Nelson
Spokane 99218

Tri-C Camping Association
Craig N. Jorgenson
17404 8th Avenue
Seattle 98155

Washington Kayak Club
Al Winters
8519 California Avenue, S.W.
Seattle 98116

West Virginia

West Virginia Wildwater Association
Ward C. Eister
Route 1, Box 97
Ravenswood 26164

Wisconsin

Wisconsin Hoofers Outing Club
Steve Ransburg
3009 Hermina Street
Madison 53714

Appendix 3

BOOKS ABOUT CANOEING

Books of a general nature are listed here; local guidebooks, pamphlets, and other sources of information about specific regions are grouped in Appendix 5. Many of the books below are stocked by mail-order equipment suppliers such as Waters, Inc., and L. L.

Bean (Appendix 9); or by the American Canoe Association. Complete addresses are given for organizations such as the Appalachian Mountain Club, whose publications are best ordered direct; books of the general publishers can be obtained through regular bookstores.

General Guidebooks

Appalachian Mountain Club. *The A. M. C. New England Canoeing Guide; A Guide to the Canoeable Waterways of New England,* 3rd ed. The Appalachian Mountain Club, 5 Joy St., Boston, Mass. 02108.

Colwell, Robert. *Introduction to Water Trails in America.* Stackpole Books. Paperback.

Fabbro, Reece and Marcy. *1,000,000 Miles of Canoe and Hiking Trails.* Ohio Canoe Adventures, Inc., P. O. Box 2092 (5128 Colorado Avenue), Sheffield Lake, O. 44054. A catalogue of books, maps, and guidebooks about canoeing in many parts of the continent, all available from the same source.

Jenkinson, Michael. *Wild Rivers of North America.* Dutton. Detailed chapters on nine routes, plus notes, many from firsthand experience, on 106 wilderness rivers; oriented as much toward rafting and kayaking as canoeing, but useful nonetheless and well illustrated; entertainingly written.

Makens, James C. *Makens' Guide to U.S. Canoe Trails.* Le Voyageur Publishing Company, 1319 Wentwood Drive, Irving, Tex. 75061. Condensed notes, state by state, on most of the canoeable rivers and lake systems of the United States.

Nickels, Nick. *Canada Canoe Routes.* Canoecanada, Lakefield KOL 2HO Ont. A not too informative summary of canoe routes, with sources for more concrete information.

Palzer, Robert J.; and Joette M. Palzer. *Whitewater, Quietwater.* Guide to river canoeing in Wisconsin, Upper Michigan, northeastern Minnesota, with photographs, maps. Paperback. Evergreen Paddleways, 1416 21st St., Two Rivers, Wis. 54241; or 1225 Richmond St., El Cerrito, Calif. 94530.

Canoeing Technique

American Red Cross. *Canoeing.* Doubleday (or American National Red Cross, 17th and D Streets, N.W., Washington D.C. 20006). A comprehensive account of everything from paddling to how to make a laminated paddle or build a birch-bark canoe; somewhat dated and all the material on paddling assumes an empty canoe, but, with these qualifications, useful and generally reliable. Paperback.

Urban, John T. *A White Water Handbook for Canoe and Kayak.* Appalachian Mountain Club. The most useful introduction to white-water technique that I've found—but no substitute for firsthand instruction. Paperback.

Background, History, Travel

Angier, Bradford. *Survival with Style.* Stackpole Books. One of many books by this prolific writer on wilderness living, this one emphasizes how to provide food and shelter in emergency situations (after losing your outfit, for instance), but many of his techniques are useful for camping in general.

Bolz, J. Arnold. *Portage into the Past; by Canoe Along the Minnesota-Ontario Boundary Waters.* University of Minnesota Press.

Burmeister, Walter F. *Appalachian Water: The Delaware River and Its Tributaries.* A detailed study, but with notes on a number of attractive canoe runs. Paperback. Appalachian Books, P. O. Box 248, Oakton, Va. 22124.

———. *Appalachian Water: The Hudson River and Its Tributaries.* Paperback. Appalachian Books.

Denis, Keith. *Canoe Trails Through the Quetico.* University of Toronto Press. Paperback.

Dietz, Lew. *The Allagash.* Holt, Rinehart & Winston. A history of the river and its people.

Goodrum, John. *Rivers of Alabama.* Strode Publishers, 6802 Jones Valley Drive, S.E., Huntsville, Ala. 35802.

Jaques, Florence. *Canoe Country.* University of Minnesota Press. A classic, superbly illustrated by Francis Lee Jaques.

———. *The Geese Fly High.* University of Minnesota Press. Illustrated by Francis Lee Jaques.

Mead, Robert Douglas. *Ultimate North.* Doubleday. Canoeing in the Mackenzie Valley from Alberta to the Arctic Ocean—the land and its people, present and past.

Morse, Eric W. *Fur Trade Canoe Routes of Canada, Then and Now.* In Canada: the Queen's Printer, Ottawa, or Canadian Government bookstores; in the United States: Minnesota Historical Society, 1500 Mississippi Street, St. Paul, Minn. 55101. An account of the canoe routes that combines history with a canoer's personal experiences.

Nickerson, E. B. *Kayaks to the Arctic.* Howell-North Books. A gossipy account of a family cruise down the Mackenzie, worth reading because current information about the region is so scarce.

Nute, Grace Lee. *The Voyageur.* Minnesota Historical Society.

———. *The Voyageurs' Highway.* Minnesota Historical Society. The border-lakes country; paperback.

————. *Rainy River Country*. Minnesota Historical Society. Stories of life on the Minnesota border.

Olson, Sigurd F. *The Lonely Land*. Knopf. The Churchill River.

————. *Runes of the North*. Knopf. Canoeing in many parts of the North, from Hudson Bay to the Camsell River.

————. *The Singing Wilderness*. Knopf. The borderlakes country.

James Reber. *Potomac Portrait*. An in-depth appreciation of the river by a white-water canoer and kayaker; well illustrated. Hard-cover or paperback. Liveright.

Severeid, Eric. *Canoeing with the Cree*. Minnesota Historical Society. An account of the famous author's boyhood trip from the border-lakes region to Hudson Bay.

Sunset Editors. *Rivers of the West*. Lane Book Company.

Sutton, Ann and Myron. *The Grand Canyon*. Lippincott. Not canoeing as such, but a splendid introduction to the natural and human history of the Grand Canyon and of the Southwest generally; handsomely illustrated.

Appendix 4

SOURCES FOR U.S. AND CANADIAN MAPS

Sources for the two countries' national map systems, with methods for ordering, are given below. In addition, a number of canoe-oriented maps—published locally or by various state and provincial government agencies—are listed in Appendix 5, along with many other kinds of canoeing information.

United States Geological Survey Maps

Free index maps for each state show maps available in three different series (7½-minute/1:24,000, 15-minute/1:62,500, and 1:250,000—see Chapter 8) and list a variety of special maps, including maps of national parks (but *not* maps of the U. S. Forest Service that happen to cover canoe routes, as in the case of the Boundary Waters Canoe Area—see Appendix 5). The index maps also list dealers and libraries in each state

that carry a comprehensive stock. For index maps and orders (generally fifty cents to one dollar per map, with discounts for large orders) *for states east of the Mississippi:* Distribution Section, U. S. Geological Survey, 1200 South Eads Street, Arlington, Virginia 22202. For index maps and orders *for states west of the Mississippi:* Distribution Section, U. S. Geological Survey, Federal Center, Denver, Colorado 80225.

Canadian Topographical Maps

The Federal Surveys and Mapping Branch publishes a free booklet (MDO 79) listing the index maps for the available series (1:125,000, 1:250,000, 1:500,000, 1:1,000,000); the same booklet includes a master index, in map form, of the eighteen index maps in the 1:50,000 series. (For maps produced by other agencies or by the provincial governments, see Appendix 5.) For index maps and orders (generally one dollar per sheet for the smaller maps), write to: Map Distribution Office, 615 Booth Street, Ottawa K1A 0E9 Ontario.

Appendix 5

LOCAL SOURCES OF CANOEING INFORMATION

Much of the most useful material is published in the area to which it pertains—by state or provincial governments, parks, canoeing and conservation organizations, enterprising individuals. Many of the publications listed below are free, the rest modestly priced, usually at two to three dollars or less, a few at around five dollars. Since prices these days change rapidly, I have not tried to quote them—you'll have to check before ordering—but all free items are identified with an asterisk (*).

United States

For New England canoeing, bear in mind that *The A. M. C. New England Canoeing Guide* (Appendix 3) is the most thorough and reliable source of information available for canoeing in all the states in the region. The background books listed in the same appendix should also be consulted for particular areas.

Alabama

*The Beautiful Cahaba River. Alabama Conservation Department, 64 N. Union St., Montgomery, Ala. 36104.

Alaska

*Alaska Canoe Trails. Twelve routes, with maps, mileages, other details. Bureau of Land Management, U. S. Department of the Interior, 555 Cordova St., Anchorage, Alas.

Don and Vangie Hart. A Guide of the Yukon River. Alaska Magazine Book Department, Box 4-EEE, Anchorage, Alas. 99509.

The Milepost. A guidebook, revised each year, to road travel in Alaska, northern Alberta, British Columbia, the Yukon Territory, and the Northwest Territories (approaches to the Alaska Highway)—all useful if you're trying to get to canoe country in these areas by car. Alaska Northwest Publishing Co., Box 4-EEE, Anchorage, Alas. 99509.

*Swan Lake Canoe Route. Bureau of Sport Fisheries and Wildlife, U. S. Fish and Wildlife Service, P. O. Box 1287, Juneau, Alas. 99801.

Arkansas

Buffalo River Canoe Guide. Ozark Society, P. O. Box 38, Fayetteville, Ark. 72701.

Kenneth L. Smith. The Buffalo River Country. Guidebook, with maps and photographs; paperback or hardbound. Ozark Society, Box 725, Hot Springs, Ark. 71901.

A Guide to Canoeing the Cossatot. Jack Wellborn, Jr., 1635 Slattery Bldg., Shreveport, La. 71101.

*Maps of the Buffalo River. Arkansas Game and Fish Commission, Little Rock, Ark. 72201; or Supervisor, Ozark National Forest, Hot Springs, Ark. 71901.

*Ouachita River Float Trip. Also, separate *map. Supervisor, Ouachita National Forest, Hot Springs, Ark. 71901.

California

Ann Dwyer. Canoeing Waters of California. Guidebook, with maps. GBH Press, 125 Upland St., Kentfield, Calif. 94904.

Connecticut

*Connecticut Canoeing Guide. Boating Commission, State Office Bldg., Hartford, Conn. 06115.

The Connecticut River Guide. Detailed coverage, with maps, of the entire river, from source to Long Island Sound. Connecticut River Watershed Council, 497 Main Street, Greenfield, Mass. 01301.

The Farmington River and Watershed Guide. Booklet, separate map. Farmington River Watershed Association, Inc., 24 E. Main Street, Avon, Conn. 06001.

Florida

*Everglades National Park, Florida. Leaflet, with map. Everglades National Park, P. O. Box 279, Homestead, Fla. 33030.

*Everglades National Park Canoe Trail Guide. Booklet. Everglades National Park, P. O. Box 279, Homestead, Fla. 33030.

*Florida Canoe Trail Guide. A booklet, with maps, covering sixteen routes; a supplement from the same source describes eight additional canoe routes. Florida Department of Natural Resources, Division of Recreation and Parks, Larson Bldg., Tallahassee, Fla. 32304.

William G. Truesdell. A Guide to the Wilderness Waterway of the Everglades National Park. University of Miami Press, Drawer 9088, Coral Gables, Fla. 33124.

Georgia

*Leaflets, with maps, on canoe routes in the Okefenokee National Wildlife Refuge and on the Alapaha, Suwannee, St. Mary's, and Saltilla rivers. Generally available from the Coastal Plain Area Tourism Council (P. O. Box 1223, Valdosta, Ga. 31601); the State of Florida Department of Natural Resources (Larson Bldg., Tallahassee, Fla. 32304); or Slash Pine Area Planning and Development Commission, P. O. Box 1276 (902 Grove Avenue), Waycross, Ga. 31501.

Idaho

*Canoeing maps and general information. Idaho Department of Commerce and Development, Room 108, Statehouse, Boise, Ida. 83707.

*Maps: Salmon River and North Fork of the Snake River. Idaho Fish and Game Department, P. O. Box 65, Boise Ida. 83701.

*Middle Fork of the Salmon. Booklet, with map. Forest Service, U. S. Department of Agriculture, Intermountain Region, Ogden, Ut.

Illinois

*Illinois Canoeing Guide. Boating Section, Illinois Department of Conservation, 106 State Office Bldg., Springfield, Ill. 62706.

Indiana

Canoeing Trails in Indiana. Indiana Department of

Natural Resources, Map Sales, Room 604, State Office Bldg., Indianapolis, Ind. 46204.

Iowa

Guide to the Upper Iowa River. G. E. Knudson, Luther College, Decorah, Ia. 52101.

*Iowa Canoe Trips. Iowa Conservation Department, E. 7th and Court Streets, Des Moines, Ia. 50309.

Kansas

*Kansas Streams. Kansas Department of Economic Development, 122-S State Office Bldg., Topeka, Kan. 66612.

Kentucky

*Daniel Boone National Forest. Canoeing guide (Red River), with map. Forest Service, U. S. Department of Agriculture, P. O. Box 727, Winchester, Ky. 40391.

*Mammoth Cave National Park. Map (park includes part of the Green River). Superintendent, Mammoth Cave National Park, Mammoth Cave, Ky. 42259.

Louisiana

*State Parks with Canoeable Waterways. Leaflet. Louisiana State Parks and Recreation Commission, Old State Capitol, Drawer 1111, Baton Rouge, La. 70821.

Maine

*Allagash Wilderness Waterway. Illustrated leaflet, with map. *Escape to Me.; Flat Water Canoeing. Summary of routes. *Wild Me.; White Water Canoeing. Summary of routes. All from Bureau of Parks & Recreation, Maine Department of Conservation, State House, Augusta, Me. 04330.

Eben Thomas. No Horns Blowing; Canoeing 10 Great Rivers in Maine. A highly personal guidebook. Hallowell Printing Company, 145 Water Street, Hallowell, Me. 04347.

Maryland

Canoeing Streams of the Potomac and Rappahannock Basins. Thomas L. Gray, 11121 Dewey Road, Kensington, Md. 20795.

See also listings under Virginia.

Massachusetts

The Connecticut River Guide. Detailed description, with maps, of the river from source to mouth.

Connecticut River Watershed Council, Box 89, Greenfield, Mass. 01301.

Michigan

*Canoeing in West Michigan. West Michigan Tourist Association, 136 Fulton East, Grand Rapids, Mich. 49502.

*Huron River Canoeing Guide. Huron-Clinton Metropolitan Authority, 1750 Guardian Bldg., Detroit, Mich. 48226.

*Huron National Forest and *Manistee National Forest. Maps. Forest Service, U. S. Department of Agriculture, Cadillac, Mich. 49601.

*Michigan Canoe Trails. Michigan Department of Natural Resources, Stevens T. Mason Bldg., Lansing, Mich. 48926.

*Michigan Guide to Easy Canoeing. Michigan Department of Natural Resources.

Minnesota

See also the general books on canoeing in Appendix 3.

*Big Fork River Canoe Trail. Box 256, Big Fork, Minn. 56628.

*Chippewa National Forest. Map. Also *canoe maps of the Turtle, Rice, and Inguadona rivers. Forest Supervisor, Chippewa National Forest, Cass Lake, Minn. 56633.

*Crow Wing River. Crow Wing Trails Association, Box 210, Sebeka, Minn. 56477.

*Kettle River Canoe Route. Pine County Soil and Water Conservation District, P. O. Box 276, Hinckley, Minn. 55037.

*The Minnesota River. Booklet, with map. City Administrator, 218 S. Main Street, Le Sueur, Minn. 56058.

Minnesota Voyageur Trails. Booklet, with maps, on the Boundary Waters Canoe Area and a number of Minnesota rivers. Division of Parks and Recreation, Minnesota Department of Conservation, 320 Centennial Bldg., St. Paul, Minn. 55101.

Mississippi River Guide. Aitkin County Park Commission, Court House, Aitkin, Minn. 56431.

*Root River Canoe Trail. Canoe Trails Association, Box 548, Rushford, Minn. 55971.

*St. Croix/Nomehagon Rivers. Muller Boat Co., Inc., Taylor Falls, Minn. 55084.

*Snake River. Minnesota State Documents Section, 140 Centennial Bldg., St. Paul, Minn. 55101.

*Superior National Forest. Planning map of canoe routes and portages, including the Boundary Waters Canoe Area. Also, booklets on the same area: *The Boundary Waters Canoe Area and *Canoeing-Camping in the BWCA. Forest Supervisor, Superior National Forest, Box 338, Duluth,

Minn. 55801 (or district rangers at Aurora, Cook, Ely, Tofte, Grand Marais, Two Harbors, Isabella, Virginia—all in Minnesota).

Superior-Quetico Canoe Maps. Set of fifteen detailed maps (scale of about one and a half miles per inch) covering border-lakes routes on both sides of the international boundary; inexpensive, printed on waterproof paper. Available from most outfitters in the area or from the publisher. W. A. Fisher Co., Virginia, Minn. 55792.

Mississippi

*Black Creek Float Trip. Leaflet. Also, a *map of this national forest. Supervisor, De Soto National Forest, Box 1291, Jackson, Miss. 39505.

Missouri

Maps, Current and Jacks Fork rivers. S. G. Adams Printing & Stationery Co., 10th and Olive Streets, St. Louis, Mo. 63101.

Oz Hawksley. *Missouri Ozark Waterways.* Detailed guide to thirty-seven canoe routes, with maps. Missouri Department of Conservation, P. O. Box 180 (North Ten Mile Drive), Jefferson, Mo. 65101.

Montana

*Montana's Popular Float Streams. Introductory notes on canoeable sections of twenty-three rivers. Also: *leaflets on the Yellowstone and Missouri rivers; and *"The Wild Missouri," reprint of a recent article in *Montana Outdoors,* with planning map. Montana Department of Fish & Game, Helena, Mont. 59601.

New Jersey

*Canoeing in New Jersey. Notes on river routes. Division of Parks, Forests, and Recreation, New Jersey Department of Economic Development, P. O. Box 400, Trenton, N.J. 08625.

James and Margaret Cawley. *Exploring the Little Rivers of New Jersey.* Paperback and hard-cover editions. Rutgers University Press, 30 College Avenue, New Brunswick, N.J. 08903.

Maps of the Delaware River. Delaware River Basin Commission, 25 Scotch Road, Trenton, N.J. 08603.

New Mexico

Rafting, Kayaking and Canoeing on the Rio Grande and Chama Rivers. C. Carnes, 130 Rover Blvd., White Rock, Los Alamos, N.M. 87544.

New York

*Adirondack Canoe Routes. Descriptive folder with planning map. New York State Department of Environmental Conservation, Albany, N.Y. 12201.

*Canoe Trips. Leaflet with brief notes on thirty-five rivers. New York State Department of Environmental Conservation.

Ohio

*Canoe Trails and **Canoe Adventures.* Ohio Department of Natural Resources, Division of Watercraft, 1350 Holly Ave., Columbus, O. 43212.

1,000,000 Miles of Canoe and Hiking Routes. Catalogue of dozens of route descriptions and maps for rivers in Ohio and elsewhere available from the same source. Ohio Canoe Adventures, Inc., P. O. Box 2092 (5128 Colorado Ave.), Sheffield Lake, O. 44054.

Oklahoma

*Scenic Rivers. Oklahoma Department of Wildlife Conservation, 1801 N. Lincoln, Oklahoma City, Okla. 73105.

Oregon

*The Rogue River. Descriptive map; also, *map of the national forest. Supervisor, Siskiyou National Forest, P. O. Box 440, Grants Pass, Ore. 97526.

Dick Schwind. *West Coast River Touring Guide— Rogue River Canyon and South.* Touring notes against a background of ecology and geological history. Paperback. Touchstone Press, P. O. Box 81, Beaverton, Ore. 97005.

Pennsylvania

See also Delaware River maps listed under *New Jersey.*

*Canoe Routes. Notes on the Allegheny, Monongahela, Ohio, Susquehanna, and Delaware rivers. Also, *leaflets on state-park boating and camping. Bureau of State Parks, Pennsylvania Department of Environmental Resources, P. O. Box 1467, Harrisburg, Pa. 17105.

*Canoeing in the Delaware and Susquehanna Watershed of Pennsylvania. Leaflet rating many rivers for difficulty and attractiveness. Pennsylvania Fish Commission, Department of Environmental Resources, P. O. Box 1673, Harrisburg, Pa. 17120.

Canoeing Guide: Western Pennsylvania/Northern West Virginia. From the same source: a large canoeing map of the area covered by this guidebook. Pittsburgh Council, American Youth Hostels, 6300 Fifth Avenue, Pittsburgh, Pa. 15232.

Select Rivers of Central Pennsylvania. Mostly white-water. John Sweet, Penn State Outing Club, 118 S. Buckhout St., University Park, Pa. 16801.

Stream Map of Pennsylvania. Oversize map, showing all streams and rivers in the state. College of Agriculture, Agricultural Experiment Station, Pennsylvania State University, University Park, Pa. 16801.

Rhode Island

*Pawcatuck River and Wood River: Division of Conservation, Rhode Island Department of Natural Resources, Veterans Memorial Bldg., Providence, R.I. 02903.

South Carolina

*Canoeing the Chattooga. Also, **Sumter National Forest* map. District Ranger, Andrew Pickens Ranger District, Walhalla, S.C. 29691.

Tennessee

*Canoeing in Tennessee. Folder listing and rating twenty-two canoeable rivers throughout the state. Tennessee Tourism Development Division, Andrew Jackson Bldg., Nashville, Tenn. 37219.

The Oneida Trail. Wild Rivers, Inc., P. O. Box 18, Oneida, Tenn. 37841.

*Tennessee Recreational Waters. Maps of the Buffalo, Duck, Harperth, and Little Tennessee rivers. Tennessee Game and Fish Commission, P. O. Box 9400, Nashville, Tenn. 37220.

Texas

*Big Bend National Park. Map. Superintendent, Big Bend National Park, Tex. 79834.

*Suggested River Trips Through the Rio Grande River Canyons. Detailed notes, multilithed, with maps, prepared by Bob Burleson, president of the Texas Explorers Club. Bob Burleson, P. O. Box 844, Temple, Tex. 76501.

Texas Rivers and Rapids, Vols. I and II. Ben Nolen, P. O. Box 673, Humble, Tex. 77338.

Vermont

*Canoeing on the Connecticut River. Descriptive booklet, with maps, of the Vermont sections of the river. Agency of Development and Community Affairs, 61 Elm Street, Montpelier, Vt., 05602

*Vermont Canoeing. Vermont Development Commission, Montpelier, Vt. 05602.

Virginia

Roger H. Corbett and Louis J. Matacia. *Blue Ridge*

Voyages, Vols. I–IV. Louis J. Matacia, Blue Ridge Voyageurs, 2700 Gallows Road, Vienna, Va. 22180.

Randy Carter. *Canoeing White Water.* Paperback guide to wild rivers in Virginia, West Virginia, North Carolina's Great Smokies, Pennsylvania. Appalachian Outfitters, Box 11, 2930 Chain Bridge Road, Oakton, Va. 22124.

*Canoe Trails of Eastern Virginia. Virginia Commission of Game and Inland Fisheries, Box 1642, Richmond, Va. 23213.

*Virginia's Scenic Rivers. Virginia Commission of Outdoor Recreation, 803 E. Broad Street, Richmond, Va. 23219.

Washington

Werner Furrer. *Kayak and Canoe Trips in Washington.* Paperback. Signpost Publications, 16812 36th Ave., Lynnwood, Wash. 98036.

———. *Watertrails of Washington.* Paperback. Signpost Publications.

Kayak and Canoe Trips in Washington. Signpost Publications, 16812 36th Ave. West, Lynnwood, Wash. 98036.

Map of Washington rivers. Angle Lake Cyclery, 20840 Pacific Highway South, Seattle, Wash. 98188.

Map of Washington rivers. Washington Kayak Club, 5622 Seaview Ave., Seattle, Wash. 98107.

West Virginia

Bob Burrell and Paul Davidson. *A Canoeist's Guide to the Whitewater Rivers of West Virginia.* West Virginia Wildwater Association, Route 1, Box 95, Ravenswood, W.Va. 26164.

See also listings under *Pennsylvania* and *Virginia.*

Wisconsin

Canoe Trails of Northeastern Wisconsin; Canoe Trails of North-Central Wisconsin; Canoe Trails of Southern Wisconsin. Three handsome and professionally produced guidebooks covering, in all, nearly sixty canoeable rivers, with maps. Wisconsin Trails, P. O. Box 5650, Madison, Wis. 53705.

Andres Peekna. *A Guide to White Water in the Wisconsin Area.* Outing Director, Wisconsin Union, University of Wisconsin, 800 Langdon Street, Madison, Wis. 53706.

*Kickapoo Canoe Trail. Kickapoo Valley Association, Inc., Route 2, Box 211, La Farge, Wis. 54639.

Northwest Wisconsin Canoe Trails. Northwest Wisconsin Canoe Trails, Inc., Gordon, Wis. 54838.

*Wisconsin Water Trails. Notes, with maps, on forty-eight short river routes suitable for canoeing (Publication 104–72). Division of Tourism and In-

formation, Wisconsin Department of Natural Resources, P. O. Box 450, Madison, Wis. 53701.

Wyoming

Bridger National Forest. Map (part of the Green River). Supervisor, Bridger National Forest, Forest Service Building, Kemmerer, Wyo. 83101.

Floating the Snake River. Superintendent, Grand Teton National Park, Moose, Wyo. 83012.

Medicine Bow National Forest. Map (part of the North Platte River). Supervisor, Medicine Bow National Forest, Box 3355, University Station, Laramie, Wyo. 82070.

Wilderness Boating on Yellowstone Lakes. Superintendent, Yellowstone National Park, Wyo. 83020.

Canada

Through its Wild Rivers Surveys, the Canadian Government has done rather more than any branch of the U. S. Government to assemble in one place information on canoeing. Since 1971, teams of canoeists have been sent out to travel and report on some of the wildest wilderness rivers on the continent. Their useful reports, usually with maps, are available in multilithed form and cover the following rivers, among others: Coppermine, Hanbury and Thelon, Hare, Mountain, Natla and Keele, South Redstone, Snare (all in the Northwest Territories); Clearwater (Saskatchewan and Alberta); Fond du Lac and Churchill (both Saskatchewan); Klondike and North Klondike, Macmillan, Nisutlin, Ogilvie and Peel, Ross, Stewart, Teslin, White (all Yukon); Goose, Lloyds-Exploits, Main, Ugjoktok, Naskaupi (all Labrador or the island of Newfoundland). In an open canoe, *all of these remote rivers are hazardous and should be attempted only by experienced, thoroughly prepared canoeists;* but the rewards are commensurate. For copies of the available reports, write to:

Information Services
Conservation Group
Department of Indian Affairs
Ottawa K1A 0H4
Ontario

Nick Nickels's *Canada Canoe Routes,* with sources of information about routes throughout Canada, is listed in Appendix 3.

For some general background information on Canadian canoeing (in Ontario, New Brunswick, and Quebec's La Vérendrye Provincial Park, among others) and for provincial and other sources, write to:

Outdoor Editor
Canadian Government Office of Tourism
150 Kent Street
Ottawa K1A 0H6
Ontario

Alberta

For information on specific canoe routes in Alberta and some other areas of the Canadian West and Northwest, the Alberta canoe club, the North West Voyageurs, can put you in touch with members who have personally traveled the routes. Write to: Mr. Robert Gilpin, Archivist, North West Voyageurs, 10922 88th Avenue, Edmonton 61, Alta.

Canoeing Alberta; a Trip Guide to Alberta's Rivers. Descriptions from firsthand experience (like the national Wild Rivers Surveys, on a smaller scale) of the province's main rivers and their tributaries: the North and South Saskatchewan and Athabasca river systems. Alberta Department of Culture, Youth, and Recreation, Canadian National Tower, 10004 104th Avenue, Edmonton T5J 0K5 Alta.

British Columbia

*Booklets on provincial parks, with canoeing information, are available from Parks Branch, Department of Recreation and Conservation, Parliament Bldgs., Victoria, B.C.

Canoe British Columbia. Trip Guide, 1606 W. Broadway, Vancouver, B.C.

Maps of the provincial parks are available from Surveys and Mapping Branch, Department of Lands, Forests and Resources, Parliament Bldgs., Victoria, B.C.

Manitoba

*Canoe route maps; also, *booklets describing corresponding canoe routes. Parks Branch, Department of Tourism, Recreation and Cultural Affairs, 409 Norquay Bldg., Winnipeg, Man.

New Brunswick

*Canoe routes, provincial maps. Request a descriptive booklet, appropriate maps, and individual guidance from New Brunswick Travel Bureau, Box 1030, Fredericton, N.B.

Newfoundland

In Labrador, Newfoundland's mainland, non-residents are required to be accompanied by a licensed guide. In addition to the surveys listed at the outset of this section, you can get information about guides and local travel conditions from

Parks Service
Newfoundland Department of Economic Development
Box 9340, Postal Station B
St. John's, Nfld.

Northwest Territories

*Canoeing in the Northwest Territories (general advice about preparations). Also: *Nahanni National Park and *The South Nahanni River (multilithed descriptive notes) and general tourist information on the North, including lists of outfitters. TravelArctic, Division of Tourism, Government of the Northwest Territories, Yellowknife X0E 1H0 N.W.T.

Ontario

*Algonquin Provincial Park. Planning map, descriptive booklet, lists of outfitters, and other materials. Superintendent and District Manager, Ontario Department of Lands and Forests, Algonquin Provincial Park, Box 219, Whitney K0J 2M0 Ont.

*Algonquin Provincial Park: canoe route booklets, maps, general information. District Forester, Ontario Department of Lands and Forests, 162 Agnes Street, Pembroke, Ont.

*Canoe route pamphlets, as available, for Beaver River, Black Lake, Burnt River system, Gull River system, Kishkebus Lake, Magnetawan River, Mississagi River, Mississippi River (Canada, not United States), Pickerel River, Rankin River, Saugeen River, Sixmile Lake Provincial Park, Smoked Pickerel River, Wolf and Pickerel rivers. Mostly short routes. Director, Park Management Branch, Ministry of Natural Resources, Parliament Bldgs., Toronto, Ont.

Northern Ontario Canoe Routes. Booklet with map and general information on 125 canoe routes and sources for specific additional information. Ask also for provincial maps of specific canoe routes. Surveys and Engineering Branch, Map Office, Ministry of Natural Resources, Parliament Bldgs., Toronto, Ont.

*Parks, descriptive booklets: *Mattawa Provincial Park; *Canoe Routes, North Georgian Bay Recreational Reserve. Chief, Parks Branch, Department of Lands and Forests, Parliament Bldgs., Toronto, Ont.

*Quetico Provincial Park, planning map; also, descriptive booklet, detailed maps (charge—see also listing for Superior-Quetico maps, under Minnesota). District Forester, Department of Lands and Forests, Fort Frances, Ont.; also, Park Superintendent, Quetico Provincial Park, Department of Lands and Forests, Atikokan, Ont.

Quebec

Guide des Rivières du Québec. In French; English edition promised. Éditions du Jour, 1651 rue Saint-Denis, Montréal, Québec (publisher of the French edition); or Fédération Québécoise de Canot-Kayak, Inc., 881 Boulevard de Maisonneuve Est, Montréal 132, Québec.

*List of Outfitters. Bilingual test, extensive list of outfitter-guides for hunting and fishing, but no identification of those that specialize in canoeing. Ministère du Tourisme, de la Chasse et de la Pêche, Direction Générale du Tourisme, Cité Parlementaire, Québec G1A 1R4 Que.

*Map-booklets on canoeing in La Vérendrye and Laurentides provincial parks (the latter, Métabétchouan River). Ministère du Tourisme.

*Quebec Parks. Two different booklets, giving rates, facilities (including canoeing), general information for all the provincial parks; illustrations, maps, bilingual text. Ministère du Tourisme.

Saskatchewan

For general information on canoeing and travel in the northern Saskatchewan wilderness and for information on Prince Albert National Park and Lac La Ronge Provincial Park, write to

Head Office
The Department of Northern Saskatchewan
La Ronge, Sask.

There are provincial government offices in the following towns, which may be contacted for local information (as a safety precaution, you are also advised to tell them your route and schedule if canoeing in the vicinity): Pierceland, Meadow Lake Provincial Park, Loon Lake, Dorintosh, Green Lake, Beauval, Île-à-La Crosse, Buffalo Narrows, La Loche, Molanosa, Pelican Narrows, Creighton, Cumberland.

*Canoe Saskatchewan. A listing of the many canoe routes within the province. Also, *individual booklets under general title of Saskatchewan Canoe Trips, detailing, so far, forty routes, with distances, portages, access points and means of getting there, map references. Get both the general booklet and the specific guide or guides. Saskatchewan Department of Tourism and Renewable Resources, P. O. Box 7105, Regina S4P 0B5 Sask.

Yukon Territory

For general information and answers to specific questions, write to

Yukon Department of Travel and Publicity
Box 1703
Whitehorse, Y.T.

Several rivers described in the Wild Rivers Surveys listed at the beginning of this section are actually in the Yukon, although the natural approaches would be from the Mackenzie River in the Northwest Territories. See also *A Guide of the Yukon River,* listed under *Alaska.*

Mad River Canoe
P. O. Box 363
(Spring Hill)
Waitsfield, Vt. 05673

Old Town Canoe Company
Old Town, Me. 04468

Sawyer Canoe Company
234 South State Street
Oscoda, Mich. 48750

Voyageur Canoe Company, Ltd.
Millbrook, Ont.

Appendix 6

CANOE MANUFACTURERS

In the following list, Great World and The Chicagoland Canoe Base are primarily dealers that also produce canoes of their own in limited quantities (Allagash and Canadien, respectively), included here because they seem to me of exceptional interest. The canoe builders listed here will furnish catalogues and specifications for their canoes and related equipment and in most cases will fill retail orders in areas where they are not represented by dealers; all can provide you with lists of their dealers and rental agencies or can refer you to nearby dealers. Grumman and Old Town canoes are generally available throughout the United States (Grumman to a limited degree in Canada); Alumacraft, Sawyer, and Mad River dealers are more scattered and regional, but all three, particularly Alumacraft, are expanding. In Canada, Chestnut seems to be the most widely available make; Voyageur's limited production is mostly sold direct.

Alumacraft Boat Co.
315 West St. Julien
St. Peter, Minn. 56082

Chestnut Canoe Co., Ltd.
P. O. Box 85
Fredericton E3B 4Y2 N.B.

The Chicagoland Canoe Base, Inc.
4019 North Narragansett Avenue
Chicago, Ill. 60634

Great World, Inc.
P. O. Box 250
(250 Farms Village Road)
West Simsbury, Conn. 06092

Grumman Boats
Grumman Allied Industries, Inc.
Marathon, N.Y. 13803

Appendix 7

PADDLES AND OTHER CANOE EQUIPMENT

Most of the canoe builders listed in Appendix 6 also produce or market paddles, carrying yokes, car-top carriers, and other equipment. The following sources are specialists in the items indicated.

Cannon Products, Inc.
P. O. Box 612
(2345 N.W. Eighth Avenue)
Faribault, Minn. 55021
(inexpensive ABS paddles; carrying yokes)

Crawford Industries
P. O. Box 31
Marshall, Mich. 49068
(snap-on car-top carriers)

Raymond A. Dodge, Importer
1025 Broadway
Niles, Mich. 49120
(Clement paddles in solid and laminated wood)

Iliad, Inc.
168 Circuit Street
Norwell, Mass. 02061
(fiberglass paddles, premium quality—and prices)

Smoker Lumber Company, Inc.
New Paris, Ind. 46553
(solid and laminated-wood paddles)

Sports Equipment, Inc.
P. O. Box T
Mantua, O. 44255
(fiberglass paddles, rubber rope)

Appendix 8

CAMPING EQUIPMENT MANUFACTURERS

Unless otherwise indicated, the following companies produce tents and sleeping bags and other equipment suitable for canoe camping. Those marked with an asterisk (*) are hospitable to retail orders by mail and in most cases handle lines other than their own; all will supply catalogues and price lists on request and can put you in touch with local dealers if there are any.

*Thomas Black & Sons Canada, Ltd.
225 Strathcona Avenue
Ottawa K1S 1X7 Ont.
or
*Thomas Black & Sons (Ogdensburg), Inc.
930 Ford Street
Ogdensburg, N.Y. 13669

*Canoe California
P. O. Box 61
Kentfield, Calif. 94904
(frameless nylon packs designed with canoeing in mind)

*Duluth Tent & Awning Co.
1610 West Superior Street
Duluth, Minn. 55806
(Duluth packs, poplin tents)

*Eureka Tent, Inc.
P. O. Box 966
(625 Conklin Road)
Binghamton, N.Y. 13902
(Draw-Tite and other tent designs, in poplin and nylon)

Gerry Division of Outdoor Sports Industries, Inc.
5450 North Valley Highway
Denver, Colo. 80216
(polyethylene bags and squeeze tubes, as well as tents and sleeping bags)

Hirsch-Weiss/White Stag
5203 S. E. Johnson Creek Boulevard
Portland, Ore. 97206

*Holubar Mountaineering, Ltd.
Box 7
Boulder, Colo. 80302
(besides tents and sleeping bags, a pretty good selection of camping equipment and clothing, with retail stores in Denver, Colorado Springs, and Fort Collins, as well as Boulder)

*Kelty Mountaineering and Mail Order
1801 Victory Boulevard
Glendale, Calif. 91201
(a source for Sierra Designs and North Face sleeping bags and tents, some hiking clothes and equipment adaptable to canoeing)

Mountain Products Corporation
123 South Wenatchee Avenue
Wenatchee, Wash. 98801

*Voyageur Enterprises
P. O. Box 512
Shawnee Mission, Kan. 66201
(waterproof plastic cargo bags that can be used in place of packs provided they don't have to be portaged; also, a source for Duluth packs and some other canoeing equipment)

*Woods Bag & Canvas Co., Ltd.
P. O. Box 118
(90 River Street)
Ogdensburg, N.Y. 13669
(sleeping bags and some quilted clothing stocked in Ogdensburg; a full range of camping equipment, including Hudson's Bay (Duluth) packs, at this Canadian firm's stores in Halifax, Quebec, Montreal, Toronto, Thunder Bay, Winnipeg, Calgary, and Vancouver)

Appendix 9

RETAIL SOURCES FOR CANOE-CAMPING EQUIPMENT

All the retail outlets listed below produce periodic catalogues that repay study and offer prompt and efficient mail-order service if you're not within reach of their stores. Since they're primarily retailers, their stock is generally much more comprehensive and varied than that of the manufacturers in Appendix 8, even when the latter do not discourage retail business (in the case of the two Canadian manufacturers, Black's and Woods, however, the distinction is less sharp).

Credit card, if indicated, or cash with order is the rule.

Eddie Bauer, Inc. Two elegant catalogues a year include a good many country-gentry superfluities, but among them you'll find tents and sleeping bags exclusive with Bauer and serviceable clothing—shirts, trousers, boots, socks, rain wear. Stores in Seattle, San Francisco, Minneapolis, Chicago (the latter two stock Duluth packs), Denver, Detroit. Master Charge, BankAmericard, American Express. Mail-order address: P. O. Box 3700, Seattle, Wash. 98124.

L. L. Bean, Inc. Three or more catalogues per year with the most comprehensive selection of canoe-oriented clothes and equipment I know of in the United States (no Duluth packs, though); including several exclusives in trousers, shirts, boots, tents, and sleeping bags; and a number of otherwise hard-to-find items, such as pack baskets, light folding grills, ax cases, candle lanterns, tableware caddies, Bon Ami scouring bars, and the polyethylene Rec-Pac, which I like. With a scattering of frivolities, the goods are generally sturdily and sensibly made, the prices comparatively reasonable; some canoes in stock but not a primary source. The store is open twenty-four hours a day and is worth a visit if you're anywhere near. Address: Freeport, Me. 04032.

Eastern Mountain Sports, Inc. Annual catalogue (one dollar cover price), informative, with technical comparisons of tents, sleeping bags, stoves, and other camping gear. Emphasis on kayaking, skiing, technical climbing, but the canoeist can find a fair amount of useful basic equipment (canoe paddles but no canoes). Prices generally stiff, but tents, sleeping bags, and small stoves can be rented from most branches. Retail stores in Boston, Mass.; South Burlington, Vt.; St. Paul, Minn.; Ardsley, N.Y.; Wellesley, Mass.; North Conway, N.H.; Amherst, Mass. Mail-order address: 1041 Commonwealth Avenue, Boston, Mass. 02215.

Great World, Inc. Two catalogues per year. Primarily a canoeing outfitter (see also Appendix 11), but sells a good range of sensible equipment, including several exclusives under its Allagash trade name; canoes and paddles and a number of items cannily designed for New England canoeing (also one of the few U.S. dealers for Canada's Chestnut canoes). Pack baskets and Duluth packs; a good selection of books on canoeing; no food or clothing. Address: P. O. Box 250 (250 Farms Village Road), West Simsbury, Conn. 06092.

Laacke & Joys Co. Annual catalogue. A long-established tentmaker, whose poplin Explorer design, with a useful front awning that can be tied down as a storm door, is the type I consider ideal as a canoeing tent for two or three people (moderate-priced and quite light). The rest of the stock is a grab bag of camping and sporting goods, to be checked through with caution, but also, a source for two sizes of medium-grade Duluth

packs and, surprisingly, for a Hudson Bay (Canadian) pack, pack basket, and the new plastic Rec-Pac, all good for canoeing, depending on the function required and one's personal preference. Master Charge, BankAmericard. Address: 1432 N. Water Street, Milwaukee, Wis. 53202.

The Outdoor Stores, Ltd. Annual catalogue. Hunting and fishing gear at cut rates, but useful equipment, including Hudson's Bay packs and freeze-dried food, for canoers who peruse the pages with care. Chargex, Master Charge. Three stores in the Toronto area. Mail-order address: 1205 Finch Avenue West, Downsview, Ont.

Stow-A-Way Sports Industries. Annual catalogue. A fair selection of hiking equipment adaptable to canoeing, but the prime recommendation is its moderate-priced freeze-dried food line. Address: 166 Cushing Highway, Cohasset, Mass. 02025.

Waters, Inc. Annual catalogue. Another canoeing outfitter, recommended for its very complete line of Duluth packs, for boots, and for a comprehensive selection of books about canoeing and the border-lakes country. American Express. Address: 111 East Sheridan Street, Ely, Minn. 55731.

Appendix 10

FREEZE-DRIED FOODS

Despite my reservations, you'll need some, and the longer the trip, the more you'll need. All the processors listed below produce catalogues and can provide some information on nutrition. Except for Wilson, they accept retail orders; most encourage them with some form of quantity discount. Rich Moor and Wilson are quite widely available in U.S. sporting-goods stores and outfitters, the former also in some Canadian outlets. (I haven't had a chance to try the two or three Canadian brands I've heard of.)

Chuck Wagon Foods
Nucro Drive
Woburn, Mass. 01801

Rich Moor Corporation
P. O. Box 2728
Van Nuys, Calif. 91404

Stow-A-Way Sports Industries
166 Cushing Highway
Cohasset, Mass. 02025

Wilson & Co., Inc.
4545 Lincoln Boulevard
Oklahoma City, Okla. 73105.

Appendix 11

OUTFITTERS

The following selected list of canoe outfitters is arranged by states and provinces. Where I've indicated the kinds of services offered, "complete outfitting" means that the outfitter can supply all necessary rental equipment for a canoe trip (usually with food as well) at a flat rate per person per day; "partial outfitting" means that he can supply food and/or such rental equipment as you don't own yourself. The remaining agencies are generally restricted to canoe rentals and sales, including such equipment as car-top carriers, paddles, yokes, and life jackets.

All rates are approximate and should be verified when you place your order.

U.S. Outfitters

Alaska

Alaska Pioneer Canoes Association, Box 16, Sterling, Alas. 99672.

Arizona

W. C. "Bob" Towbridge Canoe Trips, Roy Reynolds, Manager, Box 1882, Green Meadow Lane, Havasu City, Ariz. 86403.

Arkansas

Hedges' Canoes. Buffalo River. Address: Ponca, Ark. 72670.

California

American River Touring Association. Rafting-oriented, but some organized canoe trips on big western U.S. and Canadian rivers. Address: 1016 Jackson St., Oakland, Calif. 94607.

Canoe Trips West. Canoe rentals; canoe, paddle, and pack sales; instruction; organized canoe trips on California rivers. Address: Box 61B (Greenbrae Boardwalk), Kentfield, Calif. 94904.

Connecticut

Great World, Inc. Complete and partial outfitting; canoe and equipment sales, including Duluth packs. New England, but also organized trips to remote wilderness areas such as Alaska. Address: Box 250 (250 Farms Village Road), West Simsbury, Conn. 06092.

Florida

Bonfleur's Blackwater Wilderness Experience. Organized, fully equipped trips, with guides, on the Blackwater River. Address: P. O. Box 656, Crestview, Fla. 32536.

Col. Jack & Betty Carpenter's Camper's World. Withlacoochee River (Rutland). Address: Highway 44, Lake Panasoffkee, Fla. 33538.

Canoe Outpost, Tex Stout, Outfitter. Two locations: R. R. 2, Box 745-H, Arcadia, Fla. 33821; P. O. Box 473, Branford, Fla. 32008.

Georgia

Amplay Canoe Rentals, P. O. Box 805, Folkston, Ga. 31537.

Suwannee Canal Recreation Area, Harry Johnson, Concessionaire, Okefenokee National Wildlife Refuge, Folkston, Ga. 31537.

Illinois

The Chicagoland Canoe Base. Canoe and canoe-equipment rentals and sales; Duluth packs; books about canoeing, including some rare or hard-to-find titles. Crude but informative catalogue of this firm's extensive stock of canoes and kayaks from many sources; the owner, Ralph Frese, is also a builder, very knowledgable about the design and history of canoes and paddles. Address: 4019 North Narragansett Avenue, Chicago, Ill. 60634.

Indiana

Clements Canoe Rental & Sales, 911 Wayne Avenue, Crawfordsville, Ind. 47933.

Oldfather Canoe Center, State Road 15 North, Goshen, Ind. 46526.

Water Meister Sports Canoe and Kayak Center, 6137 Lincoln Highway East, Fort Wayne, Ind. 46803.

Kentucky

Camping World, Beech Bend Park, Bowling Green, Ky. 42101.

Louisiana

Ricky's Guide Service, Route 1, Box 375, Bogalusa, La. 70427.

Maine

Allagash Wilderness Outfitters. Complete and partial outfitting, western Maine. Address: P. O. Box 73, Millinocket, Me. 04462.

Maine Wilderness Canoe Basin. Complete and partial outfitting (complete at about twelve dollars per person per day), canoe and equipment sales (Duluth packs). Eastern Maine; lakeside camp area which can be used as a base for canoe trips in the area; organized canoe trips for young people. Address: Carrol, Me. 04420 (winter: 20 Bass Drive, Groton, Conn. 06340).

McBreairty's Service, Allagash, Me. 04774.

Old Maine Guide Wilderness Trip Outfitters. Complete and partial outfitting (about eleven dollars per person per day, complete). Eastern Maine; camp areas at Ellsworth Falls and near Millinocket; organized trips for young people and families. Address: RFD 1, Box 27B, Ellsworth Falls, Me. 04633 (winter: P. O. Box 296, Wilton, Conn. 06897).

Maryland

Appalachian Outfitters, Box 44, 8000 Main St., Ellicott City, Md. 21043.

River and Trail Outfitters, Box 246, Valley Road, Knoxville, Md. 21758.

Massachusetts

Canoe Camp Outfits, 8 Cherry St., Belmont, Mass. 02178.

Michigan

Chippewa Landing. Manistee and Pine rivers. Address: P. O. Box 245, Cadillac, Mich. 49601.

Manistee River Cruises, 354 Third Street (or 267 Arthur Street), Manistee, Mich. 49660.

Minnesota

Bear Track Outfitting Company. Complete and partial outfitting (complete, about twelve dollars per person per day); guide service about thirty dollars per day; organized trips for young people. Eastern Boundary Waters Canoe Area during the summer but also similar services on the Wisconsin River in spring and fall. Address: Box 51, Grand Marais, Minn. 55604; fall, winter, spring: Route 1, Mazomanie, Wis. 53560.

Border Lakes Outfitting Company. Complete and partial outfitting (complete, about twelve dollars per person per day, less for children and groups); guides about thirty dollars per day. Boundary Waters-Quetico.

There are many outfitters in Ely and Winton, in the heart of the border-lakes country; this one, founded nearly fifty years ago by Sigurd Olson, is small and personal, and the current proprietors, Jack Niemi and John Farkas, are great canoeists who continue a noble tradition. Address: Box 158, Winton, Minn. 55796.

Gunflint Northwoods Outfitters. Complete and partial outfitting (complete, about thirteen dollars per person per day, less by the week or for children or groups); organized group trips; camp-site or cabin rental at Gunflint Lodge at the end of the Gunflint Trail near the Canadian border. Eastern Boundary Waters Canoe Area and Quetico. Address: Grand Marais, Minn. 55604.

Waters, Inc. Complete and partial outfitting, but the emphasis is on the useful mail-order operation (Appendix 9) and the posh retail store. Boundary Waters-Quetico. Address: 111 East Sheridan St., Ely, Minn. 55731.

Missouri

Akers Ferry Resort. Canoe rentals (eight dollars per day), paddles and life jackets, shuttle service, groceries. Ozark National Scenic Riverways (Current and Jacks Fork rivers). Address: Cedar Grove Route, Salem, Mo. 65560.

Jadwin Canoe Rental. Same services, charges, and area as preceding. Address: Jadwin, Mo. 65501.

New Hampshire

Goodhue Enterprises, Route 3, Weirs Boulevard, Laconia, N.H. 03246.

New Jersey

Abbot's Marine Center. Canoe rentals and sales. Delaware River (maps available). Address: Route 29, River Road, Titusville, N.J. 08560.

New York

Adventure Outfitters, Inc., Box 332, Lyons, N.Y. 14489.

Old Forge Sports Center, Inc., Route 28, Old Forge, N.Y. 13420.

Packs & Paddles Outfitters, c/o Donald Kenyon, R. D. 1, Box 166, Cleveland, N.Y. 13042.

Taconic Sports & Camping Center. Sales (no rentals) of canoes, tents, clothing, Duluth packs, and other camping equipment. Address: Rudd Pond Road, Millerton, N.Y. 12546.

Upper Delaware Outdoor Recreation, Inc., Box 188, Creamery Road, Callicoon, N.Y. 12723.

White Water Rentals, Inc., R. D. 1, Berme Road, Port Jervis, N.Y. 12771.

North Carolina

Appalachian Outfitters, Highway 321 South, Boone, N.C. 28607.

Ohio

All Ohio Canoe, 320 South Ardmore Road, Columbus, O. 43209.

Ohio Canoe Adventures, Inc., P. O. Box 2092 (5128 Colorado Avenue), Sheffield Lake, O. 44054.

Pennsylvania

Allegheny Outfitters, 19 South Main St., Clarendon, Pa. 16313.

Point Pleasant Canoe Rental & Sales. Canoe rentals (seven dollars per day, less by the week or for groups), partial outfitting, shuttle service. Delaware River, from Hale Eddy, N.Y., on south (maps). Apparently oriented toward novices and big groups—for others, less satisfactory. Address: Box 6, Point Pleasant, Pa. 18950.

Texas

Arlington Canoe Rental. 3103 W. Pioneer Parkway, Arlington, Tex. 76015.

Comanche Outfitters, c/o Charles Keyser, Horseshoe Bay, Drawer 4, Marble Falls, Tex. 78654.

Comanche Outfitters, 2008 Bedford, Midland, Tex. 79701.

Houston Canoe Sales & Rentals, 3930 Broadway, Houston, Tex. 77017.

Vermont

Woodstock Sports, 30 Central Street, Woodstock, Vt. 05091.

Virginia

Blue Ridge Mountain Sports, 1417 Emmet Street, Charlottesville, Va. 22611.

Canoe Center, 2930 Chain Bridge Road, Oakton, Va. 22124.

Matacia Outfitters, Box 32, Oakton, Va. 22124.

Shenandoah River Outfitters. Complete and partial outfitting (complete, about seventeen dollars per person per day); guides, thirty dollars per day; organized weekend trips emphasizing white water. Address: RFD 3, Luray, Va. 22835.

Spring Valley Canoe Base, Route 2, Box 175, Berryville, Va. 22611.

Wisconsin

Bear Track Outfitting Co. See listing under *Minnesota*.

Brule River Tackle Supply, Inc., P. O. Box 200, Brule, Wis. 54820.

Outfitting Center, Wisconsin Union, University of Wisconsin, 800 Langdon Street, Madison, Wis. 53706.

Smith's Landing. Canoe rentals (six dollars per day) and sales; paddles, life jackets, shuttle service. Kickapoo River. Address: Route 2, Box 211, La Farge, Wis. 54639.

Wild River Canoe Rentals, Route 1, Box 33, Trego, Wis. 54888.

Canadian Outfitters

For information about the Hudson's Bay Company's U-Paddle service, write to:

Hudson's Bay Company
Northern Stores Department
77 Main Street
Winnipeg R3C 2R1 Man.

The Northwest Territories and the provinces of Ontario and Quebec publish free lists of outfitters, obtainable from

TravelArctic
Yellowknife X0E 1H0 N.W.T.

Department of Tourism and Information
Province of Ontario
Parliament Buildings
Toronto M7A 1T3 Ont.

Direction Générale du Tourisme
Cité Parlementaire
Québec G1A 1R4 Que.

The outfitters listed in these three sources go in for hunting and/or fishing, not necessarily canoeing as such (there are no distinct listings for canoe outfitters). In general, outfitters in this sense are government-licensed to operate in a stated area, and the provision of guide service, food, and some or all equipment (at rates from twenty-five dollars per person per day up) is a condition of the license; they can usually arrange for fly-in service (additional!) where that's appropriate. If you want a local canoeing guide (*you* make your own arrangements for food and equipment), you can usually get help by writing well in advance to the manager of the local Hudson's Bay store near the starting point or to the mayor or administrator of the nearest town.

The outfitters listed here all specialize in canoeing.

Alberta

North-West Expeditions, Ltd. Emphasis on organized guided trips, by raft or canoe, in northern Alberta and the Northwest Territories, but can also provide or arrange for conventional outfitting services in this area. Address: Box 1551, Edmonton T5J 2N7 Alta.

Manitoba

The Happy Outdoorsman, Ltd., 433 St. Mary's Road, Winnipeg R2M 3K7 Man.

Northwest Territories

Roderick Norwegian. Indian outfitter licensed for canoeing on the South Nahanni River. Address: Fort Simpson, N.W.T.

Ontario

Algonquin Outfitters. Complete and partial outfitting. Algonquin Provincial Park, from a base near the southwest corner of the park; guides available but hardly necessary. Address: R. R. 1, Dwight P0A 1H0 Ont.

Algonquin Waterways Wilderness. Youth-oriented organized trips in Algonquin Provincial Park and on some wild rivers of northern Ontario; no general outfitting. Address: 271 Danforth Avenue, Toronto M4K 1N2 Ont.

North Country Outfitters. Complete and partial outfitting (complete at about fourteen dollars per person per day, less for children), guide service (easy travel but not essential). Quetico Provincial Park, with a base on Nym Lake, one of the main entrance points to the park from the Canadian side; also, fly-in service to wilderness lakes in northern Ontario. (Atikokan, like Ely, is well provided with canoe outfitters: a complete list can be obtained by writing to the town's chamber of commerce.) Address: Box 850B, Atikokan P0T 1C0 Ont.

Northern Wilderness Outfitters, Ltd. Complete outfitting (about ten dollars per day, less for groups or extended trips), canoe rentals at about five dollars per day but no other partial outfitting; a few organized, guided trips designed to instruct the young in canoe camping. Algonquin Provincial Park from a base near the less traveled northwest section of the park. Address: Box 665, Station B, Willowdale, Toronto M2K 2P9 Ont.

Opeongo Outfitting Store. Complete and partial outfitting (complete, about ten dollars per person per day), guides (about twenty-five dollars per day plus outfitting, but not needed). Algonquin Provincial Park, near the park's East Gate, and the heavily traveled southern section. Address: Algonquin Provincial Park, Whitney P. O., Ont.

The Portage Store. Comprehensive partial outfitting (no complete daily rates). Food, bait, tackle, accommodation, and meals; inside the park, near the West Gate (southern section). Address: Algonquin Provincial Park P. O., Ont.

Quetico North, Ltd. Complete and partial outfitting (complete, about fifteen dollars per person per day, less by the week, for children, or for groups); sales of canoes, equipment, food; guides about thirty dollars per day plus outfitting (not needed). Quetico Provincial Park and lakes immediately north from a base (overnight motel accommodation) near the park headquarters on French Lake, truck service to other entrance points; can also arrange for fly-in to more remote areas to the north. Address: Box 100, Atikokan P0T 1C0 Ont.

Quetico Wilderness Outfitters. Complete and partial outfitting (complete, about twelve dollars per person per day, less for groups); guides, about twenty-five dollars per day plus outfitting. Quetico Provincial Park from a base near the northwest corner of the park; can also arrange for fly-in trips to northern Ontario, with outfitting. Address: Box 1390, Atikokan P0T 1C0 Ont.

Saskatchewan

Churchill River Canoe Outfitters, P. O. Box 26, La Ronge, Sask. (winter: 509 Douglas Park Crescent, Regina, Sask.).